CRICUT FOR BEGINNERS
4 Books in 1

The 2021 Bible on the Art of Cricut!
An Easy-to-Follow Guide to Become an
Expert User in Few Weeks.
Many Practical Tips
and Step-by-Step Projects Included.

Milly Cooper

© **Copyright 2020 by Milly Cooper - All rights reserved.**

This document is geared towards providing exact and reliable information in regard to the topic and issue covered.

- From a Declaration of Principles which was accepted and approved equally by a Committee of the American Bar Association and a Committee of Publishers and Associations.

In no way is it legal to reproduce, duplicate, or transmit any part of this document in either electronic means or in printed format. All rights reserved.

The information provided herein is stated to be truthful and consistent, in that any liability, in terms of inattention or otherwise, by any usage or abuse of any policies, processes, or directions contained within is the solitary and utter responsibility of the recipient reader. Under no circumstances will any legal responsibility or blame be held against the publisher for any reparation, damages, or monetary loss due to the information herein, either directly or indirectly.

Respective authors own all copyrights not held by the publisher.

The information herein is offered for informational purposes solely and is universal as so. The presentation of the information is without contract or any type of guarantee assurance.

The trademarks that are used are without any consent, and the publication of the trademark is without permission or backing by the trademark owner. All trademarks and brands within this book are for clarifying purposes only and are owned by the owners themselves, not affiliated with this document.

Table of Contents BOOK 1

CRICUT DESIGN SPACE 18

FOR BEGINNERS 18

Introduction 19
    Creating an account on "Cricut.com" 19
    You can utilize Design Space on Mac PCs, PC PCs, and iOS gadgets. 23

Chapter 1: Getting to Know Design Space 27
    Downloading and Installing 27
    Machine Set up 31
    Cricut Access 33
    Design Space Environment 37
    Cheat Sheets 44
    Cricut Vocabulary 44
    Tools and Accessories of Cricut 48
    Canvas Overview 51

Chapter 2: Project Design 64
    How to Realize and Edit Cricut Project Ideas 64
    Step by Step Instructions to Alter The Sharing Settings And Tweak A Venture In Cricut Design Space 66
    Including Another Venture and Venture Cautioning in Cricut Design Space App .. 68

Chapter 3: Using Images in Design Space 71
    Images and how to browse for cartridges 71
    How to purchase images and upload them 73

Knockout Text Method 82

Add Color to an Uploaded Image Outline 86

Copy and paste 94

Duplicating on the Layers Panel 94

How to convert a pdf to PNG format 94

Chapter 4: Advanced Tips and Tricks 96

Font 96

Finding That Perfect Font 97

How to Edit Fonts 101

Edit projects at Cricut design space desktop 102

Adding color to an uploaded image, and how to make multiple layer vinyl 104

How to layer vinyl with registration marks 108

How to layer vinyl with registration marks/ Weed each layer 110

How to layer vinyl with registration marks 110

How to do split lettering with a décor 111

How to edit (cut, copy, paste) in the design space 116

How to group and ungroup in Cricut design space 117

Attach 119

Color sync panel 125

Flattering an unflattering 125

How to Add text in Cricut design 128

How to edit text in Cricut design space 132

Curving Your Text 137

Attaching Text 138

Making a Shadow 139

Letter spacing.. 141

How to center your designs to cut in Cricut Design Space 142

How to write with sketch pens in Cricut Design Space 143

Working with Edit Bar in Cricut Design Space 143

The Color Sync Tool 145

Sketching on The Design Space.. 145

Troubleshoot Error codes in the cricut design space 146

Chapter 5: FAQ.. 149

Where can I use Cricut Design Space? 149

How does my machine connect to Design Space? 149

What is Cricut Access? 149

How do I install Design Space? 149

Why am I getting error messages about the Design Space plugin?...... 150

Do I need a computer to use my Cricut machine? 150

What's the difference between the Cricut Explore One and the Cricut Explore Air 2? 150

Do I use the same Cricut Design Space for the Cricut Maker? 150

How does the Cricut Maker know which blade is in the carriage? 150

What is the thickness of a material that the Cricut Maker can cut? 151

How do I get a good transfer using the Cricut EasyPress? 151

How much pressure does the Cricut EasyPress need?.......................... 151

Do I move the Cricut EasyPress around like an iron? 151

Why should I use the Cricut EasyPress? 151

How do I protect surfaces while using the Cricut EasyPress?............... 151

My material is tearing! Why? 152

Why won't my transfer tape work? 152

What type of mat should I use? 152

How do I wash my mats? 153

Why won't my blade cut all the way through the material? 153

Can I upload my own images to the Cricut Design Space? 153

What is infusible ink? 153

Does Cricut Design Space require an internet connection? 154

What weight is Cricut Cardstock? 154

What are the care instructions for Cricut Iron-on material? 154

What's a quick reference list of materials I can cut? 154

Do I have to use Cricut brand materials? 154

What pens can I use in my Cricut machine? 154

What is the Cricut Adaptive Tool System? 155

What is the scoring wheel? 155

How small can the rotary blade cut? 155

Where do I buy Cricut Blades? 155

What is the Fast Mode? 155

What is the Custom material setting for? 156

Can Cricut Design Space work on more than one mobile device or computer? 156

Do I have to have an internet connection before I use Cricut Design Space? 157

Is there a difference between digital and physical cartridges? 157

How do I find the Cricut Access fonts and images on Design Space? 157

How long do I own the images that I purchase on Design Space? 157

Is it possible to disable the grid on the Canvas area? 157

Is Design Space compatible with a Chromebook computer?............................ 158

Do I need to pay in order to use Design Space?....................................... 158

Conclusion... 159

Table of Contents BOOK 2

CRICUT EXPLORE AIR 2 161

Introduction... 162

Chapter 1: What Is Cricut Machine... 163

What is Cricut?.. 163

Cricut Machine Models 163

Which Cricut Machine Should You Purchase? 174

They change in many ways: 176

Chapter 2: Machine Setup and How to Prepare the Material........ 179

Setting up the Cricut Explore Air 2 179

Useful Tips... 179

How to Plug in the Device?.. 180

How to Load/Unload the Mat? 180

How to Load/Unload Cricut Pen? 181

How to Load/Unload Blades?.. 183

How to unmount the paper from the mat... 184

How to Load/Unload a Scoring Stylus?.. 185

How to Load or Unload Cartridges?.. 185

How to Load or Unload a Debossing Tool? 187

Linking Cartridges with the Cricut Explore Air 187

Pairing the Cricut machine through Bluetooth to the Computer 188

Unpairing or removing the Bluetooth device 189

Resetting the Cricut Explore Air 2 Machine 189

How to Cut Heavyweight and Lightweight Materials 190

Chapter 3: Cricut Design Space software For Cricut Explore Air 2 192

How to Upload Images with A Cricut Explore Air 2? 192

Making a Vinyl Sticker 195

Best Tools and Software's for Cricut Machine Explore Air 2 196

How to Cut Vinyl from A Cricut Machine? 200

How to Cut Basswood by Cricut? 201

How to design with Cricut machine 201

Finding the current firmware version on my machine 204

Finding the current version of Design Space 205

The Fast Mode of the Cricut Explore Air machine and how it is used 205

Cleaning and Care 206

Using or creating custom material settings 209

Cut Vinyl with A Cricut Machine 211

Using Snap Mat cutting multiple Colors 212

Cricut Scrapbooking 212

How do you desire to get your words onto your page? 213

Electronic and mechanical systems 215

Chapter 4: Solving the most common problem when using Cricut Explore Air 2 217

Helpful Troubleshooting Techniques 217

Chapter 5: FAQs about the Cricut Explore Air 2 224

Why does Design Space say my Cricut machine is already in use when it's not? ... 224

Why doesn't my cut match the preview in Design Space? 224

What do I do if I need to install USB drivers for my Cricut machine? 225

Why does my Cricut Maker say the blade is not detected? 225

Is Wireless Bluetooth Adapter required for All Cricut Explore machines? 226

How do you differentiate between the Cricut Explore machines? 226

Is carry bag included in Explore series machine package? 226

Is it possible to write & score with my Explore One machine? 227

Are the weights and dimensions of Explore Series machine similar? What are their dimensions? 227

Why is my Cricut machine making a grinding noise? 227

What if my Cricut is making a different loud noise? 227

Why is my mat going into the machine crooked? 227

Why isn't the Smart Set Dial changing the material in Design Space? 228

What do I do if my Cricut Maker stopped partway through a cut? 228

Why is my fabric getting caught under the rollers? 229

Why would my Cricut Maker continuously turn off during cuts? 229

What do I do about a failing or incomplete firmware update? 229

What do I do if my Cricut machine is having power issues? 230

What do I do if I'm having issues with the machine's door? 230

Where Can I Download Software for my Cricut Explore Air Machine? 230

Does My Cricut Explore Air need a Wireless Bluetooth Adapter? 231

Can I link my cartridges to more than one account? 231

Can a cartridge be unlinked after it has been linked? 231

I linked my cartridge to older software; can I still use it in Cricut Design Space? .. 231

I have linked my cartridges; how do I access them? 231

Can I use physical cartridges without linking them? 231

What type of materials can I cut with my cricut? 231

Can I upload my images? 232

What is the duration of my cutting mat? 232

Can I make use of other paper size? 232

Can I learn how to create my own customize project with cricut design software without much stress? 232

Chapter 6: Tips for beginners 233

De-tack your cutting mat! 233

Keep Your Cutting Mat Clean 233

Use the Proper Tools 233

Start Your Cricut Journey with the Sample Project 234

Always Test Cuts 234

Replace Pen Lids after Use 234

Link Your Old Cricut Cartridges 234

Bend the Cutting Mat to Get Materials off the Cutting Mat 234

Use the Deep Cut Blade for Thicker Materials 235

Always replace the pen lids after use 235

Linking your old Cricut Cartridges to your Design Space Account 235

Get materials off the Cutting mat 235

Get the Deep Cut blade 236

Always Replace the Blades 236

Keep Your Cutting Mat Clean 236
Use the Proper Tools 236
Start Your Cricut Journey with the Sample Project 237
Always Test Cuts 237
Replace Pen Lids after Use 237
Link Your Old Cricut Cartridges 237
Bend the Cutting Mat to Get Materials off the Cutting Mat 237
Use the Deep Cut Blade for Thicker Materials 238
Use Different Pens Where Necessary 238
Make Use of Free Fonts 238
Use Different Blades for Different Materials 238
Use Weeding Boxes for Intricate Patterns 239
Always Remember to Set the Dial 239
Make use of the Free SVG files 239
Other pens compatible with the Cricut Explore Air 2 239
Have the Mat correctly loaded 240
Tips on How to Do Iron-On or Heat Transfer Vinyl Project 240
Making use of different blades for different materials 243
Additional tips on Effective Use of Your Cricut Explore Air 2 245

Conclusion 247

Table of Contents BOOK 3

CRICUT MAKER FOR BEGINNERS 249

Introduction 250

Chapter 1: How to choose the right machine for your needs 252

    Criteria for Choosing a Cricut Machine 252

    Quick Overview of the Main Models 254

    Cricut Maker 255

    Cricut Joy 256

    Cricut Compare Models 258

    Difference in Models 259

Chapter 2: Cricut Maker 261

    Machine Setup and How to Prepare the Material 261

    Cartridge 263

    Loading Your Paper 264

    How to Remove Your Cuts from Cutting Mat 265

    How to design With Cricut Maker 267

    How to Clean The Cricut Maker 269

    Cricut Design Space software For Cricut Maker 270

    Making Your First Project Idea 272

    How to Upload Images with a Cricut Maker 275

    Cut Vinyl with A Cricut Maker 279

    How to Make Stickers 280

    Procedure for Making Cupcake Stickers 280

Procedures for Making Sticky Labels 281

Working With Images/Edit Panel 283

Cricut Scrapbooking... 286

Solving the most common problem when using Cricut Maker 287

Chapter 3: Cricut Joy 290

Machine Setup and How to Prepare the Material 290

Cartridge 294

Loading Your Paper 295

How to Remove Your Cuts from Cutting Mat... 297

How to design With Cricut Joy.. 298

How to Clean The Cricut Joy 299

There are many ways to clean your cutting mat... 300

Cricut Design Space software For Cricut Joy 303

Making Your First Project Idea 305

How to Upload Images with A Cricut Joy 307

Cut Vinyl with a Cricut Joy... 308

How to Make Stickers 309

Working With Images/Edit Panel 312

Cricut Scrapbooking... 313

Solving the most common problem when using Cricut Joy 315

Chapter 4: FAQs about the Cricut Maker & Joy 319

Why does Design Space say my Cricut machine is already in use when it's not? ... 319

Why doesn't my cut match the preview in Design Space? 319

What do I do if I need to install USB drivers for my Cricut machine?................. 320

Why does my Cricut Maker say the blade is not detected? 320

Why is my Cricut machine making a grinding noise? 320

Why is my mat going into the machine crooked? 321

Why isn't the Smart Set Dial changing the material in Design Space? 321

What do I do if my Cricut Maker stopped partway through a cut? 321

Why is my fabric getting caught under the rollers? 322

Why would my Cricut Maker continuously turn off during cuts? 322

Chapter 5: Tips that might Assist You To Begin 323

Make sure that you have a deep cut blade. 323

Know your glue 324

Think about a Coach 324

Exhibit Your True Talent with a Business Card for Artists 324

Give the Quality of Your Work a chance to radiate through 325

Consider Other Ways You Can Display Your Skills to the World 325

Remember to tell individuals how to connect! 325

Be Adaptable 326

Conclusion 327

Table of Contents BOOK 4

CRICUT PROJECT IDEAS 329

Introduction 330

Chapter 1: project ideas for beginners 331

1. A Simple Birthday Card 331

2. Welcome to Our Happy Home" Sign 334

2. Personalized Paper Bookmark 338

3. Fancy Leather Bookmark 340

5. Personalized Envelopes 344

6. Clear Personalized Labels 347

7. Stenciled Welcome Mat 350

8. Momma Bear on Board Keep Your Distance Car 352

9. Window Stickers 356

10. Car Keys, Wood Keyring 359

11. Planner sticker 363

12. Nama and Kiss Glitter Tumbler 365

13. Sleep Eye Mask with Eyes 368

14. Coloring Gift Wrap 370

15. Art journal 372

16. Felt Roses 375

Chapter 2: Project ideas for intermediate 378

17. Custom Coasters 378

18. Customized Doormat 380

19. 3d Paper flowers 383

20. Luminaries 385

21. Shamrock Earrings 388

22. Valentine's Day Classroom Cards 391

23. Glitter and Felt Hair Bow Supplies 394

24. Halloween T-Shirt 396

25. Hand Lettered Cake Topper 399

26. Unicorn Free Printable 402

27. Custom Back To School Supplies 405

28. Leather Keychain 408

29. Tassels 411

30. Etched Glass 414

31. Wooden Sign 417

32. Clutch purse 420

33. Thank You Card 423

Chapter 3: Project ideas for advanced 426

34. Coloring Pages 426

35. Luggage tags 428

36. A Table Lamp 430

37. Xmas Decoration 433

38. Wall Art 435

39. Print socks 438

40: Jam Jar Labels 440

41. Monogrammed Drawstring Bag 442

42. Drinks Coasters 444

43. Baby Blanket 447

44. Shoe Decals 449

45. Leather foil 451

46. Leftover Boxes 454

47. Photo Envelope Liners 456

48. Burlap **459**

49. Model Airplane **461**

50. Wedding invitation **463**

Conclusion **466**

CRICUT DESIGN SPACE FOR BEGINNERS

Learn the secrets of the most experienced DIY enthusiasts. Discover tools and accessories to get started. A complete step-by-step guide with Tips and Illustrations

Introduction

Creating an account on "Cricut.com"

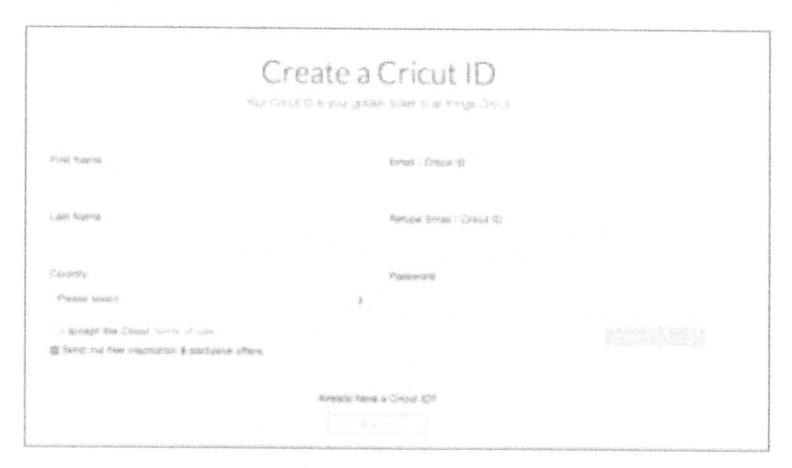

Now that you understand what "Design Space" is and how you can use to create beautiful DIY projects. Let's look at how you can get your own "Cricut ID" to log into the "Design

"Space" application.

On the official "Cricut" site, select *"Design"* from the top right corner of the screen.
A new window will open, from the bottom of the screen select *"Create A Cricut ID"*.
Now, in the window as shown in the picture below, you would need to enter your personal information, such as, first name, last name, email ID and password.
You would then need to check the box next to *"I accept the Cricut Terms of Use"* and click on *"Create a Cricut ID"*.

You will be instantly taken to the "Design Space" landing page and a message reading *"New! Set your machine mode"* will be displayed.

With the steps above you have registered your email address as your new "Cricut ID"!!!!
Now, let's see how you can complete your registration and start using "Design Space".

When you log into "Design Space" for the first time, your screen will display the message as shown in the picture below.

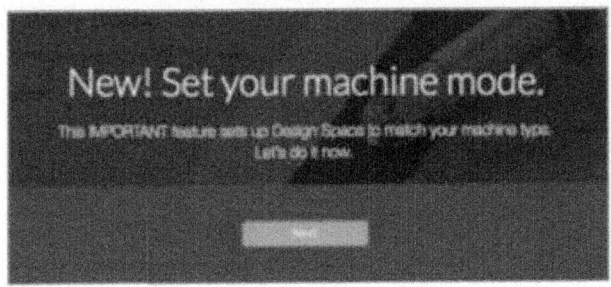

Click on *"Next"* as displayed in the picture above, a blacked-out screen with *"Machine"* on the top right corner of the screen will be displayed as shown in the picture below.

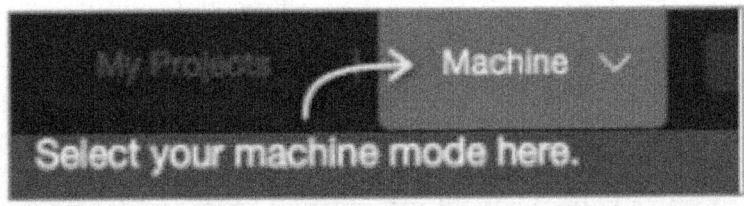

Click on *"Machine"* and the options of the "Cricut" machines will be displayed as shown below.

Cricut for Beginners

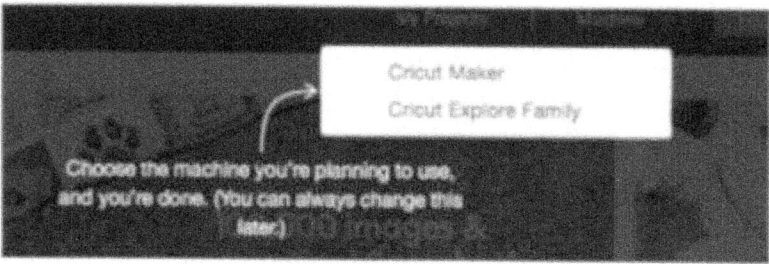

You can select your device from the two options. For this example, "Cricut Maker" was selected and upon selection, the next screen will confirm the device you selected, as shown in the picture below.

Remember, if you wish to toggle to the "Cricut Explore", all you have to do is click on the "Maker" and you will see the dropdown option for the two machines again, as shown in the picture below.

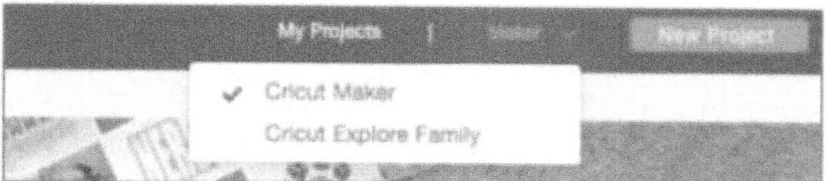

Design Space on Mobile Devices

As mentioned earlier, the "Cricut Design Space" is cloud based and you can pick up your project across various platforms. Here's how you can download the latest version (v 3.18.1) of this application on your mobile devices.

Apple App Store (iOS) – Simply search for "Cricut" on the App store from your iPhone or iPad and select "GET" to begin the download. You can then easily login with your registered "Cricut ID" to continue working on your projects on your phone.

Google Play (Android) – You can search for "Cricut" on the Google Play from your android phone and table. Then select "Install" to begin the download. Once completed use your "Cricut ID" to login and pick up your projects and ideas where you left off. Cricut Design Space is the online stage that Cricut designed to be utilized with their more up to date machines.

It's not programming – you download a module on your PC (or the application on your table/telephone), and after that, you can design however much you might want.
You can utilize designs and pictures that are now transferred into Design Space, or you can transfer your own!

Be that as it may, you can introduce your own textual styles onto your PC and transfer pictures to Design Space (that you've made, found for nothing, or obtained without anyone else).

Cricut Design Space is an online program, so you don't download it onto your PC.
Nonetheless, you should download some modules, which should auto popup and brief you to download when you experience the underlying procedure.

Any undertaking that you make in Design Space can be spared to the Cloud. You simply need to ensure you spare your venture – that catch is in the upper right-hand corner.
This enables you to see your task on any gadget where you are signed in.

Nonetheless, if you are dealing with an iPhone or an iPad, you have the choice to spare it just to your gadget. I would, for the most part, consistently propose sparing it to the Cloud, however!

You can utilize Design Space on Mac PCs, PC PCs, and iOS gadgets.

Your PC must run a Windows or Mac working framework, and hence, Google Chromebooks CANNOT be utilized, as they keep running on a Google OS.

Once in a while, when you go to cut your design, it will stop you before you get to the tangle seepage and state you have to pay.

You may have incidentally included a picture that requires instalment – you can return to your canvas and check each picture to check whether there is a dollar sign beside it (or check whether the text style you chose has a dollar sign. Remember that regardless of whether you have Cricut Access, you don't approach ALL the pictures and textual styles).

If you chose a venture from Design Space, it might have incorporated a picture or textual style that is paid. When you take a gander at the task guidelines, it should let you know if it is free or not.

Some of the time, they will convey an email when they anticipate a blackout. However, I don't generally observe this.
If it's down, I will propose not reaching their client backing and simply be quiet. You can likewise attempt another program or clear your program store, just to ensure it is anything but an issue on your end.

Cutting is one of my preferred highlights in Cricut Design Space! I cherish removing text styles and pictures in different designs.

Yet, now and then it won't work. If you are observing this to be an issue, here are a couple of thoughts:

− Make sure the picture/text style you are removing of (so that is over another picture) is totally inside the other picture. If a bit of it is standing out, it won't cut.
− Make sure everything is chosen.
− Keep as a main priority that when you cut it, you will have two layers to expel from the picture − the first picture/text style that you cut, just as the cut

For what reason isn't Print and Cut working?

Notwithstanding, the most compelling motivation why I see individuals experiencing difficulty with Print and Cut is that they didn't smooth their pictures! Before you go to print and cut, ensure you select all and press straighten.

For what reason Can't I Open Cricut Design Space?

Regularly you will get a blunder or a white screen with Design Space if you don't have the most as of late refreshed module.

If you get a clear page, take a stab at invigorating the page to check whether the module update shows up. Try not to move far from this page when it's refreshing, or it will turn white.

Cartridge

Designs are produced using parts put away on cartridges. Every cartridge accompanies a console overlay and guidance booklet. The plastic console overlay demonstrates key determinations for that cartridge as it were. Anyway, as of late Provo Craft has discharged an "All-inclusive Overlay" that is perfect with all cartridges discharged after August 1, 2013. The motivation behind the all-inclusive overlay is to simplify the way toward slicing by just learning one console overlay as opposed to learning the overlay for every individual cartridge.

Designs can be removed on a PC with the Cricut Design Studio programming, on a USB associated Gypsy machine, or can be legitimately inputted on the Cricut machine utilizing the console overlay. There are two kinds of cartridges shape and textual style. Every cartridge has an assortment of imaginative highlights which can take into consideration several different cuts from only one cartridge. There are as of now more than 275 cartridges that are accessible (independently from the machine), containing textual styles and shapes, with new ones included monthly.

The Cricut Craft Room programming empowers clients to join pictures from different cartridges, consolidate pictures, and stretch/turn pictures; it doesn't take into account the formation of discretionary designs. It additionally empowers the client to see the pictures showed onscreen before starting the cutting procedure so that the final product can be seen in advance.

Referring to Adobe's surrender of Flash, Cricut declared it would close Cricut Craft Room on 15 July 2018. Clients of "heritage" machines were offered a markdown to refresh to models good with Cricut Design Space. Starting on 16 July 2018, Design Space is the main programming accessible to do projects. Design Space isn't perfect with cartridges once in the past bought for the Cricut Mini, which was power nightfall on October 2018.

Chapter 1: Getting to Know Design Space

Downloading and Installing

The first stage of learning the Cricut Design Space is to know how to download and install it correctly. The steps are not so complicated, all you need is to have the basic computer skills, i.e., know your way around your PC or Desktop. Follow the steps below to get your Design Space downloaded, installed, and launched.

Go to your internet browser on your PC or Desktop, then open the following address to access Cricut design website; design.cricut.com.

Once you are on the platform, select "Download."

Cricut for Beginners

The download should start immediately, and the display will change once it starts downloading. However, the display could be quite different depending on the browser you are using. The screenshots being used are from Google Chrome.

Once the download has been completed, either go to your "Downloads" folder or double-click on the file that appears after the download on your browser.
You might get a popup, asking you if you want to trust the application or not, select "Yes" and wait for the next window.

Cricut for Beginners

You should have a setup window displaying the installation progress popup shortly after.

Go ahead and input your registered ID and password on Cricut to sign in.

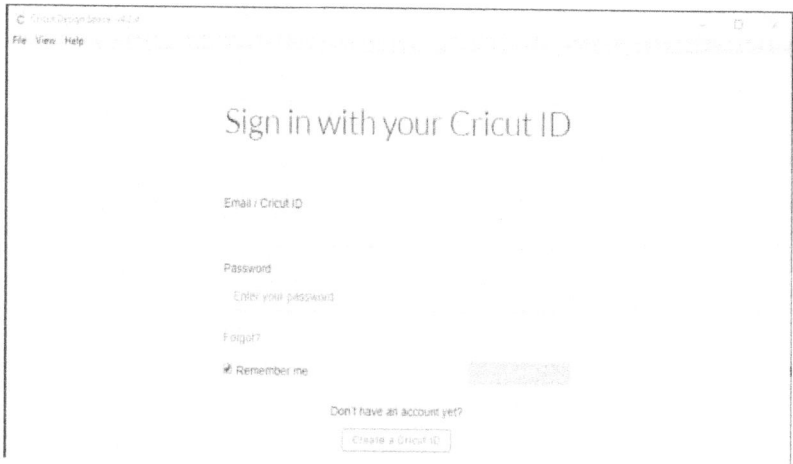

1For most computers, a Design Space icon gets added automatically to your home screen. Right-click the icon and then select "Pin to Taskbar," or get the icon dragged to the taskbar to get the shortcut pinned for easy access.

And that's it! You're done with the installation of your Design Space. That wasn't so hard, was it? You can now proceed to launch the app when you are ready. You can also share your feedback by using the feedback tab located at the lower part of the design space menu.
You should also note that the application remembers your sign-in details. You won't need to log in every time you open the app unless you intentionally logged out of your last session. Also, the application doesn't save automatically. Therefore, save your projects regularly as you work and when you are about to close the application.

Lastly, you need to ensure that your Design Space is the latest version. This will make sure you're up to date with all that Cricut offers, and you get the best results from your Cricut Machine. To find the current version of your Design Space application, follow the steps below:

Left click on the small arrow located on the Taskbar to reveal hidden icons.
Place your mouse on top of the Design Space icon (don't click.)
The Cricut Bridge version should appear.

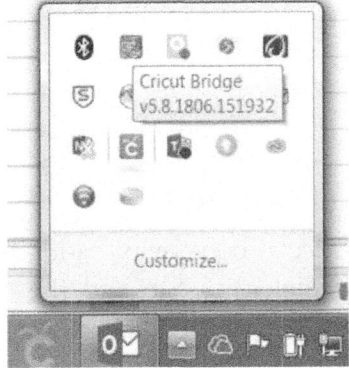

Machine Set up

Setting up your Cricut machine doesn't take too much time or stress. Although you need to be watchful while doing it, it should take you approximately an hour to finish the setup. Fortunately, you would find some tools inside the package to help you through the setup. The following are the tools you'll need to get your machine set up:

- Using Cricut Maker:
- Cricut Maker
- Power Cord and USB cable
- Fine Point Pen
- A Fine Point Blade
- Rotatory Blade with Housing
- FabricGrip Mat 12" by 12"
- LightGrip Mat 12" by 12"
- An internet-enabled computer with the basic requirements. (If you're using the Desktop platform)

Note: The computer will not come with the box.

The following are the procedures for setting up your machine:
Unbox the package, and you'll find a couple of tools placed on the machine, and the power cord should be under it all.

Cricut for Beginners

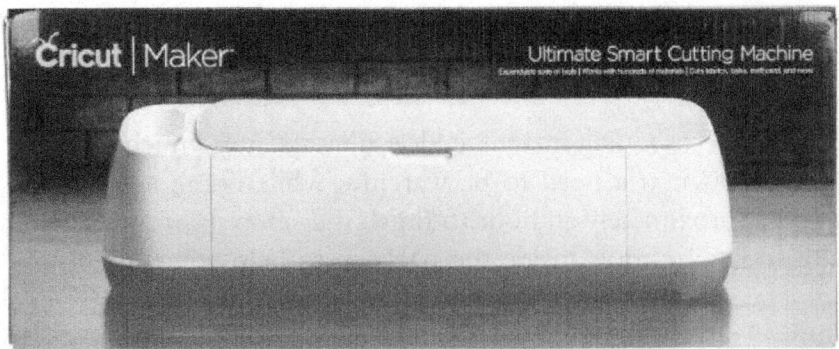

Unwrap the machines and the supplies you find inside the box.

Visit www.cricut.com/setup to set up your machine. Log in with your previous ID or create a new one if you don't have it.

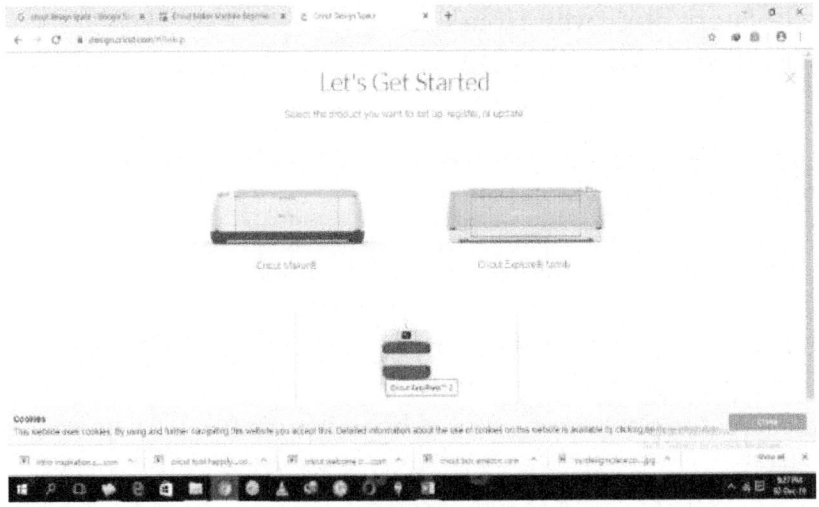

Plug all the cables in the right place; the USB cord from your machine to the computer, and the power cable to a power outlet.

And that should get your machine all set up!
Now back to our primary objective; the Cricut Design Space. Once you set up your machine and Design Space for the first time, you get a one-month free subscription to Cricut Access. Let's discuss for a while about Cricut Access.

Cricut Access

Cricut Access grants you access, either monthly or yearly, to the image library of over 50,000 unlicensed images, over a thousand projects, and over 400 fonts.
There're three diverse plans available to choose from:
Cricut Access - Monthly
Cricut Access - Annual
Cricut Access - Premium
With Cricut Access, you benefit the following from your subscription:
Unlimited Access to more than 400 attractive fonts.
Unlimited Access to more than 50,000 cut-ready, covet-worthy premium Cricut images.

10% discounts on every product you purchase on cricut.com. This includes machines, materials, accessories, and many more.
10-50% discounts on licensed images, fonts, and ready-to-make projects.
Priority member care line option.

Cricut Access (Monthly and Annual)

Unlimited Access to more than 400 attractive fonts.
Unlimited Access to more than 50,000 cut-ready, covet-worthy premium Cricut images.
10% discounts on every product you purchase on cricut.com. This includes machines, materials, accessories, and many more (including sale items.)
10% discounts on Premium licensed images, fonts, and ready-to-make projects. These projects are from brands such as Disney, Anna Griffin, and Simplicity.
Priority member care line (50% reduction in wait time.)

Cricut Access (Premium)

Unlimited Access to more than 400 attractive fonts.
Unlimited Access to more than 50,000 cut-ready, covet-worthy premium Cricut images.
10% discounts on every product you purchase on cricut.com. This includes machines, materials, accessories, and many more (including sale items.)
10% discounts on Premium licensed images, fonts, and ready-to-make projects. These projects are from brands such as Disney, Anna Griffin, and Simplicity.
About 50% discounts on licensed images, fonts, and ready-to-make projects.
Free Economy Shipping on orders worth more than $50.

Priority member care line (50% reduction in wait time.)

You either subscribe to Cricut Access through their website, www.cricut.com, or from the Design Space platform.

To purchase through Cricut.com, follow the steps below:

Go to shop.cricut.com on your internet browser.

Proceed to sign in by inputting your Cricut username and password.

Choose your desired plan, and then proceed by adding it to your Cart.

Proceed to checkout your order and complete the purchase.

Once you have successfully submitted your order, your new Cricut Access Plan should activate immediately.

Note: If you are from the UK, you can't purchase Cricut Access on www.cricut.com for now. It can only be purchased from Design Space, and this can be done on a Windows computer or Mac.

To purchase on the Design Space (Windows or Mac,) consider following the procedures below:

- Sign in by inputting your Cricut username and password on the Design Space.
- Click the menu icon on the Design Space, then click on "Cricut Access."
- Go through the available plans and choose the appropriate option.

Cricut for Beginners

Enter your Credit Card details (or just review it if you've made a purchase before), and then click "Continue."

When your payment information has been saved, enter your password to proceed with your purchase, and then click on "Authorize."

Once you have successfully authorized your purchase, your new Cricut Access Plan should activate immediately and should be available in every Design Space platform.
Design Space Environment

It is usual for a new user of Cricut Design Space to get easily confused on their first session. We'll take an overview of the general things you see when you first sign in.
We'll be discussing majorly on the Design Space menu contents. The menu serves as a way of navigating through primary screens in the Design Space such as "Home" and "Canvas." From the menu list, you can likewise get to every other feature of Design Space such as Settings, Help, Print then cut calibration, Link Cartridges, Account Details, and Manage Custom Materials.

Home

The "Home" button, when clicked, will always take the user to the Home screen. And at the Home screen, you can go through the numerous curated project lists. You can also get swift access to previous projects or start new ones. Your project won't be removed when you navigate through the Home screen until you decide to start a new one by adding it to the canvas.

Canvas

Left click on the "Canvas" button to go back to the canvas whenever you like. If any project has been opened on the canvas before, you'll be taken back to it.

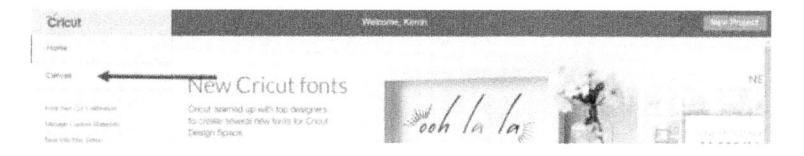

Print Then Cut Calibration

If you want your machine to make accurate cuts from images for Print then Cut, make sure you calibrate the machine.

Manage Custom Materials

Manage Custom Materials is best used for adjusting the Cut Pressure for any kind of material. It is also perfect for creating a new Cut Pressure for any new material.

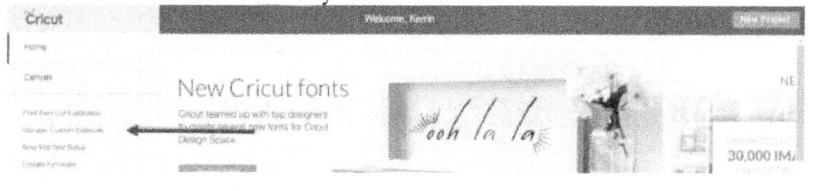

New Machine Setup

If you've got a new Cricut machine and you haven't made use of it yet, then click on "New Machine Setup" to make sure you've got the appropriate software, the right firmware, and that you're all set up and ready to begin creating.

Update Firmware

If the current Firmware on your Cricut machine needs an update, or if you desire to check if there's another update on Firmware, then click on "Update Firmware."

Account Details
If you want access to every account detail of your shopping, then click on the "Account Details" link.

Link Cartridges

If you've got cartridges you desire to make use of in your various designs, then you should click "Link Cartridges" to have them linked to your account.

Cricut Access

As discussed earlier, you can get access to more than 370 fonts, 30,000 images, and 1000 projects with just $7.99 a month. You will likewise get 10% discounts on each of your orders on Design Space and Cricut.com.

Settings

In Settings, you can learn various keyboard shortcuts, alter measurement units to centimeters or inches, and also switch the grid off or on.

Cricut for Beginners

Legal
In Legal, you can learn about things like the Cricut Privacy Policy, Patents, Terms of use, and so on.

Country Selection
You should choose your present country if you desire to know the suitable currency for different projects, fonts, and images.

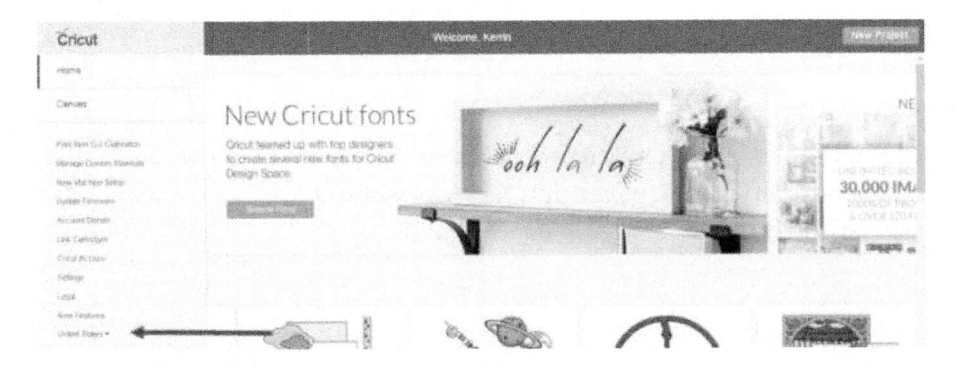

42

Help

The Help Center will give you access to the User Manual, helpful videos, as well as answers to FAQs.

Sign Out

Apparently, this enables you to log out of the Design Space anytime you want. However, you should ensure you save all your projects before ending the session.

That should be all you need to know about the Design Space interface for now. As time goes on, you get more familiar with the environment. Make sure you spend a lot of time checking out these primary functions so as to master it. By now, you should know how to set up your Cricut machine, download and install the Cricut Design Space, subscribe for a Cricut Access plan, and also know how to use all the functions available on the Design Space menu.

Before you proceed to the next chapter, ensure you already know everything that has been discussed. After this chapter, every other instruction and guideline that will be given will assume you already know these basics.

Cheat Sheets

There are many cheat sheets available on the internet and you simply need to type "Design space cheat sheets" into the search bar. You'll have many options to explore that will help you with any of the six areas mentioned above.

The cheat sheets are filled with tips and tricks from getting you up and running to doing complex projects.

The cheat sheets are free from most sites, and Pinterest has many to choose from. You can also purchase them on Etsy. They aren't expensive, but chances are you can find what you're looking for at no cost. It's just a matter of searching through the hundreds or thousands available online.

Cricut Vocabulary

These are some of the most common technical terms you'll hear when discussing Cricut. They are provided courtesy of HTV Addict, and they are written in simple terms.

Design Space
The cloud based Cricut software for making your projects accessed at https://us.cricut.com

Siser Easyweed
Most popular manufacturer of Oracal – Oracal is a manufacturer of adhesive vinyl (631, 651, 951, etc.) commonly used by crafters.

Printable vinyl
vinyl you can put through your inkjet or laser printer (make sure you use the correct type for your printer!!) usually used with Print and Cut function in Design Space.

Attach
You'll find the attach tool in Design Space. This tool holds your cuts in the same position on the cutting mat as they are on the design screen.

AutoBlade
The Silhouette cutting blade automatically adjusts to the recommended cut settings based on the

Contour
If you want to hide part of an image, the Contour tool will remove any unwanted cut lines. You can use this feature in Design Space.

Cut lines
Cut lines are the lines that outline the shape you are trying to cut. They are red or gray lines that indicate where the machine will cut.

Decal
The end result when you cut shapes into vinyl.

Edit Points
The dots on lines in a design that indicate where the line curves and moves to form a shape.

Inkscape
Inkscape is a free graphic design software that can be used to trace images, create vectors, and SVG files.

JPG & PNG Files
Types of files. You can tell if a file is a JPEG if it ends in .jpg and PNG will end in . png.

Kiss cut
When the cut made by the machine only cuts through the top layer- such as when only the top vinyl layer is cut when making a decal.

Mirrored Image
A necessary step before you cut any HTV. All images that have been mirrored will appear reversed when cut.

Offset
The act of creating an equal distance border - at any distance of your choosing - around the border of a design.

Print then cut
Home printer to print a design and your cutting machine to die cut your design.

Printable vinyl
Vinyl that can be sent through your inkjet/home printer. You can print on it from DS or Silhouette Studio and then have your machine die cut it, also called print and cut function. Comes in heat transfer and adhesive varieties.

Registration Marks
Marks that are printed on printable vinyl when using the print then cut function.

Reveal Grid
Exposing the grid lines, from the Page Set-Up window,

Sketching
An action that can be performed by your machine if the blade is replaced with a sketch pen.

Slice
The slice tool creates new cut paths from two images, resulting in three or more completely new shapes. Each of the new shapes will show up in the Layers panel as individual layers.

Software
The program that exists on your computer, whether it be Silhouette Studio or Design Space.

Spatula
A tool used to help remove small pieces of vinyl or paper from the mat.

SVG
A type of file that is a scalable vector.

Teflon
A teflon always be placed between an iron/heat press and HTV to protect your iron or heat press.

Text to Path
The action of manipulating text by forcing it to curve around another object or shape such as a circle. When the text is converted to a path, it will keep its new shape.

Transfer Tape
Transfer tape is the sticky material that is used to transfer adhesive vinyl from the carrier sheet to the surface of your project.

Weeding
Removing vinyl from decal.

Weeding Lines
Cut lines put around a design to make the weeding process easier.

A compressed file
There is a learning curve with the Cricut machine, no matter which model you choose, and there are many things with the Cricut that you'll acclimate to with time. You can't expect to learn everything at once, and a lot of it will come as you work on your projects.

Tools and Accessories of Cricut

Cricut has much to offer in the way of tools and accessories. There are machines they offer to suit different crafting purposes, which have their own accessories and tools as well.

For the Cricut cutting machines, here is what's available:

Cricut Maker Cutting Blades
In addition to the Explore Cutting blade, the Cricut Maker has additional cutting blades that allow for intricate cutting details on a variety of materials.

Cutting Mats
Cricut cutting mats come in a variety of sizes and degree of stickiness. Depending on what material you are using, you will want less or more stickiness on your mat, to hold the material in place while cutting.

The Circuit Weeder
The weeder tool, which looks similar to a dental pick, is used for removing negative space from a vinyl project. This weeder tool is a must when doing any type of project that involves vinyl.

The Cricut Scraper
The Circuit Scraper tool is essential (and a lifesaver!) when you need to rid your cutting mat of excess negative bits. This tool typically works best with paper, such as cardstock, but other materials can easily be scraped up as well. Use the flexibility of the mat to your advantage as you scrap the bits off the mat, to ensure you are not scraping up the adhesive on the mat as well.

The Cricut Spatula
A spatula is a must-have tool for a crafter who works with a lot of paper. Pulling the paper off of a Cricut cut mat can result in a lot of tearing and paper curling if you are not diligent and mindful when you are removing it.

Scissors
These sharp tools come in handy more often than you can possibly know with Cricut projects and having a dedicated pair makes it so much easier to complete your projects.

Craft Tweezers
These reverse-action tweezers have a strong grip, precise points, and alleviate cramping after prolonged use.

Spatula
Sometimes you feel like you need an extra set of hands when you're peeling or laying down a project. This tool gives you that extra support and maneuverability where you need it.

Scoring Stylus
This tool can be loaded into clamp A in your Cricut machine. This will allow the machine to draw deep lines into your project to give it texture or a precise folding point.

Portable Trimmer
This is a precision cutting tool that allows you to get fast, crisp, straight cuts on your projects 100% of the time.

Rotary Cutting Kit
This kit includes a gridded cutting mat and a rotary cutting tool. Cuts are fast, sharp, and precise.

XL Scraper/Burnishing Tool
This provides a level of control that cannot be beaten. It exerts pressure evenly and helps to eliminate uneven layering and air bubbles.

TrueControl™ Knife
This is a precision blade that is comparable to XACTO in quality and in type. For more precise freehand cuts, this knife is very helpful at any crafting station.

Cricut Explore Wireless Bluetooth Adapter
This product is to help your Cricut Explore machine connect with Bluetooth to your computer or device.

Deep-Point Replacement Blades
These help your Cricut machine to make more precise cuts with thicker materials!

Bonded Fabric Blades
These blades are meant to retain their extremely sharp point, cut after cut into fabric in your machine!

Replacement Blades
With different purposes like debossing, engraving, perforation and more, can be purchased from Cricut as well.

The Cricut Easy press
If you begin to venture into iron-on projects and want to upgrade from a traditional iron and ironing board, the Cricut Easy press is the right way to go. It will make projects so much easier than using a traditional iron.

The Cricut Brightpad
The lightweight and low-profile design of the Cricut Brightpad reduces eyestrain while making crafting easier. It is designed to illuminate fine lines for tracing, cut lines for weeding and so much more!

Canvas Overview

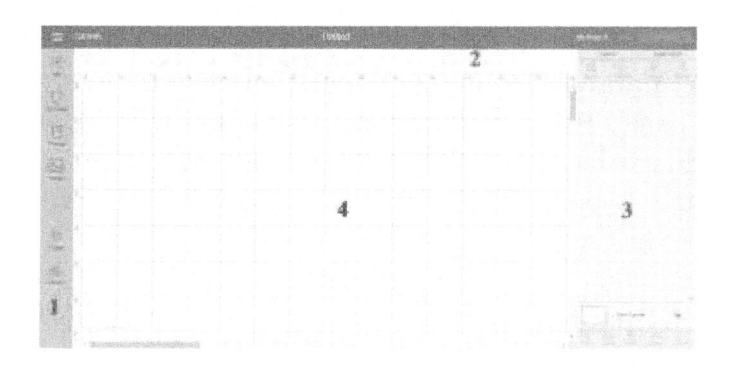

The canvas is where you will be spending the most time in this software. At first glance it appears intimidating and overwhelming however with time you'll get a clear understanding of the many icons, buttons, and option on this screen. Plus, you always have this book to guide you.

I have gone ahead and partitioned the above screen into four different sections (as you can see above) so you can understand better.

Left panel (marked 1)
this contains all the main insert area with functions such as
- New
- Templates
- Projects
- Images
- Text
- Shape
- Upload

Top menu panel (marked 2)
this is where most of the tools you need to edit your project are found. We shall study each tool in the next section of this book

Right layer panel (marked 3)
contains the layer panel. Every single object, shape, image or text you add to your design has a layer. As you add elements to your design the layer panel populates with the layers associated with the added element. (We shall see more on this in subsequent chapters).

Center canvas area (marked 4)
this is the canvas area where you'll see your design as it takes shape. As you can see from the screenshot above, it is the area with the gridlines.

I will work you through the four major section of this canvas. We shall cover every icon, every button, and every option. Keep reading. Let's start off with the left panel.

The left panel

New
This is the first option on the left panel. This option can be used to start a new project. Clicking on it would give you a new empty canvas. If you have been working on a project and click the new option, you'll see a pop up asking you if you wish to save you current work or replace it with a new canvas.

Template

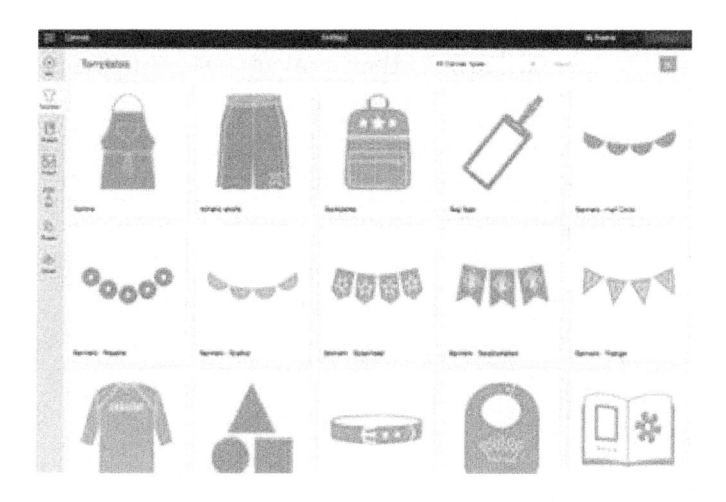

The template is the second tool on the left panel of your canvas. When you click on this icon you get a screen with lots of template to help you see exactly how your design would appear on a surface.

You can select a template of what you want to design and use it as a guide to create your own design.

So let's say you want to customize your shirt with a text. All you do is select the template of the shirts, adjust the size and dimensions and type in the text.

Next you place the text on where you want it to be on the shirt.

NOTE: the templates themselves cannot be cut out or saved. However they are useful to help you visualize and guide you in setting up the size, dimension, space, and other properties of your design. You don't need a template to start a project. But if you'll like to see how your design looks on a surface then a template is the perfect visual aid.

When working on a template you have the option to change/set the size. This can be found on the top left panel of the selected template. With a template selected, the canvas loads up the template and you see you template on the canvas. Now, if you check just above the canvas area, you'll see options to set the *'type'*, *'size'*, and *'color'* of the selected template. Use these options to set up the template as per your requirements.

Projects

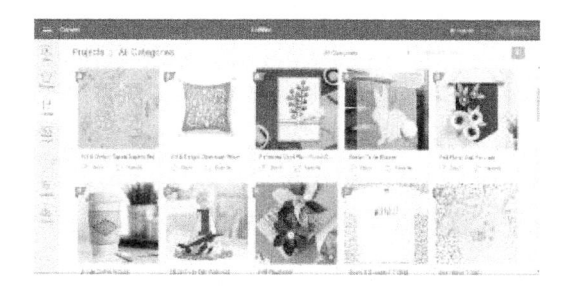

This is probably my favorite part of design space. The *'projects'* option offers you numerous design project which are already made for you. Thanks to this option, you do not have to be a design guru to craft out an awesome design.

All you need to do is click on the project icon. This will open up a screen with all the predesigned projects. Scroll down and choose any design you like and either just *make it* or *customize it*.

Note: the 'make it' button is just by the top right corner of your screen.

I like that you can decide to customize any of the projects from the list, or simple just hit make it to create the design. Awesome right!

Worthy of note is that not all the projects are free. You'll have to purchase some, however Cricut access members can use most of the projects. All projects with an '*a*' sign on a little green banner are available with your Cricut access subscription. However if you don't have a Cricut access subscription you can do a onetime purchase of any project you like. Once you purchase a design it'll be available for you to use at any time and as many times as you like.
But with Cricut you don't even have to purchase a design. There are lots of free designs that you can try as a beginner.

For beginners, I recommend you try out some of the free projects available. You can filter your search result by using the dropdown button located at the top right of the Project screen (check screenshot above).

Clicking on this drop down will help you narrow down your search by selecting from the list of project categories available.

Click on the *all categories* drop down now (top right corner of your screen) and take a look at the list of items there. They are simple inexhaustible.

Images

Going down the left panel is the images option. The image tool is useful to insert images into your design. So, let's say I want to design a tablecloth with the idea of a teddy bear on it. I'll click on the image icon and then scroll down the list of images displayed to find a picture of a teddy bear for my design.

Alternatively, you can choose to carry out a more focused search by clicking on the dropdown search button located at the top right corner of the screen. This allows you to simple type in what you're looking for (teddy bear) into the space provided.
You can also search for images using the *cartridges* or *categories* option at the top right corner of the screen.

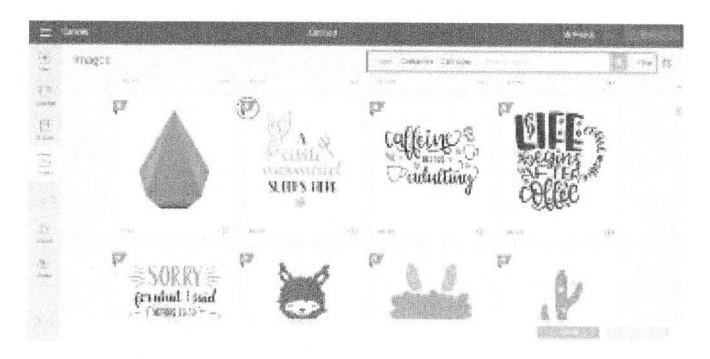

NOTE: the green "a" icon on an image tells you that the image is available if you have a Cricut access subscription. Other photos you would have to purchase.

You can also carry out your image search using the cartridges and categories option which can be seen at the top right corner of the screen, beside the search bar.

Another fantastic thing about the images option is that new images are added to the list every week. So, you never run out of ideas to use in personalizing your designs.

Text

Moving down the line is the text tool. This is a very important tool with much functionality. It may take you a while to master everything about this tool; however, it becomes easier with time and practice.

The first thing you'll notice when you click on the text tool is a blank work area with a text box. You type in your text in the box and it is seen on the blank canvas.

In the screenshot above, I typed in 'Hello World' and changed the text's color from the default black to purple. (We shall see more on how to use all of the top edit menu option later on) The second thing you'll notice is, with the text tool selected and a text typed in, a complex menu bar (edit menu) appears in the screen's top panel. This top menu panel contains all the icons and functions you'll need to edit your text.

Now permit me to work you through the top panel (text editor icons).

Located at the top left corner of the text edit panel is a drop-down button with the word '*font*'. Clicking on it allows you to change the font of your text. You can select thousands of font styles from, including Cricut fonts, system fonts (fonts installed on you PC).

You could also just decide to scroll down the list of available fonts to see which on suits your design.

Looking to the right of the same text menu panel (the top right corner), you'll see a search bar where you can simply type in the specific type of font you like, or just type in the criteria you require of the font. Doing this would give you only those fonts that fit the criteria you are looking for.

For example, if I type in 'system fonts' into the search bar, I'll only get those installed on my PC.

Now I believe you should know how to select fonts and navigate between different fonts style. Let's move on!

When working with text in design space most of the tools used in editing the book are located at the top tool menu (top panel when using the edit tool). You would find means to edit your text attributes and set how you would want them to appear in your design. These options include font size, font style, line and letter spacing, alignments, and so on.

The key to using these tools are the downward and upward pointing arrows.

So, if you want to decrease the font size of a text, you simply hit the down arrow. On the other hand, if you're going to increase the font size you hit the up arrow until you are satisfied with the result. This rule applies to most of the text editing tools.

Another tool I find useful is the isolate layer button. This is used to isolate a letter from a text, giving you the ability to edit that letter separately. So, you can choose to increase the size of a single message, change the font style, rotate it and so on.

The easiest way to isolate the letters in a text is to:
- Select the text on the canvas,
- Right click on the mouse and
- Select ungroup from the drop down.

Now you can work on each letter individually, customizing them as you like.

When you are satisfied with the outcome, you may need to regroup the letters so you can work (move, edit, rotate, etc) on the text as a whole.
To do this:
- Select the text
- Right click on the mouse button and click group.
- So far we have been going through the tools on the left panel in the canvas.
- After the text tool is the shape tool.

Are you confused about anything so far? Take a break. When you get back continue from where you stopped. Everything would be clear by the time you are done reading.

Shape

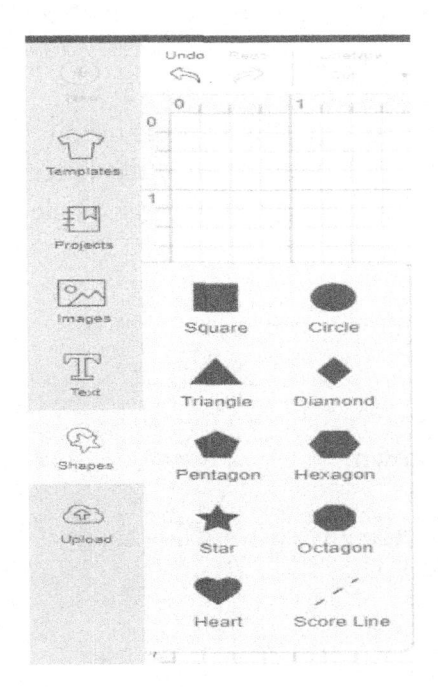

As the name suggest the shape tool can be used to place shapes into your design. There are about 9 shapes available for you to choose and mess around with: square, circles, heart shape, star shape, triangle and so on. The exciting thing about working with shape is the ability to customize them. You can add/change colors, add pattern, adjust the size, rotate, and so on.

- Click on the text tool and type in 'HELLO WORLD'
- Drag the text to the position you want.
- Resize the text using the bottom right resize handle on the selected text.
- Change the color of the text from the top menu bar
- Locate the curve tool at the top edit menu panel and drag the curve slider to the right. This action curves my text upwards as seen above.
- Click on the shape option and select the square shape.
- Resize the shape using the handle at the bottom right corner of the selected shape
- Right click the shape and select *'send to back'*. This sends the selected shape to the back of the text.
- Change the color of the shape from the top edit menu panel
- Click the images option on the left panel

- Scroll down and select an image I like.
- Resize the image using the handle and place it on the square shape.

Each individual color of the selected shape can be edited by clicking on the appropriate layer on the layer panel (right panel). More on this in the next section.

The above description is just a tip of what you can do with what you've learnt so far. We shall talk more on the *curve* tool, the *send to back* option and more as you read on.

Upload

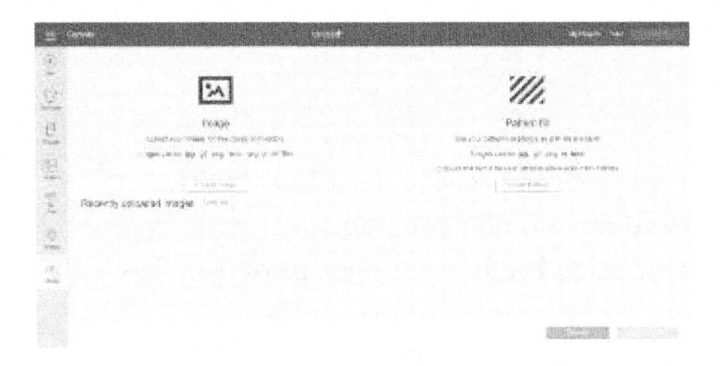

This is the last tool on the left panel of the canvas. When you click on it, it takes you to a screen where you can upload designs or images on your system to cut them with your Cricut. You could also get lots of pre-made designs from the internet, upload them into design space and cut them.

So, let's assume you have a design or a shape on your canvas. With the element selected, you'll notice that at the 4 corners of the condition are 4 different icons.

The first icon (top left edge) is a little 'x' sign. This can be used to close the shape/element at any time.

At the bottom left edge of the shape/design is an icon of a locked padlock. It is used to maintain the proportions of the element while resizing. If you do not want to keep balances, all you need to do is click on the padlock to unlock it.

At the top right edge of the shape or design is the handle for rotating the shape/element.
At the top left is the handle for resizing the shape to your desired size

Chapter 2: Project Design

How to Realize and Edit Cricut Project Ideas

Saving, accessing, and editing projects are very simple activities in Cricut Design Space.

-Saving, Accessing and Editing Projects in Cricut Design Space While Using a Desktop

Let us begin from the earliest starting point.

Saving a Job in Cricut Design Space Using a Desktop

Cricut Design Space does not offer you the luxury of autosaving your ventures, consequently (and as a decent practice), I prescribe that you save your undertaking after you place the principal piece, shape, or picture on the canvas region.

Now and again, tasks can take some time, and in the event that you don't save your activity as you work on it, your significant time and valuable work will go to the waste if Design Space Crashes.

Several people have lost numerous prior minutes working their exercise and not saving. In the end, they had to start over. Along these lines, if you don't mind, save as you work. Save changes on your ventures like clockwork or something close to that.

At the point when you start on a fresh out of the plastic new canvas, the Save option (situated on the upper right-hand corner of the window) is turned gray out, yet once you include a picture, it will enact.

To save your task, place the principal thing (picture, content, shapes, and so on.) you will use on your canvas.

At the point when you click on save, a little window will spring up, requesting that you name your task. On the off chance that you are just utilizing Cricut Images or textual styles, you will have the alternative to share your venture on Facebook or Pinterest.
Be that as it may, on the off chance that you utilize your pictures, "The public" choice won't show up. Try not to stress; however, you can even now share the things you have created from the "My projects" window.

Note: When you share ventures, you should acknowledge Cricut's Terms and Conditions; so ensure you concur with them.

In the wake of naming your undertaking, click on Save. A blue pennant will show up over the window, advising you that your project is saved.

Now, you can begin changing your plan by including content, evolving hues.
Simply make sure to save your venture each three to five minutes; trust me, you would prefer not to sit around idly if the program crashes.

If sooner or later, you need to make another venture, ensure your undertaking is saved.
<u>Opening a Project in Cricut Design Using a Desktop</u>

To open a venture you've just made, you have to have a clean and fresh out of the plastic new canvas.

You can discover your structures in two distinct ways.

The first and quickest one is tapping on the "My Projects" quick link situated on the right-hand corner of the window.

The subsequent path is by tapping on the Projects option on the left board of the canvas and going to the dropdown menu and selecting "My Projects." Check out the various options of the dropdown menu to discover ready cut activities.

From the "My Projects" view, you can alter, erase, modify, and cut your as of now made ventures.

There are better places you can tap on a specific task; in the event that you click on the "share" option, you will be provoked to include a depiction, photographs, and so forth. Also, in the event that you click on the three dots (base right of each undertaking), you will have the option to erase it.

Step by Step Instructions to Alter The Sharing Settings And Tweak A Venture In Cricut Design Space

You should tap on the included picture of your structure on the off chance that you need to tweak your venture or project or remove it right.

After clicking, a little window will open, and you'll have the option to share and observe the entirety of the data about the task, including the text styles, shapes, and pictures you utilized.
In particular, you can redo your venture from this window or send it to cut; this "Make it" quick route is incredible. Supposing that your task has been made, you can skirt all the Design Space process and immediately go to the Mat preview.

If you need to alter the presence of your plan, click on redo.
Presently, let us see how to alter your venture

Alter Projects in Cricut Design Space Using a Desktop
When you click on to alter for any venture, you will have the option to alter and change things around.

Welding and Slicing a picture in Cricut
Include Shape: Add a hover in the canvas and change color.
Weld: Select the first picture and snap on the weld device (base of the Layers Panel) to have the entirety of your plan in a solitary layer.
Slice: Place the welded picture in the circle and select both the circle and image and click on the Slice device (by the weld apparatus).
Keep the purple hover with the cut-out picture.
This altering is easy, I am certain you can improve, but what I need to tell you is the best way to continue in the wake of altering a task.
Pay attention to this; if you click on save, you will supersede your unique plan, and if that is the thing that you need, then that is alright. However, in the event that despite everything, you need to keep the undertaking you began with, click on save, and pick the option "Save As."

Saving an Undertaking with An Alternate Name in Cricut Design Space
At the point when you click on "Save As" you will be incited to change the name of your unique undertaking; for this situation, you can just include a "two" to the title.
Simple, isn't that so?

Presently, if you choose to utilize either plan once more, return to your activities and see that any of them are accessible.

Saving, Accessing and Editing Projects in Cricut Design Space While Using a Tablet, Ipad or Phone

The ways you take to spare, alter, and open a Project in Cricut's App are fundamentally the same as those you would use from your computer.

You can make sense of it rapidly, yet here I am to make it simple for you.
Note: On this little learning segment of the book, I accept you know a few nuts and bolts from Cricut's App, for example, change color, weld, slice, and so forth.

Including Another Venture and Venture Cautioning in Cricut Design Space App

Go to the "Home" view and tap on "New Project." If, despite everything you have unsaved changes, the application will bring an admonition. Select previews and save the entirety of the progressions and rehash a similar procedure to dispose of any sign.
Try not to mess with this notice; in the event that you don't save, your task will be lost.

Opening/Accessing a Project in Cricut Design Space App

To open a previously made undertaking, first, ensure your canvas is perfect (no different activities, text, pattern, or shapes and go to the "Home" perspective on the application.
On this view, and beneath your profile picture, there's a dropdown menu, click here and select where your undertaking is (Cloud or Ipad/iPhone).

Note: From this dropdown (and on the off chance that you are connected to the Internet) menu, you can likewise discover ready to cut activities, free undertakings for your machine, and so forth.

If the entirety of your activities is in the cloud, you should choose "My Projects on the Cloud."

From this view, "Home/My Projects in the Cloud," you can accomplish a few things on each venture.

If you tap on the "share" option, you will be incited to include a depiction, photographs, and so on of your venture. Furthermore, if you click on the three dots (base right of each venture), you will have the option to erase it.

You should tap on the highlighted picture of your plan on the off chance that you need to tweak your project or remove it right.

Tweaking A Made Task in Cricut Design Space App
After tapping, the perspective on your telephone will change, and you'll have the option to see the entirety of the data about the undertaking, including the textual styles, shapes, and pictures you utilized.

In particular, from this window, you can modify your project or send it to cut; this "Make it" quick link is extraordinary in such a case that your undertaking has been made, you can avoid all the Design Space process and go to the Mat preview immediately.

By and by, on the off chance that you need to alter the appearance of your structure, click on edit.

Presently we should see how to edit your undertaking.

Editing Projects in Cricut Design Space App
At the point when you tap on edit for any task, you will have the option to edit and change things around.

Editing a Picture in Cricut Design Space App
Select the entirety of the letters within the "daydream outline."
Weld the entirety of the inside letters.
Slice the outline of the layer using the welded letters.
Note: Slice and Weld are inside the activity's menu.
If you tap on save, you will override your unique structure, and if that is the thing that you need, incredible. Yet, if despite everything you need to keep the undertaking you began with, click on save and pick the choice "Save As."

Saving A Venture from A Previous One In Cricut Design Space App
At the point when you click on "Save As" you will be provoked to change the name of your unique task; for this situation, you can just include a "two" to the title.
Checking the entirety of the ventures in the cloud in the Cricut Design Space App
Presently, in case you choose to utilize either structure once more, return to the "Home" view and see that both of them are accessible.

Chapter 3: Using Images in Design Space

Images and how to browse for cartridges

Designs are made of elements hold on cartridges. Every cartridge comes with a keyboard overlay and instruction brochure. The plastic keyboard overlay indicates key alternatives for that cartridge solely. But recently urban center Craft has free a "Universal Overlay" that's compatible with all cartridges released when Lammas Day, 2013. The aim of the universal overlay is to modify the method of cutting by solely having to be told one keyboard overlay rather than having to learn the overlay for every individual cartridge. Styles will be cut out on a laptop with the Cricut style Studio software system, on a USB connected Traveler machine, or will be directly entered on the Cricut machine by using the keyboard connection.

There are 2 varieties of cartridges form and font. Every cartridge incorporates creative options that may give many different cuts from only 1 cartridge. There are presently many cartridges on the market, containing fonts and shapes, with new ones additional monthly.

Whereas some cartridges are introductory in content.

The Cricut line incorporates various costs; however, the cartridges are interchangeable, though not all choices on a cartridge could also be on the market with the smaller machines. All cartridges work solely with Cricut software system. They should be registered to one user to be used and can't be sold or given away. A casing learnt for a out of print machine is perhaps going to become useless at the purpose the machine is finished. Cricut stashes the correct to discontinue support for a few versions of their software system at any time, which may create some cartridges now obsolete.

How to purchase images and upload them

There are more than 50,000 images in the Cricut Library. With the Design space, you have permission to try these images for free in order to confirm its suitability in your desired project or projects and then after that you can purchase it.

www.cricut.com
You can also upload personal images unto the Canvas.

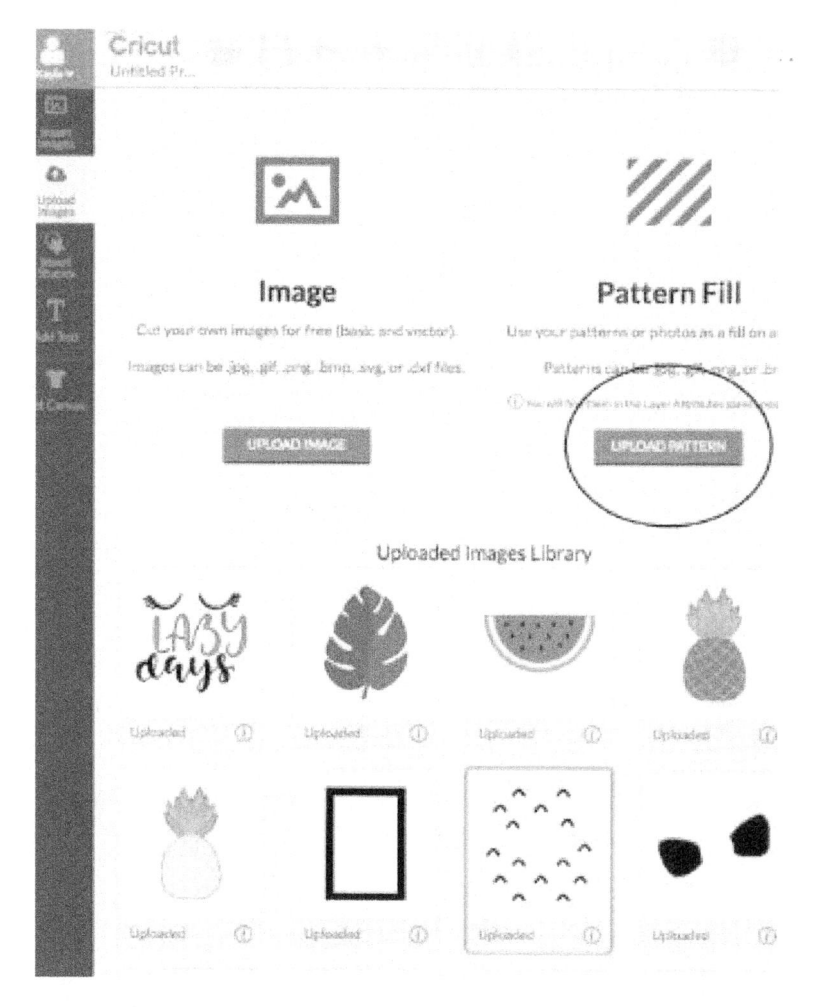

So, how do you use images in Cricut Design Space? Here are simple steps on how to use images in your project:

Create a new project by signing into your Design Space

Click on Images located at the left-hand side of the design screen if you are using Windows/Mac computer or tap on Image button situated at the bottom left corner of the design screen if you are using iOS/Android device.

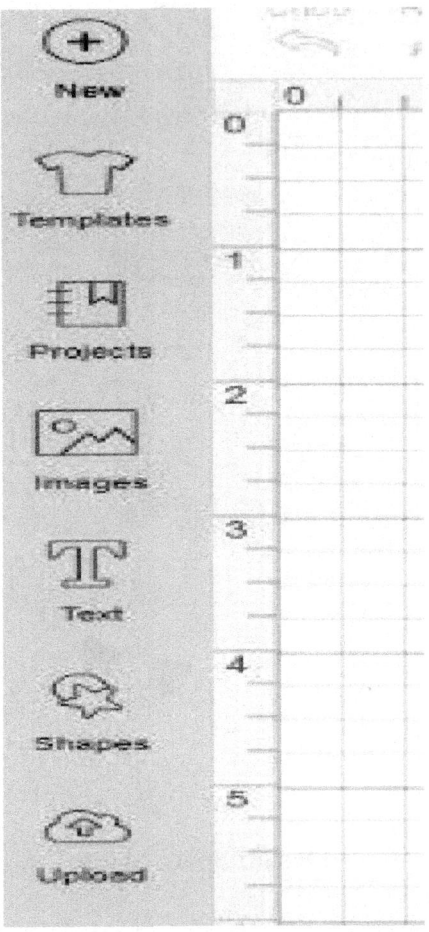

You can also browse, filter and search the images to choose the ones you intend to use in your project:

- All Images—use this option to search for a particular image in your Cricut Library or even view featured images

- Categories—use this option is more like filter tool. It is used to browse images by selecting any one of the image categories.

- Cartridges—use this option to search through the list of 400+ Cricut cartridges alphabetically or even search for a specific one.

Insert the desired image(s) into your project
Edit the images as much as you like.

How to Edit and Upload images in the cricut machine

In this part, we are going to learn how to edit or separate an uploaded picture into separate layers. Once you learn this technique you will be able to edit an image of your choice without problems.

First, you will need to browse the image on your computer and upload it using the "Upload" command. After that, you will want to choose, from the three image options, the "Complex" type. Once you have done all that just select "Continue".

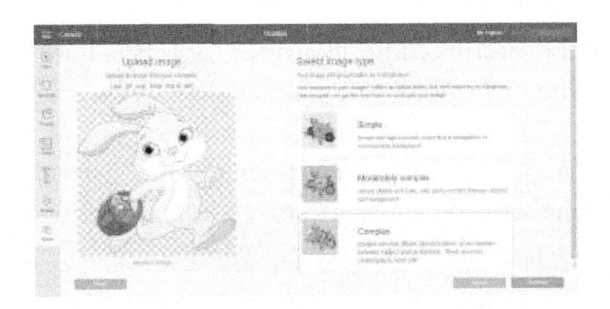

On the right part of the screen, you will have the option Undo/Redo any action or Zoom in/Zoom out from the image (1). On the left side you will have the most important tools for this job: "Select & erase", "Erase" and "Crop" (2). In this example, we will be using all three of these tools so you can get the full set of information from this technique. First, we will separate the basket from the rabbit and after that, we will separate the rabbit from the basket.

Step 1: If necessary, zoom out to be able to view the entire picture.

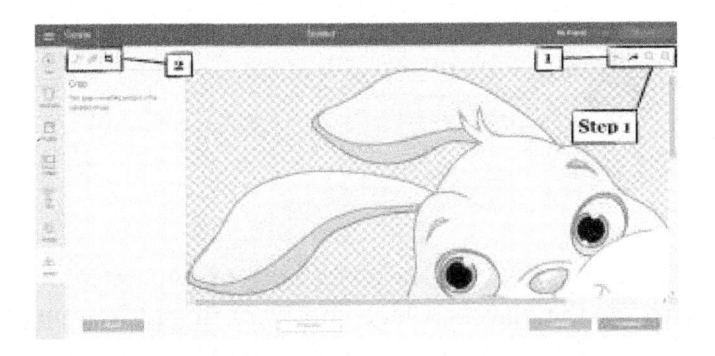

Step 2: If you want to separate a small part of a larger picture, use the "Crop" tool to isolate the targeted area. In this case, we need only the basket so most of the image can be cropped out.

Step 3: Once the rest of the image is cropped, we need to remove any part of the remaining picture that we don't want. To do that we can use the "Select & erase" tool.

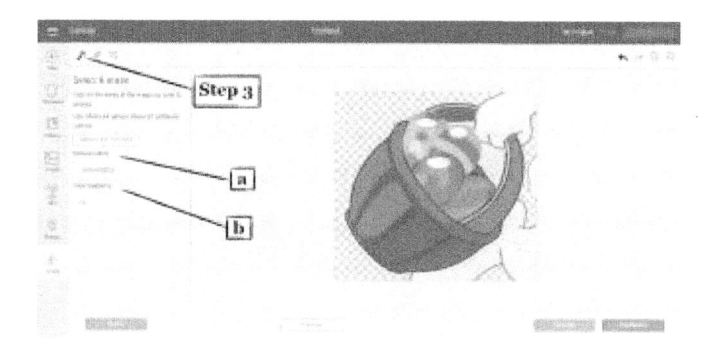

By selecting "Advanced Options" you can directly remove the color by using the "Reduce colors" tab (a). You can also increase the "Color tolerance" (b) which allows you to clear large portions more easily with the "select" method.

Step 4: To remove the fine lines and small details we can use the "Erase" tool.
Depending on your image you can increase or decrease the size of the eraser by moving the slider left or right.

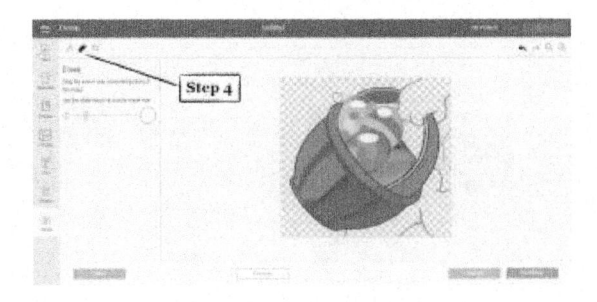

Step 5: Once you are satisfied with the result you can use the "Continue" button.

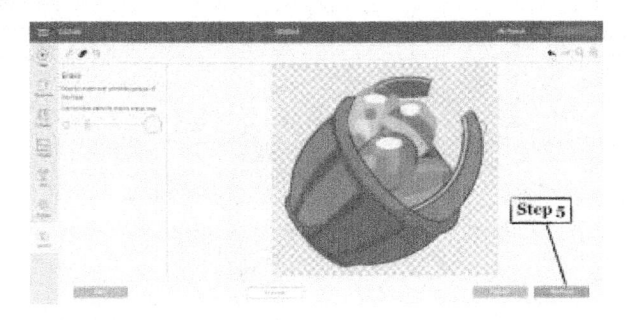

Step 6: Select the type of image that you want to save and click "Save". Here you can choose between a "Print then cut image" or "Cut image".

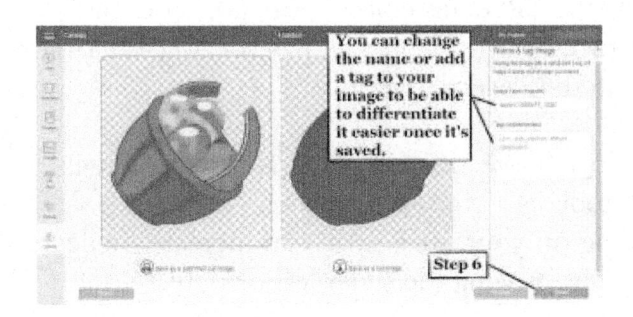

Step 7: Once we have our first part separated (the basket) we can move on to the rabbit. To do that we need to upload the image again and repeat the process.

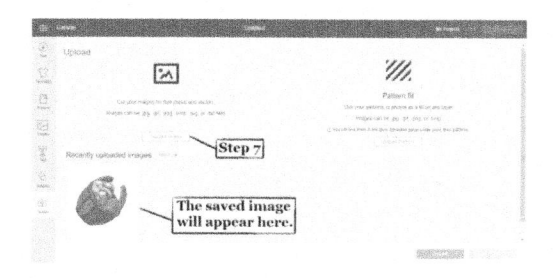

Step 8: Follow the same steps as before but now remove the basket using the "Select & erase" and the "Erase" tool again.

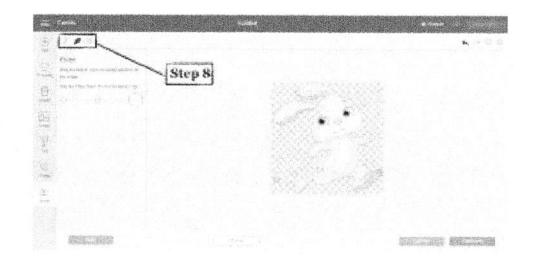

Step 9: Once the image is saved, we can add our separated pictures on our canvas. First, you have to select each image and then use the "Insert Images" button.

Each image is now considered as its own layer and can be resized, moved and edited to your liking.

Knockout Text Method

You've probably heard about this method or read about it on different forums. In the following example, we will take a step by step look at how to use it in your designs. However, this method is only limited by your imagination and as your skills progress you will quickly realize that it can be used in multiple ways to enhance your projects.

In this example, we will use it on a text object and by the end of it, you will learn how to add a personalized twist to any text you want.

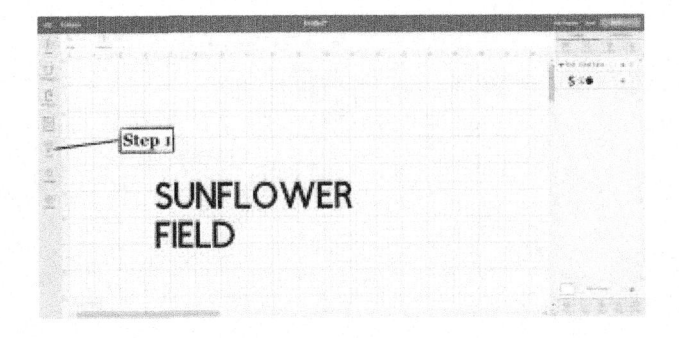

Step 1: It should go without saying but first you'll have to write your text on the canvas.

Step 2: This part is very important. Here we will edit the text in such a way that will allow the editing to be visible. You have to choose a font with thick letters. After that, you can change the spacing between the letters and the text rows. Depending on your design you might want to make sure that the letters won't touch each other. But this can vary from project to project.

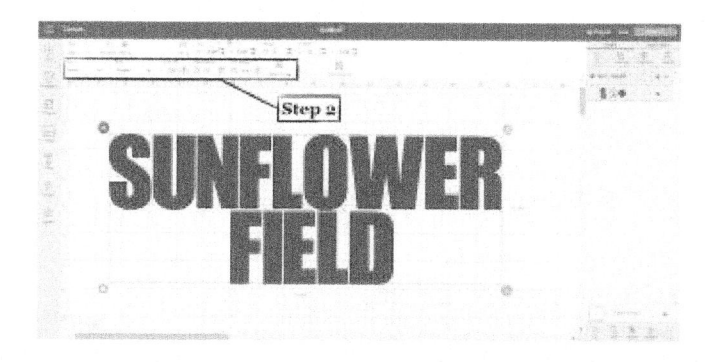

Step 3: Once you are satisfied with your text you can begin adding images that will later be embedded into the final design. In this step, you can let your creativity shine. You can choose pictures added to single letters or images that will be spread across multiple messages.

Decided whatever you think fits best.

Cricut for Beginners

Step 4: Since the images contain multiple layers, they have to be welded together. That is why you have to select all images, except the text, and use the "Weld" tool.

Even if you add a single image, if that image contains multiple layers, it still has to be welded so you can continue with this method.

Step 5: Once the images are welded together, select both remaining objects (text and welded image) and use the "Slice" tool.

Step 6: Don't be alarmed if after the "Slice" the result will look confusing. In this part, it's best first to select the sliced text and move it to the back of the canvas. That way you will know not to delete that layer.

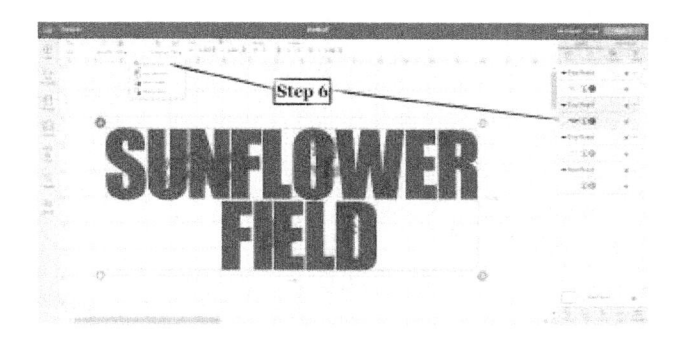

Step 7: All that remained now is to delete the extra objects that resulted after the "Slice".

You can use the on/off visibility option (eye symbol) for each layer to see if it actually has to be deleted or not.

As you can see in the final image the flower objects are now part of the text and the extra parts have been removed from the canvas.

This was just an example to illustrate how you can learn to use the "knockout" method. It's worth mentioning that this method is extremely versatile and can create a lot of different designs. Depending on your style and imagination you can adapt it and let your creativity run free.

In the next image, you can see a few more examples of this method.

Add Color to an Uploaded Image Outline

This method might seem a bit tricky at the beginning since it has a lot of steps. However, the idea is very simple, once you understand the concept you will be able to master it pretty quickly.

Cricut for Beginners

Step 1: Upload your image. It should have a clear and defined outline. Also, note that the more complex the image the more work you'll have to do to color each part. But more on that later.

Step 2: Select the image type as "Complex" and click "Continue".

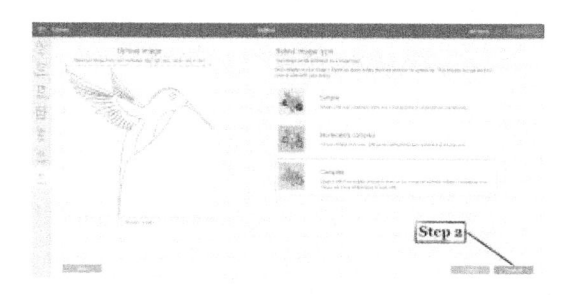

Step 3: If your image is not a .png file it will have a white background. For this method to work, you'll have to remove that background by using the "Select & erase" tool.

Cricut for Beginners

Step 4: Once you removed the background you should be left only with the outline of your picture.

Step 5: Select the type of the image to be and click "Continue". For this example, we saved it as a "Cut" image.

88

Cricut for Beginners

Step 6: After the image is uploaded and saved, add it to your canvas.

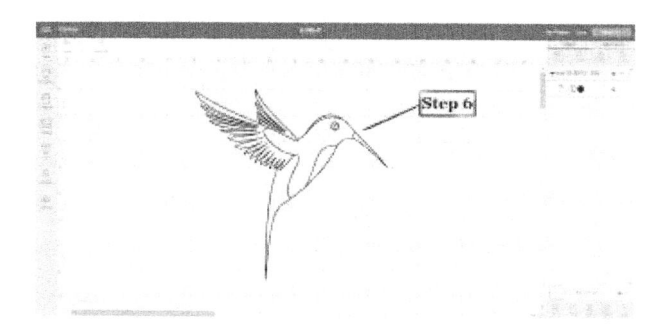

Step 7: In this step, you want to copy and paste your image. You can do that by using the combinations on your keyboard Ctrl + C and Ctrl + V. It's essential not to use the same function since it will not save the image in the system's memory. This will be important later on.

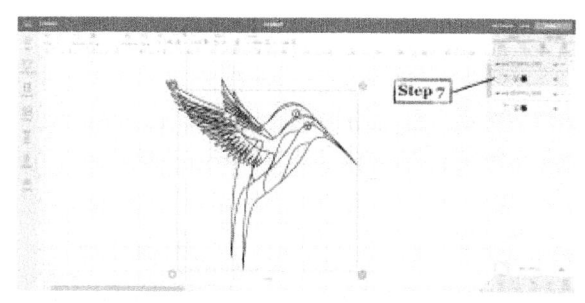

Step 8: Select both images and use the "Align" (Center) tool.

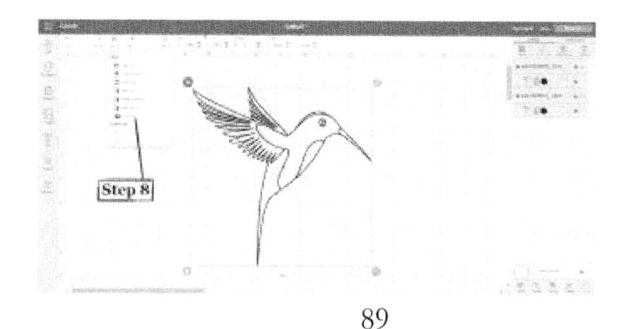

Step 9: Select the lowest image on the Layers tab and use the "Contour" tool.

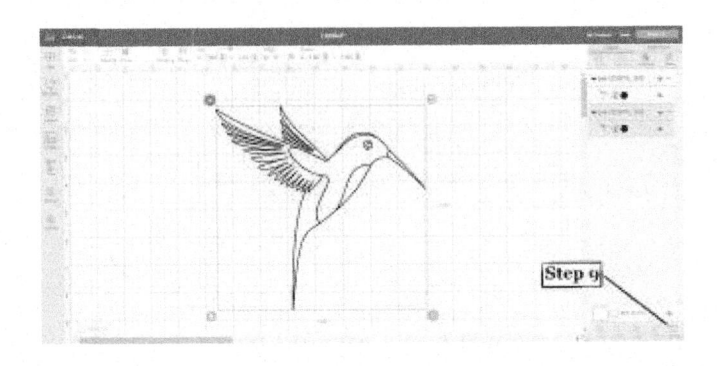

Step 10: This step is very important since from this window you will be selecting the part of the image you want to fill. To make it easier, here is a strategy you can follow for this step:
1. In the bottom right corner select "Hide All Contours".
2. Select the part of the image you want to fill.
3. Click somewhere outside the outer border of your image.
This way you will be left with the inside contour you want to color.

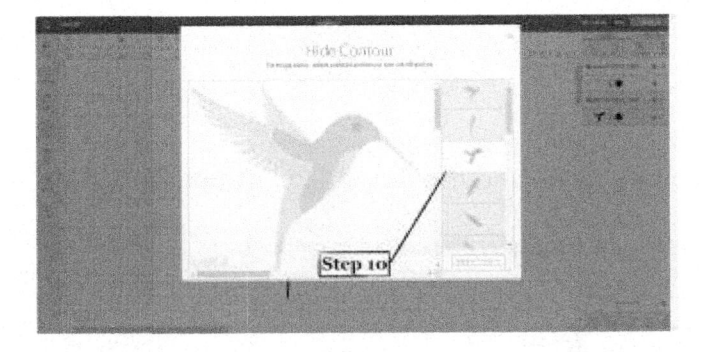

Step 11: Select the new image, that should be the inside contour and change it to the desired color.

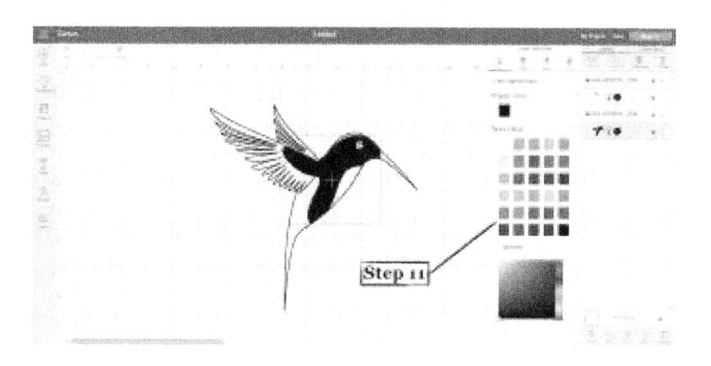

Step 12: The method to go smoothly from here now on it's better if the images are grouped. Therefore, you should select both images and use the "Group" command.

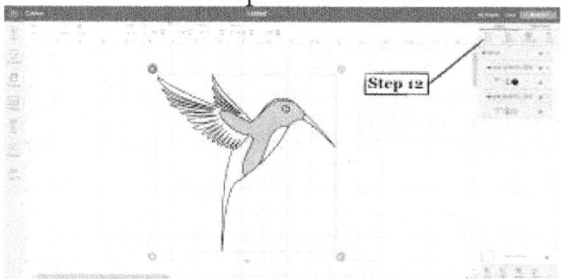

Step 13: If you used the Copy + Paste method, in the beginning, you can now just press Ctrl + V and paste another image outline.

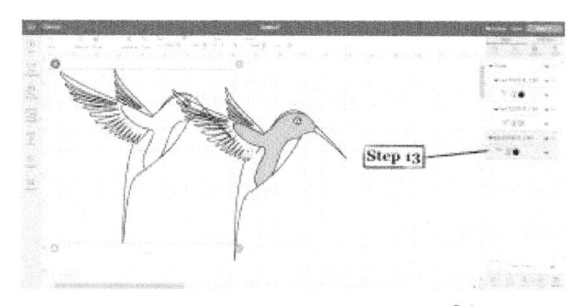

Cricut for Beginners

Step 14: Since our initial images are grouped, they can now be easily aligned with the newly added image outline. Select the group and the new image and use the "Align" (Center) tool.

Step 15: Once the images are aligned select the lowest image on the layers tab and use the "Contour" tool again.

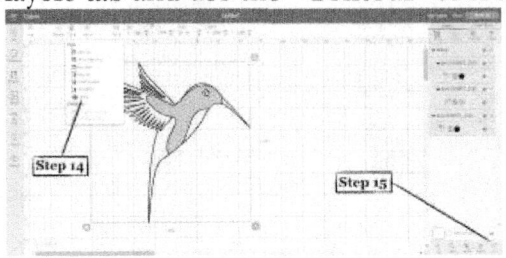

Step 16: Right now, you want to select another part of the image you want to fill. You can use the strategy from Step 10.

Step 17: Once you colored another part of the image you need to "Ungroup" the first group. That way you can avoid having a group within a group within a group later on.

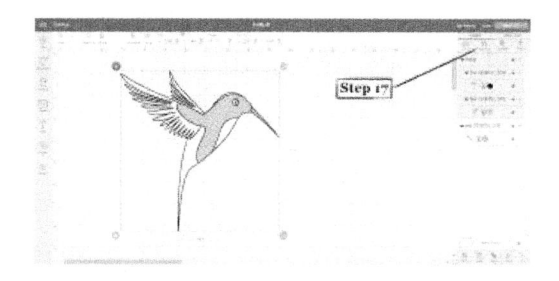

Step 18: Once all layers are ungrouped you can now use the "Group" tool on all existing layers.

Step 19: From now on you can just repeat Steps 13-18 until you filled every part of your image.

The result should be a fully colored image with a separate layer for each area.

Copy and paste

Step 1-On the canvas, pick the image, when you do this, the bounding Box will appear.
Step 2-in the edit bar menu; tap Edit, the tap Copy to copy the selected image to your clipboard.

Tip-You can also follow another method, by make use of your Pc or Mac keyboard (Use "Ctrl + C (PC) or ⌘ + C (Mac) to copy.

Step 3-In the Edit bar menu, tap Edit and go on to paste the image by clicking Paste from your clipboard, after that on the canvas, the copy of the image will be added, there will be a slim offset from the principal/original image, you can also check the new idea in the layers panel.
Tip-You can also follow another method, by make use of your Pc or Mac keyboard (Use "Ctrl + C (PC) or ⌘ + C (Mac) to copy.

Duplicating on the Layers Panel

Step1-On the canvas, pick the image, when you do this the bounding Box will appear.
Step 2 - At the top of the layers panel, tap on the duplicate button, duplicated copy of the original image will appear with a slight offset. You can also check the new idea in the layers panel.

How to convert a pdf to PNG format

After downloading the PDF document to your computer, open your browser and go to png2pdf.com.
Click on the upload files

The "Open File" dialog box starts. Locate the PDF file to convert (probably in the Downloads folder), click the PDF file and click the file is uploaded. You should see a progress bar. Once the file has been uploaded and converted, a Download button appears below the small image of the uploaded file.

Click on the download the file is downloaded as a ZIP file and appears in the status bar at the bottom of the screen. Just click on the filename to open the ZIP file.

The Open File dialog opens, and the downloaded file should be displayed. Since the file is still in ZIP format, you must first unzip or unzip it. Just click Extract All Files.

The Open File dialog opens, and your newly converted PDF file should be displayed in PNG file. You can open the file with a double-click if you only want to see what the file looks like. Close the window now by clicking on the red X.

After you have converted your PDF file to PNG format, you must upload the PNG file to Cricut® Design Space so that you can use the Print and Cut functions.

Chapter 4: Advanced Tips and Tricks

Font

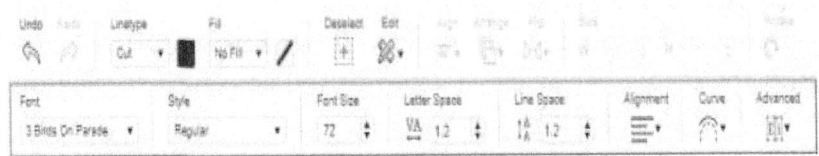

This tool lets you choose from the many font styles available for your design project. You can either use your system fonts or use the font available for those with a Cricut access subscription.

There is a search bar at the top right where you can enter in specific font name or filter the fonts result shown by either system fonts, or access fonts.

Fonts with a little green 'a' sign indicate that the font is only available to Cricut access members. If you must use one of those fonts without an access subscription, you'll have to pay for them.

Style
This is used to select the style you'll like your fonts written in. there are 4 available option to choose from:

Regular
Default font style

Bold
Increase the thickness of the font

Italic
Font appears a little bit tilted

Bold italic
Font thickness increases and is also tilted

Font size
This can be set using the resize icon of the selected text in your canvas. However, you can also set the font size from the top panel's font size option. The downward pointing arrow reduces the font size and the upward pointing arrow increases it. You can also choose to enter a number in the box provided to set the font size.

Finding That Perfect Font

After you click that "Text" button on the Design Panel and type the text you're going to type it into the textbox, it's time to choose what font you're going to use. We already talked about how to choose your font using the Text Edit Bar. I want to discuss the specifics.

Choices, Choices
When you click on the dropdown menu under "Font" on the Text Edit Menu, you'll get a new bar like this:
This bar allows you to choose which font you want to use, which is pretty obvious. The thing that might not be as obvious is, "What do I do with these three options at the top — 'All,' 'System,' and 'Cricut?'"

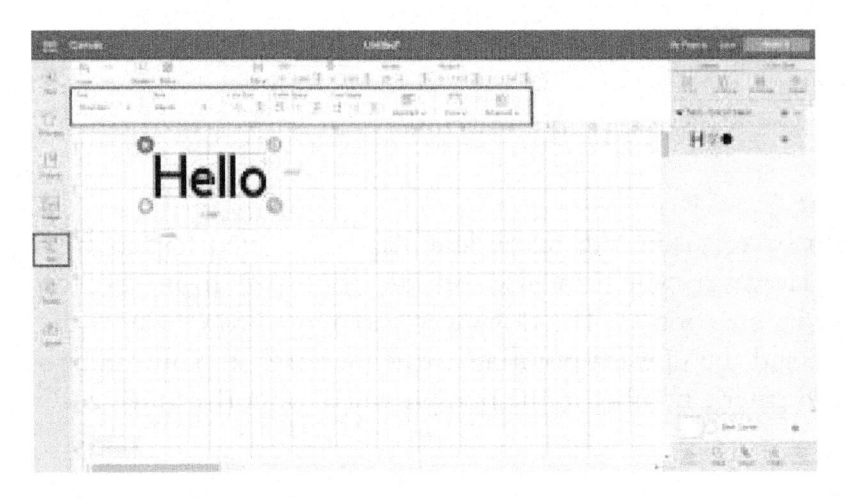

Pressing "All" brings up every font available to be used in Cricut Design Space. Clicking "System" will show you only the fonts that already downloaded on your PC. If you click "Cricut," Design Space will show you only the fonts that are available through Cricut Design Space.

Filter
Because there are so many different types of fonts available through Cricut, they created a few simple ways to find the one you want. One way is by using the "Search Bar." This, of course works for searching for your system's font as well as for a font in the Cricut system.
The other way is through the "Filter" option. You'll see the clickable word, "Filter," to the right of the "Search" bar.

Under "Filter" is "My Fonts," "MultiLayer," "Single-Layer," and "Writing." These groups are pretty self-explanatory.

"My Fonts" are fonts that you own. They are fonts that are on your system, yes. Still, they also include any fonts you uploaded to Cricut, fonts Cricut offers for free, and fonts that you've already purchased.

"MultiLayer" fonts are fonts that have more than one layer. If you were to use any multilayer fonts on your Canvas, they'd show up as two or more layers that could be separated and dealt with individually at will.

"Single Layer" fonts are fonts that show up as only one layer in your Layers Panel. "Single Layer" fonts and "Writing" fonts are the only fonts that can be sliced.

"Writing" fonts are the fonts that are specifically made for the Cricut to be able to write out instead of cut out. Most of the Cricut fonts — and most fonts, as far as that goes, are made thick. Cricut fonts have to be thick so that they can be cut out. System fonts are often on the thicker side for good visibility.

Because of the thickness of most fonts, Cricut was sure to designate a category for "Writing" fonts and even to create some anew. In the picture below, I included a Single Layered "Writing" font.

To make it even better, they allow you to choose more than one at one time. In the screenshot below, I have "Peace" written twice. With the top "Peace," I used a multilayer font. For the bottom "Peace," I searched for a font using the filters "Writing," "My Fonts," and "MultiLayered." Both "Peace's" are out of the same font. The second is simply formatted for "Writing."

Notice the multiple layers listed beside the top "Peace." The bottom "Peace," though taken from a "MultiLayer" font, is "Single Layered" since it is chosen as a "Writing" style.
There are some neat writing fonts, too. They don't all merely look like lines. Consider the following two. I think these have to be my two favorite "Writing" fonts.

Style

Some "MultiLayered" fonts can be easily made into "Writing" fonts with a click of the mouse. Others, however, do not have that option. Let me explain.

If you look next door to "Font" on the Text Edit Bar, you'll see "Style." The drop-box there can be sneaky. It changes things up with every font. Some fonts have more styles available to it than others. The possible styles are:

· Regular
· Bold
· Italic
· Bold Italic
· Writing
· Writing Italic

Some fonts can be manipulated more thoroughly than others. Some cannot be italicized or made bold. In the same way, some fonts cannot be made into "Writing" fonts, but you'd be surprised at some of them that can be! Take the following for example:

This is a "MultiLayer" font. You wouldn't expect to be able to change this font into a "Writing" font. However, you will notice that Cricut Design Space altered the look of the font to make it happen.

I changed this "MultiLayered" font into a "Writing" font by clicking the drop menu for "Styles" and selecting "Writing."

You will notice, though, that this font is only manipulatable to the point of changing to a "Writing" font. It cannot be changed to "Bold," "Italic," or "Bold Italic."

Here's an example of one more manipulatable "MultiLayer" font. This one is the opposite. It cannot be made a "Writing" font. It can, however, be made "Bold," "Italic," and "Bold Italic."

Notice how the available selections in the dropdown menu changed. These selections may differ with every font to some degree.

How to Edit Fonts

The Edit bar in Cricut design Space, grants you access to edit the features of particular images or text. These features include Linetype, Size, Rotate, Fill, Position and Mirror. In the Text layers, there are additional options in the Text layers including Line Spacing, font styles and letter spacing. So how do you edit the font? Here, I will show you.

Select the text object you want to edit on the Canvas or you can insert text from design panel, or select a text layer from the Layers Panel. Once it is selected, the Text Edit Bar will pop up directly below Standard Edit Bar. Note that the Standard Edit Bar will be hidden when you are not interacting with the text.

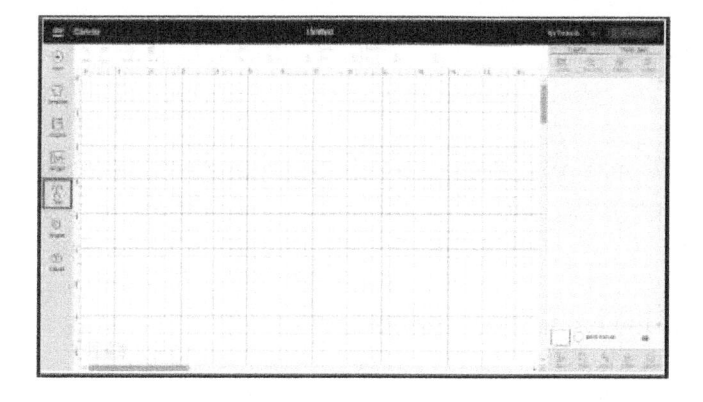

When the Text Edit Bar pops up, you can begin to manipulate the font using the options described below. Simple right?

Edit projects at Cricut design space desktop

After you click to customize for any job, you may be able to edit and switch things about.
Insert form: insert a circle at the picture and change color.
Weld: choose the original picture and click the welding instrument (base of the Layers panel) to have everyone our layout in one layer.

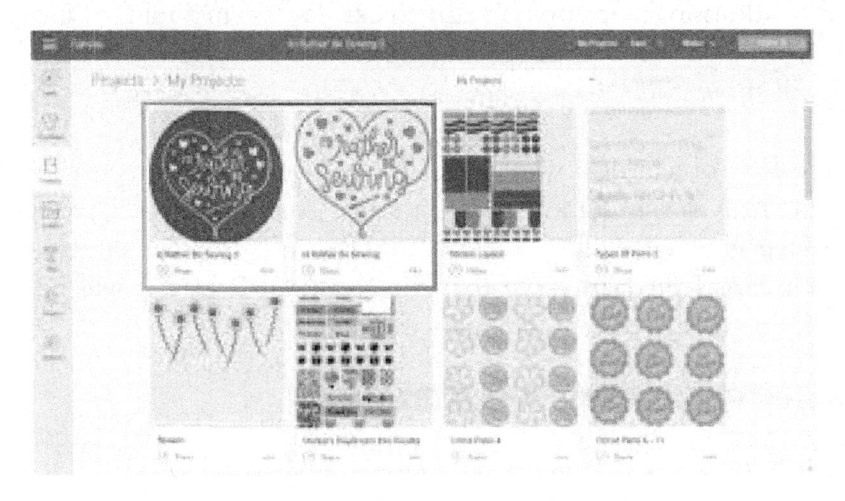

Twist: set the plotted picture in the centre of the ring and then pick either the circle, listen to it, and click the slice tool (alongside the welding instrument).

Maintain the purple ring using a cut-out image.

Here is the item, should you click save you may re-evaluate your initial layout and what you need right. However, if you still need to maintain the job you began with, click save and pick the option "save."

After you click "save," you'll be motivated to change the title of your first job

But if you choose to use either layout again, return to your jobs and see any available information.

Save the project in the Cricut design space app

Even the Cricut design space app includes three unique views, home, canvas, and create.

Usually, when you open the program, the opinion will be put into "home." to begin focusing on a new job, click the large blue square using all the plus sign tap "canvas."

After you tap saves, a small window will pop up in which you can enter the title of your job, and in which you would like to save your undertaking.

Choose "save on the cloud" in case you wish to get into your jobs from your pc, and you've got a trusted online connection. Choose "save iPad/iPhone" in case you do not have imagined the internet and enjoy having the ability to operate offline.

When choosing "save iPad," you will not have the ability to see those jobs in your pc. But you're going to have the ability to utilize that job again and again with no world wide web.

Save changes as you work in your style because if the program crashes, you may drop all your hard labor.

Proceed to the "house" perspective and tap "new project." should you have unsaved changes; the program provides a warning. Select previews and rescue everyone the adjustments and repeat the identical procedure to eliminate any hint.

Do not take this warning lightly; if you do not save, your project will be most likely.

Open a job in Cricut design space app.

First, to start an already established endeavor, be sure that your canvas is blank (no additional endeavors, text, layout, or contours) and proceed to the "house" perspective of this program.

With this perspective, and bellow your profile image, there is a dropdown menu, then click and choose where your job is (cloud or iPad/iPhone).

Notice: from that dropdown (also if you're linked to the web) menu, then you could even locate prepared to lower jobs, no-cost jobs on your system, *etc*.

If you tap the "chat" option, you'll be motivated to add a description, photographs, *etc*. Your undertaking. And, in case you click the three dots (bottom-right of every job), then you'll have the ability to delete it manually.

If you would like to customize your job or reduce it right away, then you'll have to tap the featured picture of your design.
Upon tapping on the perspective of your telephone will alter, and you will be in a position to observe all the info regarding the job, such as the fonts, shapes, and graphics you've got.

Most of all, from that window, you can personalize your job or ship it to reduce this "make it" shortcut is excellent as if your post was produced, it is possible to skip all of the design space procedures and visit the mat preview straight away.
But if you would like to edit the look of your layout, click customize.

Adding color to an uploaded image, and how to make multiple layer vinyl

Select it and resize it to whatever size you need for your venture once the layout is put on the canvas. Once you have the volume, you need to go to the board of parts and choose' ungroup.' Ungrouping enables us to transfer each layer in place of the entire layout independently.

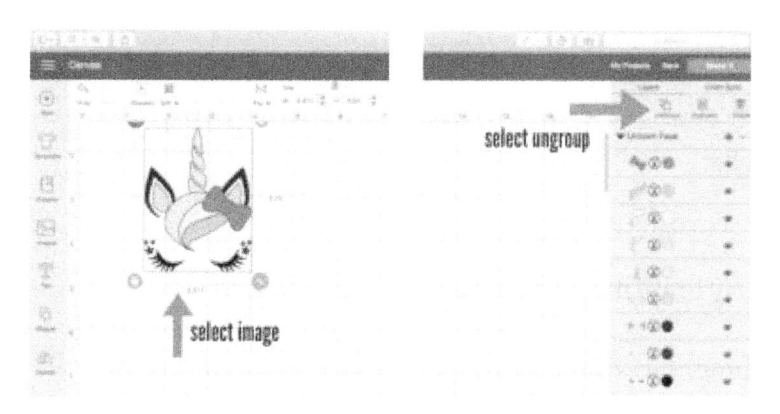

Insert a Shape as a Registration Mark

Next, put a shape in it. I used a square, but with stars and triangles, I also saw it. Insert the court and click on the 'unlock' button to manipulate the image in a rectangle. Duplicate it once you have the box size you want it to be.

Line up each rectangle below the original image. These are your registration marks to keep the design aligned on every layer.

Cricut for Beginners

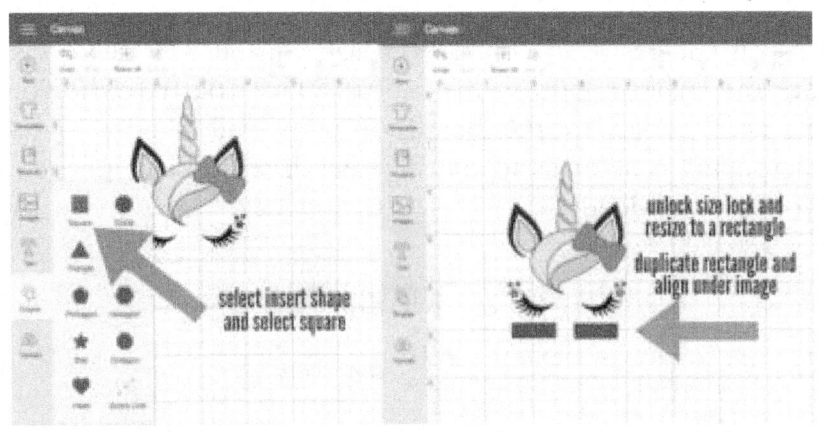

[Screenshot: select insert shape and select square; unlock size lock and resize to a rectangle, duplicate rectangle and align under image]

Duplicate Original Image and Registration Marks

Select everything and duplicate it after the original image has the registration marks under it. You're going to do this for every color you have. If you have six colors, you're going to double six times.

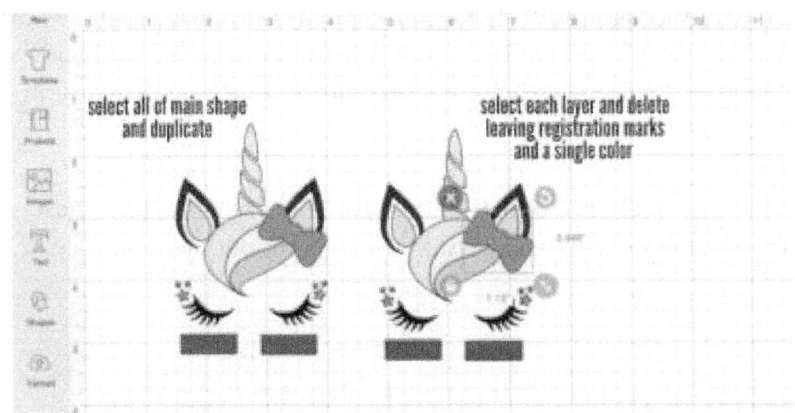

[Screenshot: select all of main shape and duplicate; select each layer and delete leaving registration marks and a single color]

Delete Layers Leaving A Single Color Delete each layer at the moment, leaving only one color for each picture you duplicated. For the inner ears, I didn't have light purple, so I chose not to trim that portion.

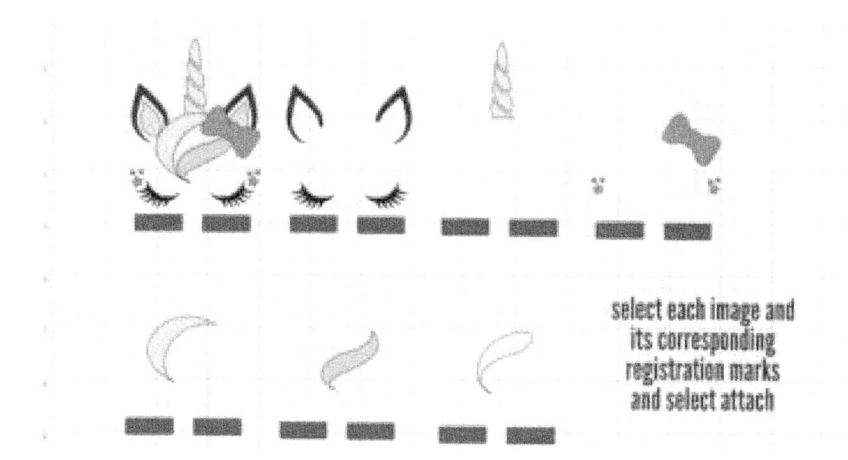

select each image and
its corresponding
registration marks
and select attach

Attach each Set of Images

Choose each layer picture and its respective registration marks (not the primary picture) and then pick' add.' When you go to trim, this will hold the image and the registration marks in position. Otherwise, by putting them as near as feasible, Design Space will attempt to save your equipment. It's not going to assist us!

You will realize that the registration marks shift to the color of your layer if you pick' add.'

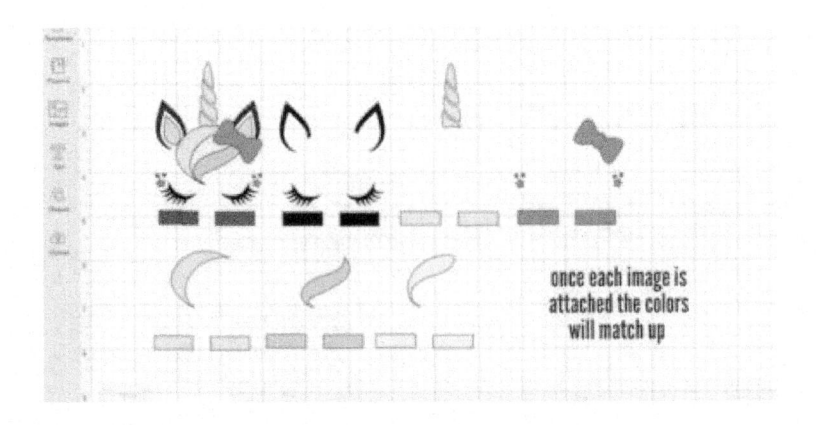

once each image is attached the colors will match up

How to layer vinyl with registration marks

Hide and hide the main image!

We need to conceal the primary picture before the plates are effectively sliced. If not, it will also attempt to split each of its parts. Select the registry marks and the primary image. Select' band' and then press the little eyeball in the layer's cabinet. It is supposed to hide that primary picture, and it will not be trimmed.

To send the project to the mat, select' Make it.' Every color is going to be on its mat. Cut every color, then weed the picture.

SIDE NOTE*: If you prefer to use scraps instead of charging and reloading each color, pick all pictures and grab' add' after hiding the primary image. They're all going to change gray, so you're going to have to remember the color you wished for each chip. It's all going to be on one mat when it comes to the folding board. Each of your color scraps can be placed where the paper demonstrates they are cutting.

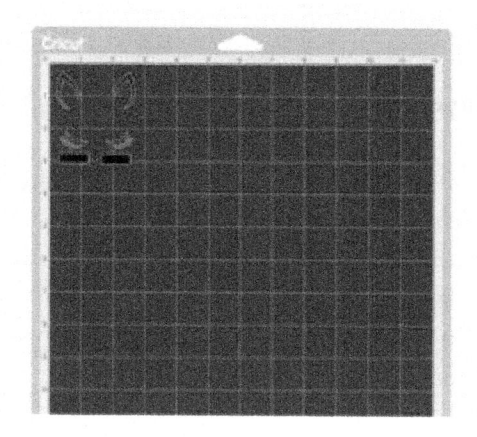

Weed Vinyl Pieces and Apply Transfer Tape

Weed leaving only the design and register marks on each layer.

How to layer vinyl with registration marks/ Weed each layer

Add each layer to the Top Layer Down Transfer Tape
The only thing you need to care about is the rectangles as you operate through the layers. Everything else will be as soon as they're lined up. I want to say it's so easy, but it wasn't really for me. It helped tremendously but knowing that you may not line up every rectangle perfectly. It's all right. Adjust and stay tuned!

How to layer vinyl with registration marks

I just folded back the paper support where only the rectangles appear, instead of separating the whole paper base of the vinyl and then layering. This can assist you more correctly line up the rectangles. It's okay whatever direction it operates for you. There is no way to' correct' or' false.'

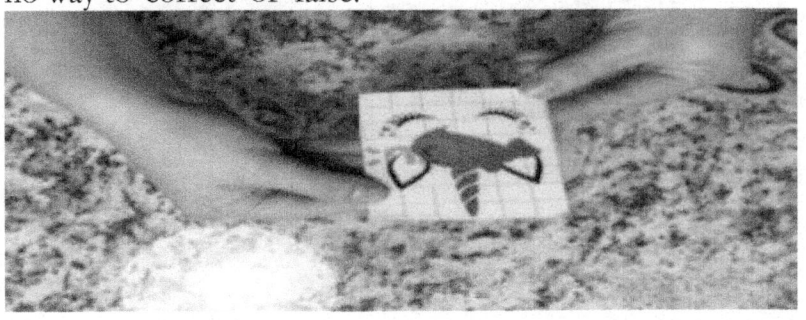

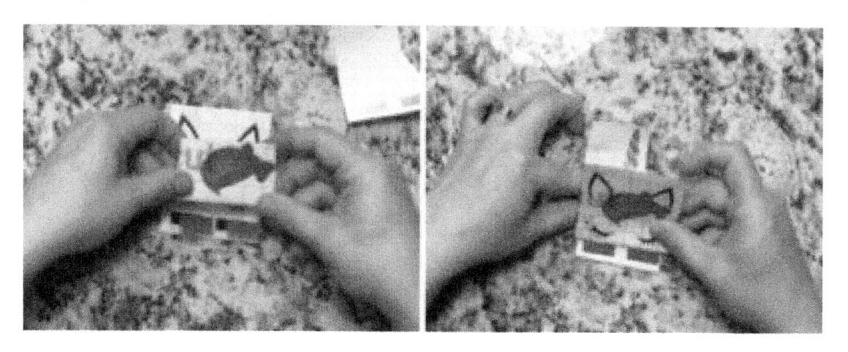

How to do split lettering with a décor

Use this monogram split-level tutorial on vinyl, heat transfer vinyl, and more in Cricut Design Space! The monogram on the split level is likely my favorite right now. I don't just like the look, but I believe it's less used than other traditional kinds of a monogram. Did you understand that in Cricut Design Space, you can create a split-level monogram? It's easy, but a few steps and the use of the slice tool are required. Open the design space for Cricut, and let's create one!

To start with, type the letter you want to split (or letters). Change it to the font you'd like. At the very end, for your project, you can resize it to the size, so do not worry about it right now. I use the font below for Cake Basics.

On the left-hand menu, select "insert shapes" and add a square. Click the lock icon on the square's lower left hand, so it turns to unlock.

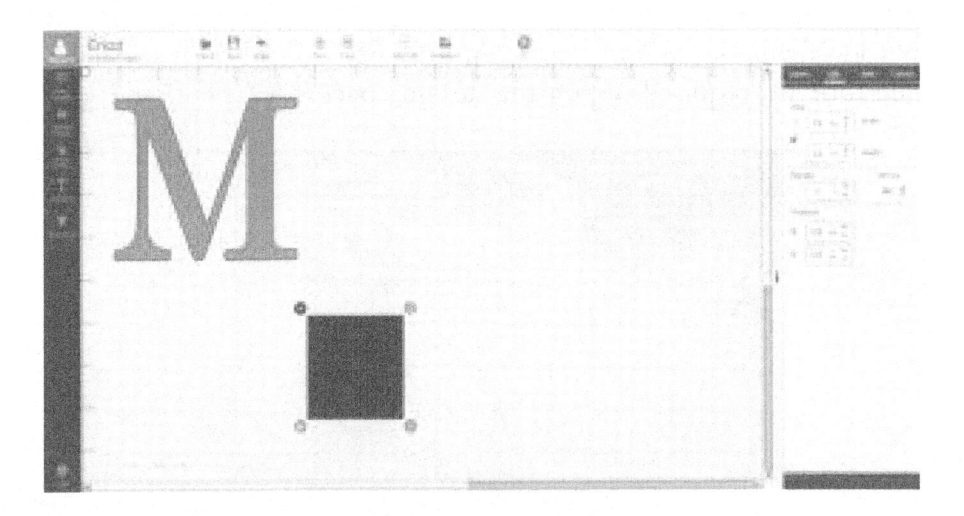

To make a rectangle, pull the circle. This rectangle will be the divided row (see the completed illustration-the row about the complete title and below it).

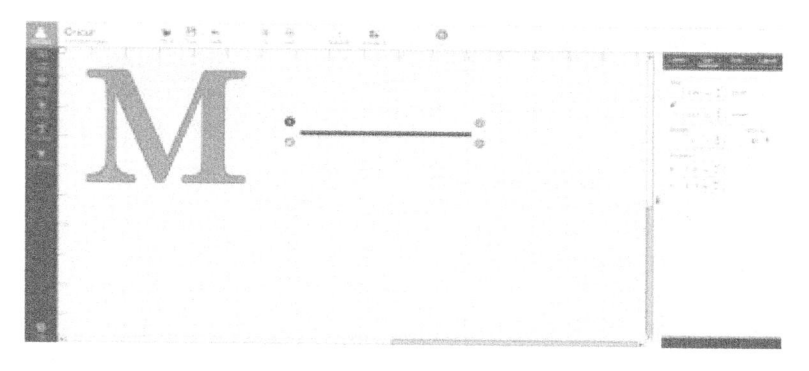

To generate a copy, copy, and paste this rectangle.

Pullover the large letter one rectangle. Keep in mind that the bottom part of the divided column is determined wherever you position the row. Select the rectangle and the large letter once the rectangle is placed and then press "Weld" on the board of the correct side parts.

Pull the second rectangle over and SPLIT the FIRST RECTANGLE.

Check to open the lock button and then draw down the SECOND rectangle to cover the text's upper part. Select the second rectangle and the letter that has been welded. Click the "slice" button.

Delete all the components except for the large letter's bottom and the upper quarter.

Add the word/name to the center.

Make sure all layers are aligned and centered as you want. Select all of them, then press "Attach" on the board of correct layers.

You can resize the whole item to suit your design once the parts are connected. Then submit it for cutting. All performed! All accomplished!

How to edit (cut, copy, paste) in the design space

To duplicate an image on the design screen is done in two ways copy and paste Duplicate on the layer Panel
After you have completed your entire project, you may wish to have multiple copies of the project, this can be done by changing the number of projects on the mat preview, and this applied the changes by clicking 'Apply'

Option 1 Copy and paste
*Step 1-*On the canvas, pick the image, when you do this, the bounding Box will appear.
Step 2- in the edit bar menu; tap Edit, the tap Copy to copy the selected image to your clipboard.
You can also follow another method, by make use of your Pc or Mac keyboard (Use "Ctrl + C (PC) or ⌘ + C (Mac) to copy.

***Step 3*-**In the Edit bar menu, tap Edit and go on to paste the image by clicking Paste from your clipboard, after that on the canvas, the copy of the image will be added, there will be a slim offset from the main/original image, you can also check the new image in the layers panel.

You can also follow another method, by make use of your Pc or Mac keyboard (Use "Ctrl + C (PC) or ⌘ + C (Mac) to copy.

Option two Duplicating on the Layers Panel

***Step1*-** On the canvas, pick the image, when you do this the bounding Box will appear.

***Step 2* -** At the top of the layers panel, tap on the duplicate button, duplicated copy of the original image will appear with a slim offset. You can also check the new image in the layers panel.

Grouping and ungrouping

How to group and ungroup in Cricut design space

***Step 1*-** This give you the opportunity to size, move, and, the rotate different/multiple images on the canvas as a single object. Grouping of images on canvas is done to make it easy to work with images on the design screen. Group will not affect the image's appearance on the cutting mat; grouping of single or many images together is possible.

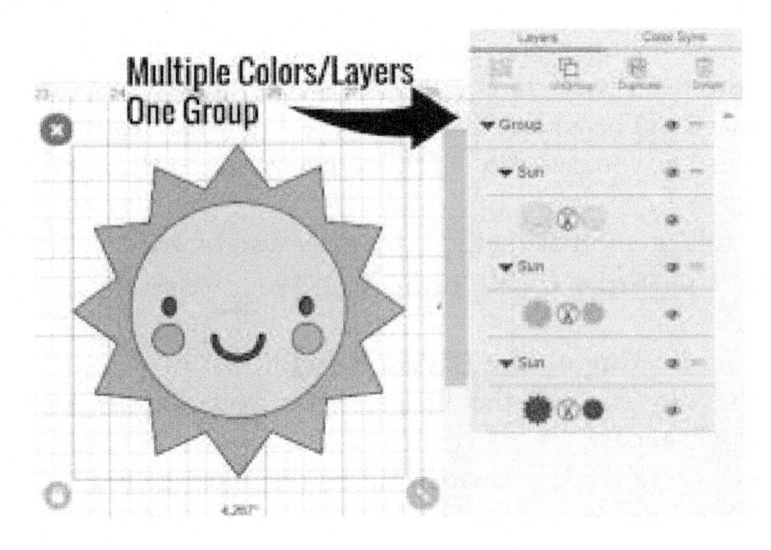

Step 2- Layers of a particular image automatically are grouped together. If you insert multilayered images to the canvas, every layer will be highlighted in grey. When you change a multilayered image on the canvas, this shows that highlighted layers is a group image.

You cannot edit (individual layers) within a set of grouped images. Editing includes changing the layer color, Layer line type, and hiding layer.

Step 3- Ungrouping an image gives you the access to work with individual layer. Choose the image on the design screen, at the top of the layers panel, choose the ungrouped button m

Step 4- You can move, sized, and rotate individual layers separately. It will appear as separate collapsible section in the layer panel.

Step 5- You can regroup layers by taking or choosing both layers on the design screen at the top of the layers panel, click group. Your newly group image will be shown in the layer panel.

Attach

Attached to hold cut placement

This tool can do two things. 1-It helps you hold your cut in the same position on the cutting mat and the way they appear on the design screen. two-It helps to quicking your write or score line to a cut layer. Below are the instructions on how to use your attached to in holding your images in place.

First of all, you need to know that all projects are cut in paper size mode, so all images are automatically placed together to conserve material on the cut mat. You need to hold your cuts ***imposition***. This allows your image on the cutting mats to position as they appear on the design screen.

When using transfer material such as vinyl, attach helps you keep images and keep text positioned relative to each other.

Step 1- Start by adding images and text to a canvas, notes arrange the images and text the way you want them to be as this is your choice.

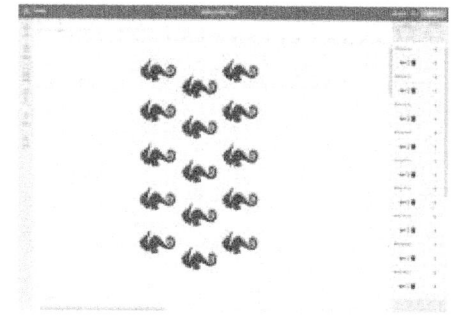

Whenever an image as more than one color, you must first ungroup them. The attach tool will help you convert or change all chosen layers or all selected layers into a single color that can be put on the same mat.

As soon as the layers attached, you can group them with other layers, it will not affect how the project cut on the mat.

You must choose two or more layers before you can attach.
Step 2- Every image you love to hold in specific position select them then going to click unattached in the layer panel.

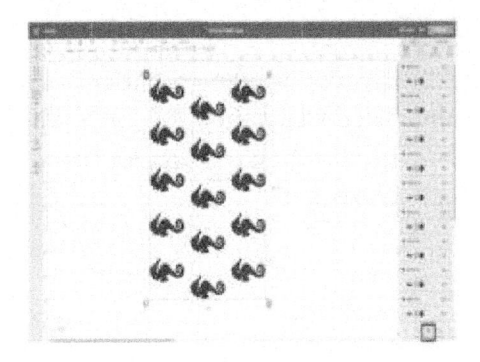

When are you feel like changing the placement of the image after you have attached the images, you can detached an image, by selecting detach in layers panel.

Note- you can make use of detach option when editing an attached text.

Step 3- For you to know if your images are attached, go to the layers panel, the attached image will be labeled Attach. Whenever you are ready to cut, select "Make it".

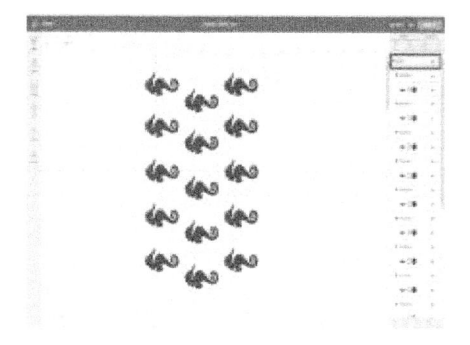

Step 4- How you want your project to be arranged the images will be shown on the match preview, go on to click "make it" the follow instructions on the design screen to cut your project.

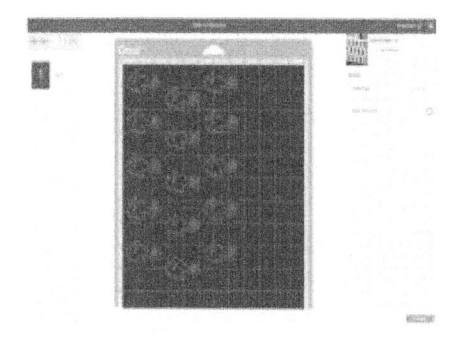

Attach different line type

This attach features are very important in Cricut design space. It is used to help fasten a write or score line to a cut layer. In a situation where you are working with more than one layer in a project, the right or score lines is needed to attach to a different or separate layer, in order for it to be written on a particular place or Location.

The Cricut machines have the capacity to write or draw ***on different materials.*** The cited examples (candy wrapped) have a cut-out text including images that are removed and all written. The written needs or anything that is drawn should be attached to a different layer.

The Cricut machines have the ability to add score lines to a project. The cited example below contains score Lines. Remember or projects having a container score line should have the score line attached to a different layer in the Cricut design space.

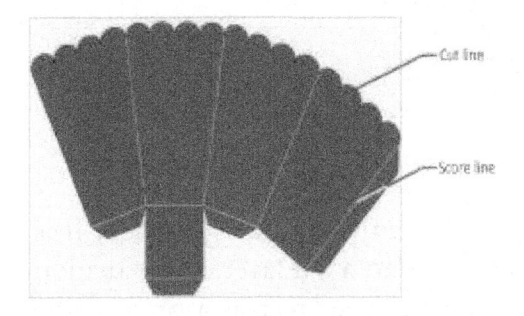

Whenever items in design space and not attached, it (design space) will cuts in paper save mode, this tells us that automatically design space replace objects on their own cutting mat in order to conserve material.

For you to easily fastening write to cut layers, images on the mat are positioned correctly as they appear on the canvas, we help of attaching, because attaching helps you to your cut in position.

In order for you to fasten alright or Score line in cutting a layer follow the instructions below.

Attach a writer score line to a cut layer
Step 1- Customize your image.

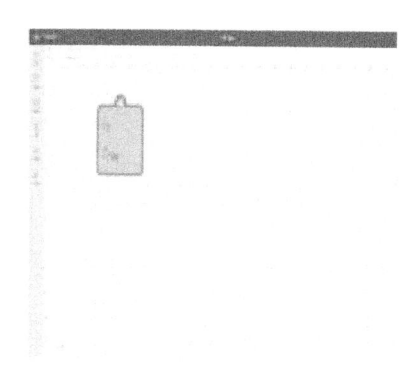

Before you can attach a right or score line to a multilayer image the first thing you do is to include the multilayer image this will help you to avoid attaching all the layers

Step two- You need to choose a Score line, write, or draw and the layer, you want to write on or score.

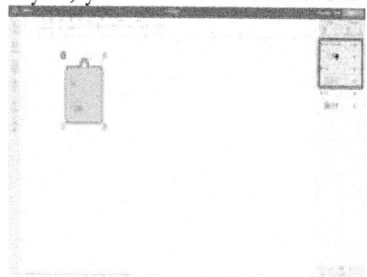

Step 3- At the bottom of the layers panel, select attach after you must have choose all images you want. The text B changed to a

photo and the text or score line will be placed on the layer that is attached to

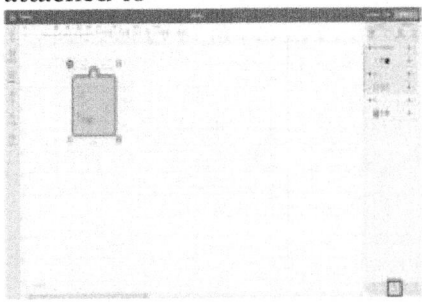

Step 4- In the layer panel all attached image will be labeled as attached. To begin cutting, click on make it.

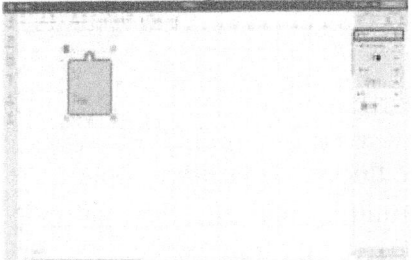

Step 5- *The* way they were arranged i.e. images, on the canvas that is all it will appear on the mat.

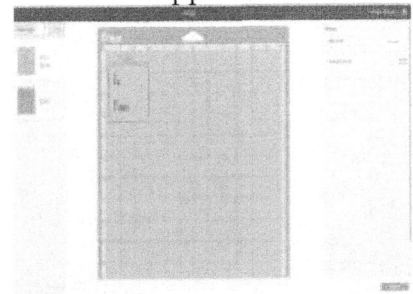

Whenever you are cutting, you will be asked to insert your Cricut pen all scoring stylus, when you need it.

Color sync panel

This allows you to sync up layer colors to decrease the amount of materials you have decided to use in your current projects. Sync color is when you drag a layer and a drop it on another layer.

Step 1- to open the color sync panel, click on the sync button.
Step 2- click and hold a layer handle, going to drag the layer on top of another layer and then release it.
Step 3- after you have followed the step 1 and step two processes the first layer color will transform or change to the second layer.

Flattering an unflattering

In design space using flattering tool give you the access to change any image to printed image for the print then cut feature. The flattering to help to flatten turn image into a single layer.

Unflatten tool
Unflatten tool on the other hand, helps to separate flattened layers, if the image is multilayered, unflatten tool also help to separate layers of an enhanced picture image.

The app does not support printing of layer, i.e. you cannot print layer from the app. But the app supports the design of Project with print layer. So, to complete the project you need to make use of design space on your PC or Mac system

To change individual layers into printable image, you can change the line type it to achieve this aim. The print will be printed separately. For more information [visit changing line type located in layer panel] you can use the flatten tool to join two or more images into a single printed image.

How to flatter images and layers
Positive images make it possible for you to transform/change standard images into a printable image. You can as well flatter both standard and enhanced printable image together.

***Step 1*-**Open the image panel, by clicking the image button, then select standard image (of any kind) from the Cricut image library, then put in/insert it into your current Project.
If you have flattened image, it can be uploaded making use of design space.

Step 2- Make use of the layer button to open layer panel, by clicking on the button. Use the action button to open the action panel.

Step 3- Pick the Layers (two or more) you would like to flatten, go on to select them.

Step 4- Flatten layers for printing in the action panel, by clicking on the flatten button.

When the layer is flattened, it will show as a single layer in the layer panel, you'll also see the label "flattened sets "showing the layers flattened. You will also notice a printer icon next to

Layer thumbnail, the printer icon shows you can print and cut.

Before flattering, the line layer of the image must be set to cut, for more information" click changing line type" located in the layer panel.

How to unflatter standard images

In Cricut design space, you can separate flattered standard images, into individual layers, when you are unflattering them.

Step 1- To open the layer panel and action panel, click on the layer button and action button respectively.

Step 2- The image you want to flatten, select it

Step 3- In layers panel, tap the unflatten button to separate the flattened image into single layers.

How to unflatter multilayered enhanced printable images

In Design space, you can separate multilayered enhanced printable images into single layer when you unflatten them.

Step 1- Open the insert image panel, by clicking image button. Go to the filter menu, open it and click on multilayer". Select enhanced printable images in the cricket image library. To identify (an enhanced printable images) you will notice a printable icon, located at the top left corner of the image tile, add it to your project by clicking insert.

Step 2- choose the image

Step 3- to separate the flattened image into single layers as shown in Layer panel, select the on floating button in the action panel to achieve this aim.

In the layers panel some layers might have icon that depicts an eye with a line through it, notes-they are hidden layers. For more clarification" click hiding and unhiding "located in layers panel.

How to Add text in Cricut design

In circuit design space to personalize your project using text and different fronts is very easy and convenient Visit the following steps to personalize text

Step 1- For you to slot in book onto the design screen, select the tab for book, which is on the left area of the canvas [located in the design panel], once you click on it, an empty text box with a text edit field will pop up on the device on a design screen.

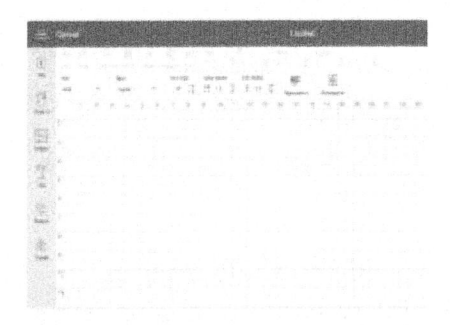

Step 2- Then you can type in your text in the text edit field then wait as it appears in a textbox for you to create line breaks you can use the keyboard return key to do that.

The first few letters of text in the layer panel represents the name of the group. Also, the individual layers is represented by the first letter of a text

Step 3- On the canvas, you cannot conveniently move, size, and rotate the fix as you wish and for you to do this click on the black area of any letter that is click on the black site of any message to move it on the canvas conveniently.

Bounding box
This is a box that appears around your text whenever it is selected by you the corners in a bounding box, let's you to make a fast and quick edit. In order for you to view the bounding box choose the text by selecting all the solid area of all of the letters

Red x (top left)
You can remove the text from the design screen when you click the red x on the top of the left corner of the bounding box after you

have done that the text you will disappear on the design screen and it will never appear automatically to be deleted from a layers panel.

Rotation handle (top right)
You can rotate the text by clicking and holding the circular arrow icon on the left corner of the bounding box and then drag it in any position as you wish whenever you make changes the text location will be reflected in the grey army Decatur near the image.

Lock (bottom left)
You will notice a closed lock icon on the bottom left corner of the volume box this shows you will be able to change the width and height at a constant ratio as well as saving the text proportional. For you to unlock the aspect ratio all you have to do is click the aspect ratio wrong to open it. InDesign space when you're not the aspect ratio this helps you to resize image and independently change weight and height freely.

Sizing Handle (bottom right)
This allows you to censor text with locked or unlocked proportion do this by clicking and holding the season handle on the bottom right corner of the bounding box and then drag in any Direction to see how the text will change automatically.

Step 4- For you to change the size of text, all you have to do is click and drag the season handle on the bottom right corner of the bounding box.

Keep in mind that whenever you are doing this the result of the vertical Dimension of a text appears to the bottom and right of burning books will definitely change as you are dragging the sizing Handle

How to size detect with lock proportions. Click and then holder season 1 do then drag it diagonally we locked closed.

For you to size the text with unlocked proportion. Press the lock to open position the news a season handle to drag diagonally. As soon as you release the sizing handle, note that the following selected numbers will be updated in the Edit bar on the top of the canvas. The font size, width (W), height (H) numbers Step 5- *For you to change your rotation of the text select the cycle handle these are the following shortcuts to rotate your text in the 45 degrees increments*

The undo button is used to make any changes, if you don't like the results of the rotation.

How to edit text in Cricut design space

Step 1- When you select the text on the canvas, the text editor will appear at the top of the canvas

Step two- You can make use of the front menu to select any of 370 fonts available for you to use. Keep in mind that for you to make use of some font, you need to join the Cricut access membership.

We can identify Cricut access fonts with a green "a" symbol which is located on the left-hand side. For you to use some fonts you have to purchase them. And to know the fonts that are available, you can make use of the filters at the top of the front menu, e.g. all font, system fonts, or Cricut fonts. At the upper right-hand corner, you can type into the search bar to search any font's name you feel like using.

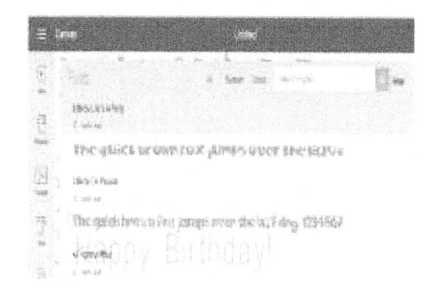

Sometimes when your mouse moves a string of text (sample), it will move to the left automatically which enables you to preview all the letters and symbol instantly.

In order for you to avoid causing letters in the samples scream to scroll automatically, when you scroll with the mouse to the list vertically, make sure your mouse is moved to the far-left corner or right corner, before you begin scrolling up and down.

Step 3- In the style menu you can access all applicable Styles e.g. bold italic, italic regular bold). Note that, every font definitely has its own styles, some fonts have the ***everyday Style*** while others are the ***bold style***.

Step 4- For you to adjust the size of the font, you are to make use of the font size menu, by clicking the font size, and then changing it, by typing new numbers i.e. [12,13, or 14]. And you can also make use of the up and down arrows to adjust your font size anytime you want.

Step 5- Also to adjust the spacing in between each letter in a text make use of the letters space menu to achieve this, and for you to increase and decrease the amount of space between the letters, you can make use of the up and down arrows.

Step 6- In a paragraph of text, you can adjust the spacing between each row by making use of the line space menu. And the amount of space between each row can be increased or decreased by making use of the up and down arrows.

Step 7- For you to align a paragraph of text either to the left to the right or justified, you can make use of the alignment menu to achieve this aim.

Step 8 -You can separate text of group into small units with the advanced menu that allows you to edit on the canvas. A string of text can be separated into separate letters (i.e. ungrouped to letters), different rows of text (i.e. ungrouped to lines), also into separate layers (ungrouped to layers).

Ungrouped to letters
Separation of each letter of text into his own letters makes it quick to rotate resize or delete individual letters that will not affect others.

Ungroup to lines
Separation of a true love text into its own layer makes it quick and fast to rotate color, resize or delete individual rows of text that do not affect others.

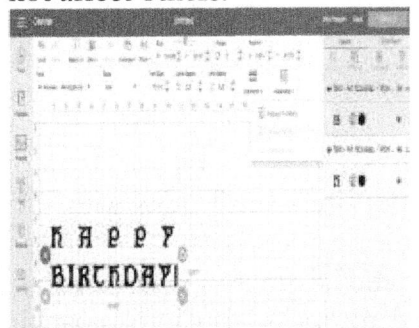

Ungroup to Layers
When you separate each layer of multi-colored text into its own layer makes it's to resize color, rotate or delete in the lower layers.

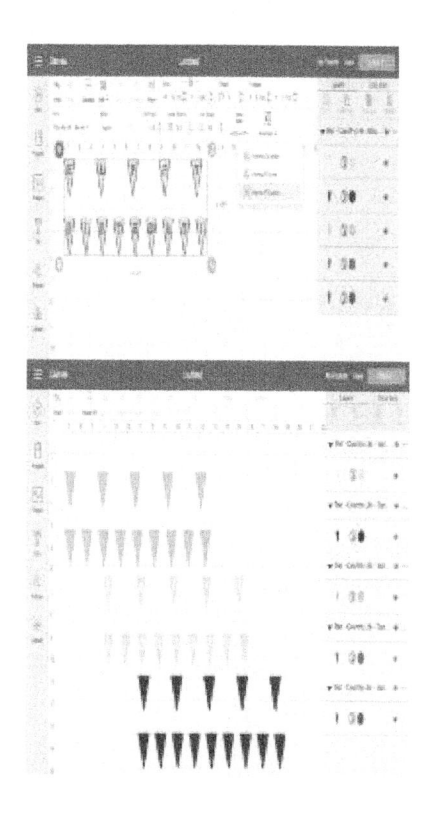

Curving Your Text

Another fun tool in Cricut Design Space is "Curve." You'll find "Curve" between "Alignment" and "Advanced." When you click on "Curve," it throws down a slide bar for you. You slide the bar to the right to curve the ends of the words down and left to curve them up.

If you thought curving that little bit of text was fun, you don't have to stop there. You can curve, un-curve, and recurve as many times as you want!

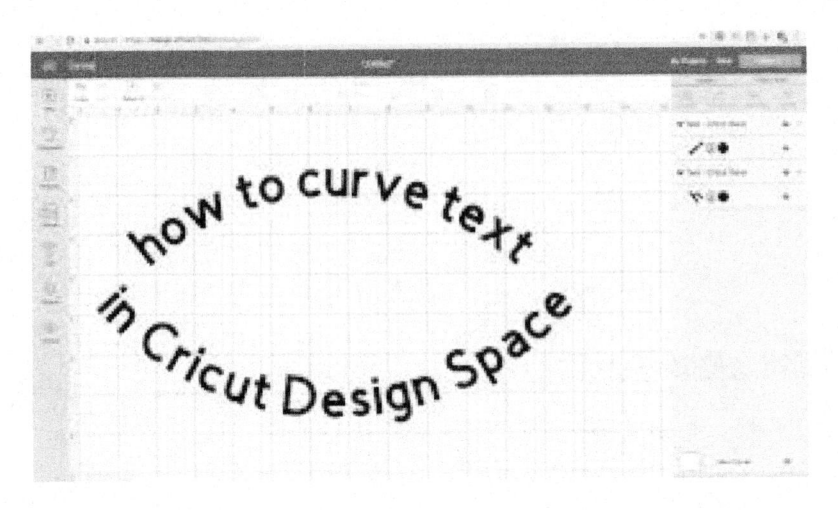

When you unlock your image by pressing the padlock in the lower, left-hand side, you can squeeze it so thin that it actually inverts.

Attaching Text

You know how to attach images. Attaching text is exactly the same. The only difference is that you're going to take a few more steps to get there. Now you could just put the word there and attach it. Presto! Done! But, what's the fun in that? Instead, try Ungrouping your letters and placing them exactly where and how you want them. Then attach them!

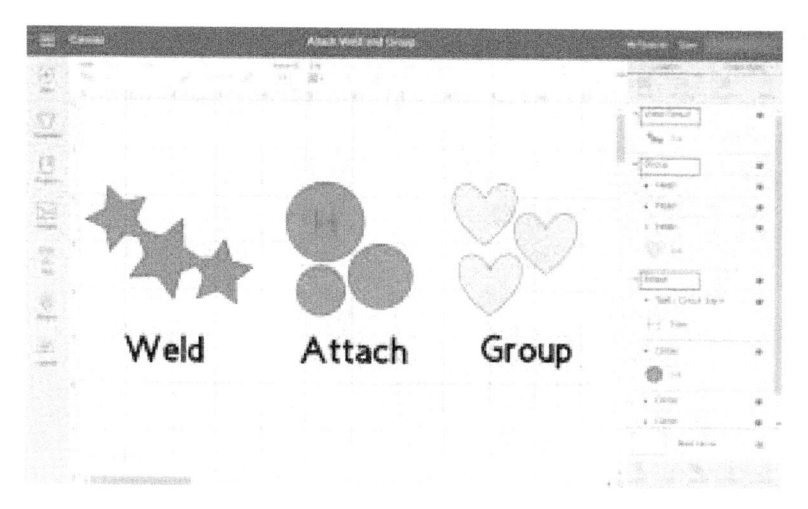

Another thing you want to remember: If you plan for your words to stay just like that to be cut out or printed instead of being thrown on their own mats and cut out individually, be sure to Attach them or Weld them together!

Making a Shadow

It's very simple to do. There's actually two different ways I'm going to show you. The easy way and the hard way. I'll show you the hard way first since the easy way is my little shortcut.
· Both ways start out the same:
· Click "Text" and type in what you'd like. I'm using my name.
· Choose your font.
· Make it bold.

- Move the letters as close together as you want them. Remember that you can "Ungroup to Letters" to get them lined up just perfect if you want to.
- Weld them together.
- Drag your text until it's as close to 9 inches across the top as you can get it.
- Change the "Fill" dropdown box on the Text Edit Bar from "No Fill" to "Print."
- Click "Make It" in the top, right-hand corner.
- After you click on "Make It," you're going to click on "Continue."
- When you do, it will bring up this next box:
- Click the toggle to turn "Use System Dialog" on.
- Click "Print." This screen will pop up:
- In the bottom, left-hand corner, you'll see a dropdown box that says, "PDF." Click that and tell your computer to "Open in Preview."
- In the Preview screen, click "File" and "Save." When it asks you to name the file, change the format from PDF to PNG by clicking on the drop-box by "Format."
- Save the file to your desktop for easy finding.
- Close out of the program you're previewing your file on.

- Go back to Cricut Design Space. Cancel the print and the cut.
- Click "Upload File" on the Design Panel.
- Click "Simple Image" since that's what you're uploading.
- Click "Insert."
- Select "Save As Cut Image."
- Once your word is on your Canvas, you'll have to rotate it. Place the word on top of it that it originally came from.
- Make sure you have your "Original Word" the color you want it.
- Group the two layers together. Viola!

Letter spacing

If you feel the space between each letter of your selected font is too much, you can use the letter spacing to reduce or increase the gap between each letter.

Let's assume you have 2 lines of text on you canvas. The line spacing option help you reduce or increase the gap between the first and second line.

Alignment

This alignment option is applicable to text. If you have used Microsoft word or any text editor you should find this easy. You can choose to align you text or paragraphs to left, right or center

Left
Paragraph is left justified

Right
Paragraph is right justified

Center
Paragraph is center justified

How to center your designs to cut in Cricut Design Space

- Sign in to the Cricut Design section. Click on the new project.
- Click Download.
- Click Upload Picture.
- Click Browse.
- Save your picture
- Select the saved image and insert an image.
- Select the picture. Click on it.
- As you can see, the picture is automatically moved to the upper left corner.
- To prevent this, you can fool the software by placing the image in the center of your design area and the mat. This is useful if you want to create openings in the middle of a page.
- Click on the shape tool.
- Create a shape of 11.5 x 11.5 inches.
- Select the square and change the setting to cut it in the drawing.
- The square now appears as an outline.
- Click Align and Center with the selected pattern and square.
- Click the arrow of the size of your square and resize it without moving the top left corner to reduce the size of the square.
- Select the square and pattern, then click Attach. Click on it.

As you can see now, the design is centered.

How to write with sketch pens in Cricut Design Space

- Sign in to the Cricut Design section. Create a new project.
- Click Download.
- Select upload a picture.
- Click Browse.
- open your file. Then save To get a good effect, use a file with thin lines and no large spaces.
- Click on the pattern and paste it.
- Select the pattern.
- Change the drawing to a drawing.
- You will now see the drawing as an outline drawn.
- Click on it.
- Your drawing will now be displayed on the cutting screen. Click on Continue.
- If you change your drawing to draw, the software automatically selects the pen tool. Insert the pen or marker into the recommended clip. Insert paper and click on the start icon.

The pen now draws your pattern.

Working with Edit Bar in Cricut Design Space

Here are important terminologies to help our understanding of the Design Space Edit Bar will have to be defined. A word of caution though, is that some of the terms used here are common tools for everyday use on the computer so it shouldn't be difficult to understand but our level of computer literacy is not the same.

Therefore, pardon me if you already know many of them. This has been done for the sake of those who do not know. The terms are as follows: *Undo/Redo-* refers to undoing any change made to the layer or redo any previously taken undone action.

Linetype
Refers to how the machine will interact with the material on the mat including cut, draw and score as described below.

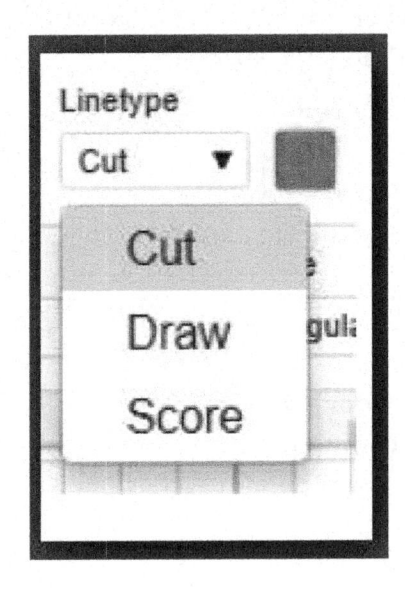

Cut
Refers to cutting layer with the aid of a blade from your material.

Draw
Refers to drawing the layer with the aid of a Cricut pen.

Score
Refers to scoring the layer using a Scoring Stylus or Scoring Wheel.

Linetype Swatch

Refers to choosing additional attributes that your layer will use. There are different types of options you can select from based on the selected Linetype (cut, draw, and score).

The Color Sync Tool

Like the Flatten tool, the Color Sync tool also has more than one function for Design Space users who know their way around it. Below are some of its functions:
The Color Sync tool can be used to recolor shapes, layers, *etc.*
It can be used to match the colors of all layers on the Canvas.
It is very useful for consolidating material colors.
It saves a user so much time and materials.
This feature wasn't available in the old version of the Design Space. But now that it is available in the new version, why not make exploits with it? This tool makes it much more comfortable to synchronize colors in a project so a user can cut them all on a single material. All you have to do is open the "Color Sync" panel located at the right side of the screen, and then start dragging and dropping all the shapes respectively into the selected layer you wish for it to synchronize to. If you desire to cut every star in chartreuse, for example, then just drag every other star to that same layer at the "Color Sync" panel. It feels so much easier to do this, and knowing they are all going to have the same color is comforting!

Sketching on The Design Space

One of the coolest facts about the using Cricut Explore model is that users can't only upload images, but they can also upload images they've drawn themselves! There are two techniques of doing this, one is by making use of Illustrator, and the other is by making use of the Design Space. And since we're discussing about the Design Space, I'll only mention how to do so on the latter. The following are the processes:

You first need to have the intended image on your computer by importing it. So, if you've hand-drawn what you want on a piece of paper or your tablet, the next step is to scan it to your computer, snap it with your mobile device and send it to your computer, or save and send it to the computer through your tablet. Whichever way you want to do it, ensure you save it as a PNG or JPEG file.

Convert the sketch using the Design Space by first uploading the image, making use of the "Upload" tab by the left side.

You will be requested to choose the image type; you should select the option that fits your image background. Proceed by clicking "Continue" and let your image be saved as a Cut image, and then click "Save." You will notice that your image is now a Cut file.

And that's how you upload and work with your sketch on the Design Space. With this function, you can let your creativity run wild! There are so many things you can do with your hands! Since you're not limited by the Design Space platform, don't ever let your imagination be limited!

Troubleshoot Error codes in the cricut design space

Every electronic device pops up error when there is a conflict with its program. The Cricut Design Space is no exception because it is also a program running on your device and will also complain if something is missing from its chain of command. As a user interface, it will report this error to you for correction in order to complete its current task.

Let us describe some of these errors and how to troubleshoot them. If you still cannot solve the problem after going through these steps or the error is not treated here, please feel free to contact Customer Care.

There are different error codes which have been discussed below:

Error (0)
Restart your computer and machine.
If your device is short of that then, ensure that your computer or device satisfy these minimum requirements or try to use another computer or device that meet the requirements.
Clear your cache, browser history, cookies and ensure that your browser is updated to the current version.
Recreate the project if only one and not multiple project is affected.
Use another computer or device if the above troubleshooting options fail.

Error (-11): "Device Authentication" error
Close all background programs on your computer or device and then try again.
Check to see that your browser is updated to the current version.

Error (-18): "Device Timeout" error
Switch off your computer or device
Close Design Space
restart the Design Space
Power on the Cricut maker and then try to cut again.
If no solution, contact Member Care

Error (-21): "data transmission" error
Clear your cache, browser history and cookies
Close your browser, re-launch it again and then try cutting
Use a different browser to try cut

Check your internet speed and ensure that it meets the minimum requirement Contact your Internet Service Provider (ISP) for assistance

Error (-24): "Ping Timeout" error
Recreate the project because it is possible that the project file is too large or is not properly saved Try another USB port on the computer or make use of Bluetooth
Use a different USB cable.
Check your internet speed
If nothing works, try a different computer

Error (-32): Firmware Not Available" error
Since this error pops up only when there is compatibility problem, check the connectivity of your device to the Cricut machine.
if you arc 100% sure that the connectivity is correct, then contact Member Care for assistance .

Error (-33): "Invalid Material Setting"
Check the Smart Set Dial. This error appears when there is no selected material from the Design space and the Smart Set Dial is set to "Custom". Therefore, ensure that a material is selected from the Design space material drop down menu.
Try a different material setting.
Contact Member Care for assistance.

Chapter 5: FAQ

Where can I use Cricut Design Space?
You can use Cricut Design Space through your web browser on PC or Mac after downloading the plugin. You can also download the app on your tablet or smartphone on iOS or Android.

How does my machine connect to Design Space?
Explore Air 2 has built-in Bluetooth, so it can connect to any device that has that capability. The Explore One has to be connected directly to your computer, or you can purchase a Cricut Wireless Bluetooth Adapter.

What is Cricut Access?
This is Cricut's subscription service to their library of images and fonts in Cricut Design Space. It gives access to more than 30,000 images, 370 fonts, and premium project ideas, as well as 10% off all purchases on the Cricut website. There are different types of plans available, ranging from $4.99 to $9.99 per month.

How do I install Design Space?
Design Space will give you a prompt to download and install the plugin. Click Download and wait for it to finish. Once it does, click the file to install the plugin. You might get a box asking for permission; if so, allow it. Follow the prompts through the installer. You're now ready to use Design Space!

Why am I getting error messages about the Design Space plugin?
If you're getting error messages or having difficulty using Design Space, you may need to reinstall the plugin. Expand your computer's system tray in the lower right-hand side of the screen and locate the Cricut icon. Right-click on it and click Exit. Open your web browser and navigate to design.cricut.com and sign in with your Cricut ID. Once prompted, download and install the plugin again.

Do I need a computer to use my Cricut machine?
No! If you have the Cricut Explore Air or the Cricut Maker, you can utilize the built-in Bluetooth to connect to your mobile device and download the Design Space app on it.

What's the difference between the Cricut Explore One and the Cricut Explore Air 2?
The Cricut Explore One has a single tool carriage, so if you do more than one action (cut and write or cut and score), it will need to do it in two steps, and you'll need to switch out the tools between them. The Cricut Explore Air 2 has two tool carriages, so it can do both functions in one step with no need to switch tools. Explore Air 2 also has built-in Bluetooth connectivity.

Do I use the same Cricut Design Space for the Cricut Maker?
Yes! The only difference is that you'll have the option to adjust the material settings in the Design Space since the Maker does not have the dial on the machine itself.

How does the Cricut Maker know which blade is in the carriage?
The machine scans the blade before it cuts a project.

What is the thickness of a material that the Cricut Maker can cut?
3/32" of an inch or 2.4mm when using the rotary blade or the knife blade.

How do I get a good transfer using the Cricut EasyPress?
Use the EasyPress on a firm and even surface. Check the iron-on material and the base material for the recommended settings and use those. Be sure to apply heat to both the front and back of the project for the recommended amount of time.

How much pressure does the Cricut EasyPress need?
Check the recommendations for the material you're using. Some will call for "firm" pressure, meaning you should use two hands and about 15–20 lbs of body weight. Others need "gentle" pressure, meaning you should use one hand with about 5–10 lbs of body weight. Use your EasyPress on a waist-high table for the easiest way to apply pressure.

Do I move the Cricut EasyPress around like an iron?
Keep the EasyPress in one spot for the recommended amount of time. Moving it might smear or warp the design.

Why should I use the Cricut EasyPress?
It heats more evenly and more quickly than iron and is easy to use. It will give you more professional-looking iron-ons and takes 60 seconds or less.

How do I protect surfaces while using the Cricut EasyPress?
Cricut recommends using the Cricut EasyPress mat, which comes in three different sizes. However, you can also use a cotton bath

towel with an even texture folded to about 3 inches thick. Do not use an ironing board, as the surface isn't even enough, and it's too unsteady to apply appropriate pressure. Silicone baking mats and aluminum foil don't provide enough insulation and can get dangerously hot.

My material is tearing! Why?
The most common reason is that your mat isn't sticky enough. It could have lost its stickiness, or you aren't using the right mat for the material. It could also be that the blade needs to be replaced or sharpened, or you're using the wrong type of blade. Materials can also tear if the machine is on the wrong setting.

Why won't my transfer tape work?
More often than not, it's not working when you try to use standard transfer tape with glitter vinyl. It requires the Cricut Strong Grip transfer tape. It's too strong to use with regular vinyl, though, so keep using the regular transfer tape for that.

What type of mat should I use?
Each mat has a specific use. Here's each one and some suggestions of what material to use with them.

Blue
Light Grip Mat – Thinner paper, vellum, construction paper, sticky notes, light vinyl, and wrapping paper

Green
Standard Grip Mat – Cardstock, thicker paper, washi paper, vinyl, and bonded fabric

Purple
Strong Grip Mat – Thick cardstock, magnet sheets, chipboard, poster board, fabric with stiffener, aluminum foil, foam, leather, and suede

Pink
Fabric Grip Mat – Fabric, bonded fabric, and crepe paper

How do I wash my mats?
Place the mat in the sink, supported by a firm flat surface. Running lukewarm water over it, use a hard-bristled brush to scrub it gently in circles until the mat is clean. Pat dry with a paper towel, and let it air dry for the stickiness to return.

Why won't my blade cut all the way through the material?
Make sure that the blade is completely in the carriage, and make sure there's no debris around it. Check that your settings are for the correct material. If you're still having trouble, slowly increase the pressure and do test cuts until it gets all the way through.

Can I upload my own images to the Cricut Design Space?
Yes! It's easy to upload your own image and create a design with it. On the left side of Design Space, there is an option for "Upload Images."

What is infusible ink?
Infusible ink is a new system from Cricut that infuses ink directly into compatible Cricut blanks. There are infusible ink transfer sheets and infusible ink Pens and Markers. They are applied using heat, such as with the Cricut Easy Press.

Does Cricut Design Space require an internet connection?
Yes.

What weight is Cricut Cardstock?
80 lb

What are the care instructions for Cricut Iron-on material?
Wash and dry the item inside out on the delicate style. If you notice areas of the iron-on material coming off after being washed, iron it again, following the full application instructions.

What's a quick reference list of materials I can cut?
For the Explore machines: all paper, all cardstock, vinyl, bonded fabrics, corrugated paper, sticker paper, and parchment paper. For the Maker machine: all of the above, plus fabric and textiles and thin wood.

Do I have to use Cricut brand materials?
No! You can use any brand of materials that you want. Thickness and quality are the only things that matter.

What pens can I use in my Cricut machine?
The Cricut brand pens will, of course, fit into your machine. However, some others will fit in the pen holder as well. Some users have found ways to adapt other pens, but the pens and markers in the following list don't require any adjustments.
• Wal-Mart Leisure Arts Markers
• Target Dual Tip Markers
• Pilot Precise V5 pens

- Thin Crayola markers
- Dollar Tree Jot markers
- Bic Round Stic pen

What is the Cricut Adaptive Tool System?
This is a new feature in the Cricut Maker. It adjusts the direction and pressure of the blades throughout the cutting process. It allows for much more precise cuts and much higher cutting pressure.

What is the scoring wheel?
A scoring wheel is a tool for the Cricut Maker, as it uses the Adaptive Tool System. It creates fold lines in thicker materials. The Scoring Stylus also makes fold lines, but the Scoring

How small can the rotary blade cut?
Cricut recommends keeping designs above ¾". Any smaller than that, the blade might gouge into your mat as it turns, damaging the mat and dulling the blade.

Where do I buy Cricut Blades?
You can buy blades where Cricut brand products are sold, including craft stores, superstores, Cricut's website, and other online stores.

What is the Fast Mode?
This is a feature on the Cricut Explore Air 2 and Cricut Maker. It allows you to cut and write twice as fast when the machine is set to vinyl, iron-on, or cardstock.

What is the Custom material setting for?
If you're cutting something besides paper, vinyl, iron-on, cardstock, fabric, or poster board on the Cricut Explore or Cricut Maker, you can choose Custom. This will open the material menu in Cricut Design Space. Select "Browse All Materials" and select the correct one. If you don't see your material listed, you can choose something close or create your own. If you create a custom material, you'll adjust the cut pressure, set if it uses multi-cut, and select the blade type. For help, you can look at the settings for something close to the material you're using. If you have enough of the material, do several tests with different settings to see what works best.

Can Cricut Design Space work on more than one mobile device or computer?
Yes, it can! Cricut Design Space, as mentioned earlier, is cloud-based. No matter where you are or the kind of device that you are using, you can always use this application as long as it is compatible. If you're logged in at home, you can also log in on your phone if you're on the go.

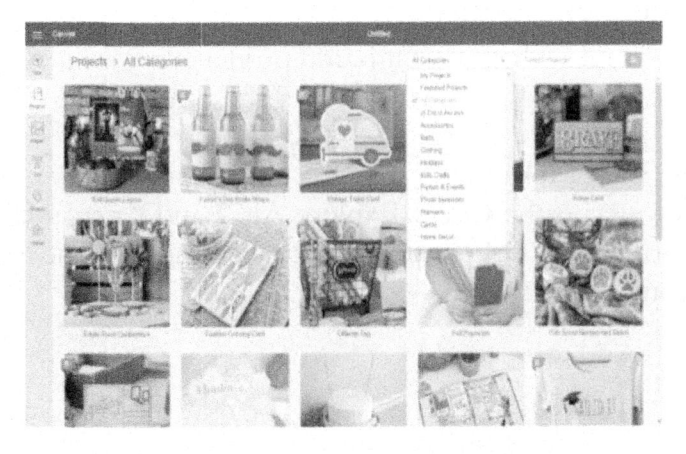

Do I have to have an internet connection before I use Cricut Design Space?
Using Cricut Design Space on a laptop or a computer requires a high-speed internet connection. The internet must be high-speed broadband if you want your designing to go smoothly. iOS users can get the offline version of the app if they have the latest version of the Design Space.

Is there a difference between digital and physical cartridges?
A cartridge, in the Cricut sense, generally refers to image sets. So, a cartridge is made up of images that have the same theme. Cartridges can be either digital or physical, although a lot of the physical cartridges have been retired. You can purchase the digital cartridges on cricut.com.

How do I find the Cricut Access fonts and images on Design Space?
With their new update, everything that is available on Cricut Access has a green 'a' marking. This means that while you explore images and fonts, you can easily distinguish which one is from Cricut Access and which isn't. When searching for something, use filters too to narrow your search.

How long do I own the images that I purchase on Design Space?
Cricut images don't expire! That's right. Once you pay for them, you own them, and they remain in your library until you don't need them anymore.

Is it possible to disable the grid on the Canvas area?
Yes, you can! If you're not comfortable or you don't want to use the gridlines, you can toggle them in your settings.

To do this, you open your Account menu and click on Settings. Click on Canvas Grid and from there, you can turn the grid lines off.

For those using an iOS device, Settings have been provided for you at the bottom of the screen. With them, you can turn the grid line on and off.

Is Design Space compatible with a Chromebook computer?
No, it isn't. The latest version of Cricut Design Space only works with Windows or a Mac operating system.

Do I need to pay in order to use Design Space?
No, you don't. Design Space comes completely free. You only need a subscription if you plan on using Cricut Access. But, if you need the basics, then you can open a Design Space account for free.

Conclusion

It's been quite an exciting journey, and here we are. Although this book has given you a lot of information on how to work better on the Design Space, don't forget to start small. Even if you have so many crazy ideas running through your head right now, you should start with small projects first to practice and get used to the platform. This doesn't mean you should limit yourself. Just ensure you build yourself to professionalism steadily.

You have almost all the information and knowledge at your fingertips, and no one's taking that away from you. However, you need to practice consistently. A little break and you might forget what's important. You might get a bit frustrated at some points while practicing, but that doesn't mean you should stop trying. Cricut is offering you much more than it's demanding.

To ensure you get better faster, you can hang on to this book till you can handle things yourself. Even after mastering the content, you should keep it close for reference purposes.

The Cricut cutting machine is as astonishing as it is because of Cricut Design Space, the free application that causes the enchantment to occur. And keeping in mind that Cricut Design Space is entirely simple and easy to use, acing it doesn't occur without any forethought. That is for what reason I'm here to share my most loved Cricut Design Space instructional exercises, tips, and traps with you! These will change your Cricut life!

The bright side of this book is that beyond being easy to understand, it is a guide that you can always come back to whenever you need them or whenever you seem to be forgetting something important about Cricut.

Cheers!!!

CRICUT EXPLORE AIR 2

*Everything you need to know to set up Your Cutting Machine successfully.
A complete guide full of Tips and Tricks to quickly create your first innovative Project Ideas*

Introduction

The Cricut Explore Air 2 can be regarded as an electronic cutter or a personal crafting machine which can be used in the cutting of different materials such as the cardstock, vinyl, Faux leather, Magnet sheets, sticker paper, Vellum, Fabric, Sticker Paper, etc.

The Cricut Explore Air 2 can make use of the pen and markers in writing, drawing as well as scoring your project with a nifty score tool. The machine can also be used in printing and cutting, as well.

One unique thing about Cricut Explore Air 2 is that its tools are made of high quality and has two cutting modes: fast and normal modes, to deliver your project with precision.

The Cricut Explore Air 2 is an electronic cutting machine that makes use of a precise blade as well as series of rollers in cutting out images, just anything you can imagine. It is used in cutting out fancy paper shapes as well as fonts that came on cartridges.

Chapter 1: What Is Cricut Machine

What is Cricut?
Cricut is a brand name for a variety of products referred to as home die cutting machines. These machines are used for scrapbooking and other countless creative projects. Cricut is one of the most popular among several electronic die cutters used by scrapbookers, paper crafters, and card makers. Cricut machines are designed to cut paper, vinyl, felt, balsa wood, and various types of fabrics. The Cricut logo is a play on an animated cricket bug, which the name closely represents. The Cricut logo is used throughout their different design offerings, including Cricut Design Space, and Cricut Access.

When the Cricut was introduced, it gave crafters all over the world a long sought-after tool for Do It Yourself project in a new, fun, and innovative way. It gave people a new opportunity to approach their projects and creativity. Cricut now influences passion and originality in a way that people truly enjoy! People all over the world have been able to make successful businesses from their Cricut design which brings more and more people to the world of Cricut crafting each and every year. Now is the perfect time to get started using the Circuit machine if this is something you want to obtain for yourself, and this book will help you get there.

Cricut Machine Models

There are various Cricut models to look over. In the event that you are planning to buy a Cricut to use at home or for your business at that point let this Cricut machines examination help you out.

Cricut Maker

The Cricut Maker is Circuits' most up to date machine. Cricut considers it a definitive smart cutting machine, and I can't help but agree. It is a best in class digital die the cutting machine that conveys proficient quality outcomes at an individual machine cost. It can cut many materials, from the most delicate fabric and paper to mat board, balsa wood, and leather.

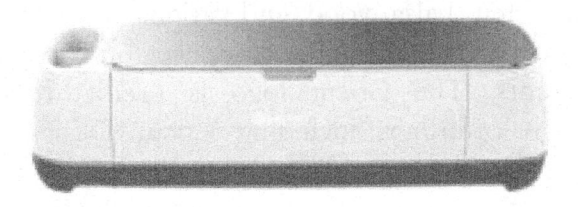

The Cricut Maker utilizes the fresh out of the box new Adaptive Tool System, which takes into account progressively precise control over the instruments, including pivoting, lifting, and shifting weight all through the whole cut. The Adaptive Tool System also enables the machine to use new kinds of devices later on as Cricut grows its device contributions.

Other than the Fine-Point Blade, Deep Cut Blade, and Bonded Fabric Blade that are good with all Cricut machines, the Maker can also utilize the accompanying apparatuses that are perfect with the Adaptive Tool System:

Rotating Blade – This gives you a chance to cut fabric with a Cricut Maker and it's a tremendous improvement over-utilizing the standard Fine-Point cutting edge. You can cut intense fabric like burlap or denim, and furthermore delicate materials like crepe paper or glossy silk. This cutting edge gives you a chance to make intricate cuts on fabric without fraying or clustering (which is the reason you need a stabilizer backing when utilizing the Fine-Point blade).

Knife Blade
This lets you effectively cut through thicker and denser materials, for example, balsa wood, leather, mat board, and Cricut Chipboard. You can make some quite complex cuts without worrying that the sharp edge will snap.

Scoring Wheels
These apparatuses make crisp creases on slender, thick, and even covered paper materials. They enable you to make extra-deep score lines on any material that doesn't break when you fold it.

The Explore machines can't utilize these new sharp edges and instruments since they depend on the Adaptive Tool System. The standard instrument holder carriage in the Explore machines simply doesn't have the necessary exactness or power.

As the name suggests, the Adaptive Tool System is intended to easily switch between devices, adjusting the drive framework to whichever device is loaded into it. This considers TONS of new kinds of instruments to be made, later on, to do new sorts of arts with the machine that we never could. I think the Adaptive Tool System is a HUGE advantage and I think it makes the Maker increasingly "future-verification"; I suspect we'll see a huge amount of cool new devices for the Adaptive Tool System soon!

Features
With expandable devices: revolving cutting edge, pens, and knife blade
With fine point pen, 12 x 12 inches cutting mats

The rotational cutting edge can cut quickly and precisely
Accompanies several computerized sewing designs
The knife blade can deal with meager and thick materials
With simple structure application; load extends on a PC or cell phone
With a gadget docking space
You can utilize your own plans
With a USB port to charge your gadget while being used
With Bluetooth remote innovation

Pros
Enables you to work at various materials
You can utilize various structures from its database
Accompanies expandable devices
Gadget dock gives you a chance to work intimately with the machine
Utilize your PC or cell phone with the Cricut

Cons
Objections that it won't work with an iPad
The blade edge is sold independently

Cricut Explore Air
The Cricut Explore Air is the subsequent stage up from the Explore One. It also comes the standard Fine-Point Blade which enables you to cut several materials, and it's good with the Deep Point Blade and the Bonded Fabric Blade (sold independently) to enable you to cut considerably more materials.

One major redesign over the Explore One is that the Cricut Explore Air has a double apparatus holder; it is intended to hold a cutting edge in one clamp and a pen, scoring stylus, or another embellishment in the other clip. This implies if you have a project that has both writing and cutting, you can stack a sharp edge and a pen into the machine, and it will cut and write across the board go without stopping for you to change between instruments. Far better, the second clasp is perfect with tools like the Scoring Stylus, Cricut Pens, and so on so there's no reason to buy an extra connector.

The Cricut Explore Air also offers worked in Bluetooth abilities. For the initial step, you should associate utilizing the USB link gave, yet after the underlying matching, you'll have the option to interface with your machine and cut remotely.

Features
With double cartridge to cut, compose or score simultaneously
With inserted Bluetooth, so you can work remotely
Will cut in excess of 60 distinct materials
With incorporated stockpiling segments
Good with .svg, .jpg, .png, .bmp, .gif, .dxf documents
Will take a shot at all Cricut cartridges

Pros
Cut and compose, cut and score simultaneously

You can work remotely
Store pens, blades and different frill away compartments
You can utilize your very own pictures or utilize any picture from the tremendous library
Works with Cricut cartridges

Cons
You have to buy extra apparatuses and accessories
You have to buy fonts and designs

Cricut Explore Air 2
The Cricut Explore Air 2 is the following stage up from the Explore Air, and it has one significant update: Fast Mode. This is extremely useful for individuals who make various duplicates of their tasks (like educators) or individuals who make things to sell who will value the measure of time they spare.

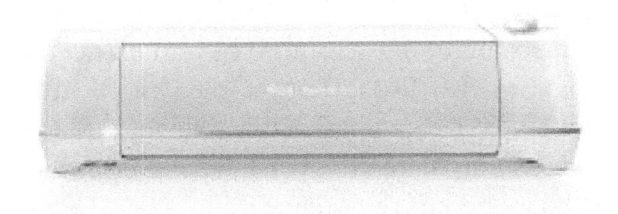

The Cricut Explore Air 2 accompanies the standard Fine-Point Blade which enables you to cut several materials, and it's perfect with the Deep Point Blade and the Bonded Fabric Blade (sold independently) to enable you to cut considerably more materials.
The Cricut Explore Air 2 additionally has worked in Bluetooth abilities so you can cut remotely and a double tool holder so you can cut and compose all in a solitary pass. Furthermore, similar to the Explore Air, the second clamp is good with frill like the Scoring

Stylus, Cricut Pens, and so on so there's no compelling reason to buy an extra connector.

Personally, I don't really utilize Fast Mode all that frequently, so the progression up from the Explore Air is definitely not a huge deal for me, however, it can spare you time if you do a ton of cardstock, vinyl, and iron-on projects!

Features
With Cricut Pens to make "written by hand" cards and different projects
Cut multifaceted subtleties with extreme exactness
With Scoring Stylus to crease cards, boxes, envelopes, acetic acid derivation and to make 3D paper specialties
With Fast Mode for 2X quicker cutting
You can work with more than 100+ sorts of materials
Within excess of 370 textual styles to look over
Can work with an Android or iOS gadget
Remote cutting with Bluetooth
Utilizations Design Space to deal with records from any gadget
With Cricut Image Library

Pros
Scoring Stylus folds lines for various projects
Cuts with extreme accuracy
Works with more than 100+ materials
Writes more than 370 text styles
Structure anyplace with Design Space
Associates with gadgets by means of Bluetooth
Cut and write multiple times quicker

Cons
Issues with Design Space
Disconnected Design Space accessible for iOS clients

Cricut Explore One

The Cricut Explore One is Circuits' entrance level spending machine; it's ideal for any individual who needs to begin with a digital die cutting machine yet wouldn't like to spend a huge amount of cash. It accompanies the standard Fine-Point Blade which enables you to cut several materials, and it's perfect with the Deep Point Blade and the Bonded Fabric Blade (sold independently) to enable you to cut considerably more materials.

As its name suggests, the Explore One has a single apparatus holder, so if you need to cut and write in a similar project you should change out the sharp edge for a pen mid-route through the cut. It's extremely simple to change out the accessory or blade, and the Design Space programming will stop the slice and walk you through it when now is the right time, yet if you do a lot of tasks that join cutting, composing, or scoring, it can get tiresome sooner or later.

Moreover, really, the single tools holder is good with the standard estimated edges (Fine-Point, Deep Point, and Bonded Fabric), however, to utilize different instruments and extras, you'll have to buy a different connector to fit in the single device holder.

The Explore One doesn't have worked in Bluetooth capacities, so you need to connect the machine to your gadget with the USB link gave. Or then again you can buy a Bluetooth connector independently to enable the machine to cut remotely.

Features
Utilize the Cricut Design Space for PC, Mac, iPad or iPhone
Transfer your own plans for nothing or pick one from the Cricut Image Library
Use text styles introduced from your PC
Work on various materials from flimsy paper to thick vinyl
With helpful device and extras holder
Works remotely by including a remote Bluetooth connector
No compelling reason to set with the Smart Set dial or make your very own custom settings
Make extends in minutes

Pros
Works remotely with Bluetooth connector
Transfer your very own pictures and structures for nothing
With 50,000+ pictures and text styles from Cricut Image Library
No settings required with the Smart Set dial
Prints and cuts quick
Structure with your very own gadget or PC utilizing Design Space

Cons
It expenses to utilize pictures beginning at $0.99
Bluetooth connector sold independently

Cricut Expression 1
You can make more customizations for various projects with the Cricut Expression 1. This electronic cutting machine works with the Cricut Craft Room where you can alter plans and improve your output even more. With its six modes and four capacities, you will have the option to make a variety of projects. You can also appreciate quick cutting and plotting speeds which imply that you can make extends quicker, perfect for business use. Expression 1 is

additionally portable you can take it any place you should be; at school, at home or at the workplace. It has an LCD screen however touchscreen isn't.

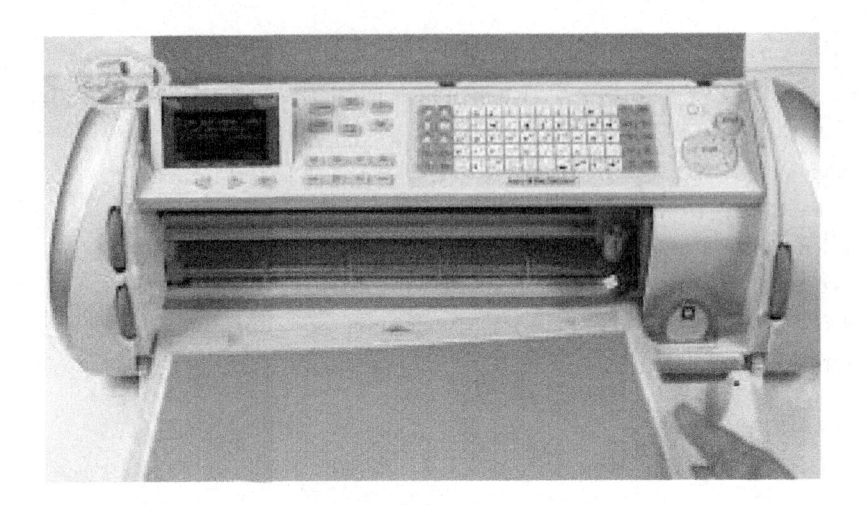

Your buy accompanies a 12" x 12" cutting mat so there is no compelling reason to buy.

The Cricut Expression 1 is portable and woks productively; you can make numerous kinds of activities any way you have to buy cartridges since this one doesn't accompany one. In fact, you can't make any projects yet when this comes out of the box.

Features
Can cut moment 0.25" pictures to 23.5" plans
Will work with the Cricut Craft Room
With ordinary LCD screen
With 6 modes and 4 distinct capacities to improve customization
Buy accompanies a 12" x 12" cutting mat
Compact structure
Cuts rapidly and productively

Pros
Totally adaptable to make better plans
With six modes and four capacities
Accompanies a 12" x 12" cutting mat
Works with Cricut Craft Room
With a convenient plan

Cons
Issues with the sticky mat
No cartridges included with buy
Isn't perfect with different cartridges
Cricut Easy Press Machine

Cricut Easy Press

Another cutting machine that worth is the Cricut Easy Press. I state that it worth the investment due to the home-accommodating structure and star level execution. It accompanies a major handle, a security base, and an auto-shutoff include so as to keep your home, workspace, and office very protected. In the event that you request this workhorse, you will get a compact, lightweight and simple to store with a giant, clay-covered warmth plate that gives the definite temperature you need. It is ideal for layered or enormous iron-on projects. It accompanies a reference diagram that will assist you in deciding time and temperature.

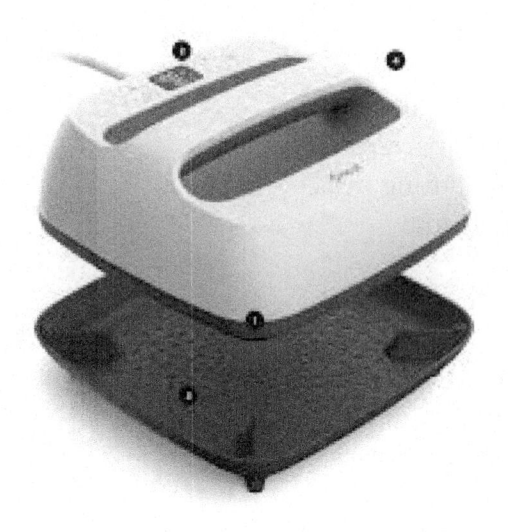

Pros
Ace level execution
Home-accommodating structure
Portable and compact
Reference graph included
Auto-shutoff highlight

Cons
Manual warmth temperature and clock settings
Conflicting weight and little cutting zone
Which Cricut Machine Should You Purchase?

There are 3 versions of this Cricut system, popular private die cutters produced available by the Provo Craft business. With three great possibilities, it can be hard to choose which to purchase. In the event you start little and purchase the first Personal Electronics Cutter? Or is your Expression model value the additional investment? How can the Generate, the hybrid version now being exclusively offered by Michael's Craft Store, stand against both of the other machines?

In numerous ways, all 3 die cut machines will be precisely the same:

All three versions are cartridge-based.
You can only create cutouts depending upon the capsules you possess. Each cartridge includes a computer keyboard overlay, which can be employed in choosing special cuts. The cartridges aren't machine-specific - they may be utilized in any of those 3 versions.

Fundamental performance of three machines is exactly the exact same.
If you have the personal electronic cutter, then you'll not have any trouble working on the Cricut expression or produce (along with vice-versa). Why? The fundamental operation of three die cutters would be exactly the exact same.

Here is a fast rundown of this procedure. After plugging in the chosen cartridge and accompanying computer keyboard overlay and turning to the machine, then you're prepared to begin making die cuts. Materials, like paper or cardstock, are set on a particular cutting edge mat, which is subsequently loaded to the machine using all the press of a switch. With another press on this button, the chosen design is selected. All that is left is to choose "cut". The device does the remainder of the job.

All three Cricut machine versions utilize the very same accessories.
It was mentioned that the capsules aren't machine-specific, but in addition, this is true with the majority of the additional accessories. It isn't important which version you have - that the replacement blades, blades, different instruments, like the Cricut spatula, and

design studio applications, may be utilized with almost any version. The 1 exception is that the cutting mats. The machines take various sizes of their mats, and you need to get one that's compatible with your particular machine.

Now that you understand the way the Cricut machines are alike, you're most likely wondering how they're different.

They change in many ways:

The dimensions of die cuts made by every machine are distinct.
The personal electronic cutter has the capacity of earning cutouts ranging from 1 inch to 5-1/2 inches in dimension, in half inch increments. The generate can create die cuts that range from 1/4 inch to 11-1/2 inches in dimension, per inch increments. The expression provides users the maximum flexibility, making cutouts out of 1/4 inch to 23-1/2 inches in dimension, per quarter inch increments.

They size and weight of these machines change.
The personal electronic cutter and produce are equally small, mobile machines. These versions are great for crafters who prefer to shoot their jobs on the street and make record layouts and other jobs in class settings. They're also suited for people who don't own a particular place in their house place aside for crafting, since these die cutters are easy to package up and set away between applications. The expression, on the other hand, is considerably heavier and bigger. In case you've got a crafting corner or room, and don't have the worries of transferring it regularly, it is a fantastic option.

The three Cricut machine versions have various functions and modes.
There are many distinct modes and purposes. By way of instance, the match to page style will automatically correct the dimensions of this die cut predicated upon the dimensions of this material loaded from the system. The middle point function lets you align with the cutting blade across the middle of this substance, so the cut is created about it. The expression machine gets the most flexibility so much as the access to functions and modes. Next in line would be the produce, and third place belongs to the personal electronic cutter. More info could be found regarding such functions and modes in the system handbooks, which can be found in pdf format on cricut.com.

The cost differs for every version.
The personal electronic cutter is the most inexpensive Cricut cutter, having an estimated retail price of $299.99. The generate is $100.00 longer, at $399.99, as well as the rake is $499.99. Please be aware that all 3 machines can be bought at substantial savings. Many retailers operate particular sales or possess a lesser regular cost compared to suggested retail cost. It is a fantastic idea to look around when purchasing your very first Cricut machine.

What projects can be done with a Cricut machine?
We cannot talk about all projects that can be done with a Cricut machine because there are so many. However, for all creative minds to enter the guide, here are some of the popular projects that can be done with a Cricut machine.
Creation, custom handmade cards
Cut letters or shapes for scrapbooking. Addressing an envelope.
I am creating a leather bracelet.

Design and creation of decorations or email for holidays. Design and production of Christmas decorations and ornaments. Design t-shirts or other tissues.
Templates are making paint and creating vinyl stickers.
We are creating labels.
Design and creation of symbolic pillows.
Design registration plates, cups, glasses, or cups. Engraved designs on glass.
Creating decorations and stickers for your walls. Creating designs in wood or wood samples.
Cutting pieces of fabric to plant another fabric or quilt squares.
Creating decorative stickers.
We are creating mountains of felt.
We are creating designs for water bottles.
Design and creation of custom bags.

Chapter 2: Machine Setup and How to Prepare the Material

Setting up the Cricut Explore Air 2

Once you can set up your Cricut Explore Air 2, it will lead to the automatic registration of the machine to your account. To set up there Cricut Explore Air 2, you will need to take the following steps: - Get the device plugged in and turn it on.
- Make use of the USB cord in connecting or the Bluetooth in pairing the Cricut Explore Air 2 to your computer.
- On the computer, visit design.cricut.com/setup.
- You will be prompted by On-screen instructions to create your Cricut ID and getting signed in.
- When prompted, download and install the Design Space plug-in.
- Once you are prompted to begin your first project, the setup is complete.

Useful Tips

Once you go through this process of getting your machine setup, the machine will be registered automatically.
In a situation where you couldn't go through with the setup when the Cricut was connected to your PC at first, you will need to get the machine reconnected and visit the design portal on the Cricut website, or visit the Design Space Account menu, select New Machine Setup and follow the on-screen instructions that come up.

How to Plug in the Device?

First, the Cricut machine needs to be plugged into the computer and also the power outlet. Use the USB cable provided to connect the computer to the machine. Next to the USB cable, the power port should be connected to both the outlet and the device, also provided in the packaging. Now press the ON button on the machine. It will illuminate to indicate that it is working.

How to Load/Unload the Mat?

For placing your material to cut it on the mat, it's important to know the placement. First, the mat's cover should be removed and placed elsewhere. The Cricut maker comes with a blue LightGrip mat, which is used for cutting paper mainly. The match will be slightly sticky for good placement of the material. When loading, the material should be placed in the top left corner of the mat. Be sure to press down gently so that the material could be evened out. Place the top of the mat in the guides of the machine. Gently press on the rollers and press the load/to unload the button on top of the Cricut. Once loaded up, the software will tell you the next step. After the project has been finished, the material needs to be unloaded. Press on the load/unload button and take out the mat from the machine. The right way to remove the material from the mat is that it should be placed on a straight surface, and the mat should be peeled off. The remaining scraps can be peeled off by a scrapper or a tweezer.

How to Load/Unload Cricut Pen?

For loading a pen, the machine needs to be opened to show the two clamps. For placement of the pen, clamp A needs to be opened up. Remove the cap on the pen and place it so that the arrow on the pen is facing the front. Gently pull clamp an upwards when placing the pen. Place the pen inside clamp until the arrow disappears, and a click sound is heard. To unload a pen, simply open up clamp A and remove the pen by upward motion. If you do not remove the pen, the machine will not be close, and the pen's cap cannot be put on.
Recently, new specialized pens are available called the Infusible Ink Pen and markers.

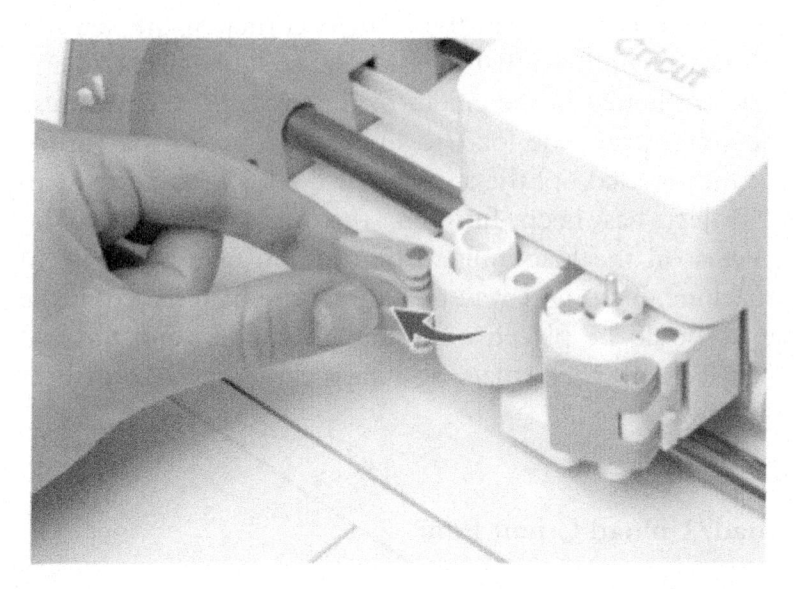

They work in by sublimation process, completely fusing the ink onto the material. It is best for Iron-on. The difference between it and regular pens is that they leave a thicker line. They also come in in two variations: traditional and neon. Heating is required to use this instrument, which can be achieved by Cricut Easy Press. For using it, first select a blank slot and fit in pen, any blank slot can fit the pens. Then draw your design on design space or by hand. Make sure the image size is according to the Cricut Easy Press. Then place a laser paper on to the Cricut Maker or Cricut Explorer. Now use the Infusible Ink to draw in the design. Now transfer the image to Cricut Easy Press and follow its guidelines.

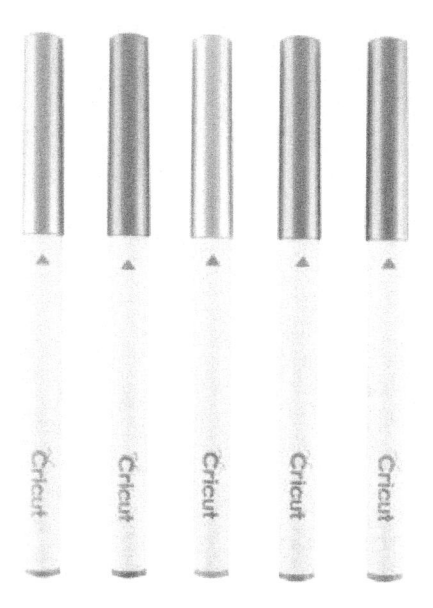

How to Load/Unload Blades?

A Fine point blade comes already place inside the machine when the package is opened. If the project requires a changing of the blade, then first, you need to unload the blade. Open up accessory clamp B and pull it upwards gently. Then pull the blade out of the machine. When putting another blade, i.e., rotary blade, make sure that the gears fit evenly. Once placed, it will give a click sound. Whenever someone is doing a project, the Cricut Maker automatically checks if the right blade is placed. With QuickSwap housing available, it is easier to change blades. Simply press on the housing tip to loosen its grip, and then slide or remove the blades.

Driving House ⬅

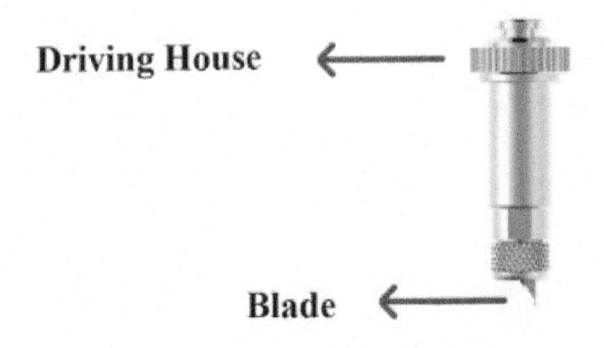

Blade ⬅

How to unmount the paper from the mat

8. Bend the paper until it pops out a little bit and uses your finger to remove the paper from the mat. You can also use the tools provided to make a little bit easier.

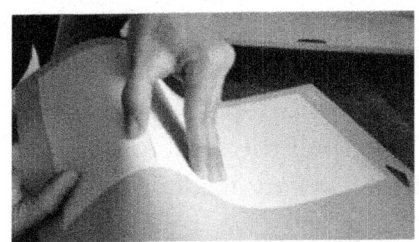

When you remove the paper and fold it this is what you should have.

When you open it, you will find a space that you could write your message on.

9. Once you get to this stage, you have to head back to the computer and click on continue.

10. The computer will keep on guiding you if you want to add more design to the one you have already done.

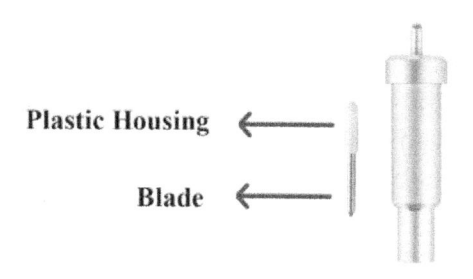

Plastic Housing ←

Blade ←

How to Load/Unload a Scoring Stylus?

To load and unload a scoring stylus is just as loading and uploading the pen. Open up the accessory clamp A and put the pen tip downwards, while holding up the clamp gently. Place it in until the arrow disappears, and a click sound is made. Now close the clamp and follow the instructions in the software. Once the scoring is completed, the scoring pen needs to be unloaded. Open up the clamp and remove the pen by pulling it upwards.

How to Load or Unload Cartridges?

What are Cricut Cartridges? Cricut cartridges are a library of images that users can buy to use in creating their projects on their Cricut machine. Usually, these cartridges collect images focusing on a

season (e. g Christmas or Easter), characters, or concept. A certain common trait links all the content of a cartridge together.
The Cartridges are physical devices that you plug into your Cricut Explore Air. You plug the cartridge into the cartridge port.

Within Cricut Access there are lots of "Cricut cartridges". These cartridges are not physical cartridges; they are digital libraries just like the physical cartridges. Once you purchase a cartridge, you can use it even without a subscription to Cricut Access. You can use Cartridges from your older machine on your Cricut Explore Air. Once linked to your account, you can have access to the content of the cartridge without even the physical unit.

With Cricut Access there is little need to get physical cartridges.
Cricut Explorer comes with the feature of using cartridges. To use a cartridge first, you need to open up Design Space using our Cricut account. Open up the green account button and click on the link cartridge option. A new page will open, which is the link cartridge window. Now turn on the Cricut Explorer and put the cartridge in the cartridge slot. The cartridge label should be facing forward, and it should be fully set. When the software air recognizes the cartridge in the device, then click 'link cartridge' at the lower right corner of the screen.

The screen will confirm whether the cartridge has been linked or not. Now the cartridge can be safely removed. To access the cartridges files, first, you should open Design Space with your Cricut ID. Then click on the ownership icon and select purchased. Now find the cartridge that you are looking for. To insert the items in your cartridge onto a design, on the Design Space window, click on insert and search for the cartridge by name or click on the cartridge icon.

How to Load or Unload a Debossing Tool?

Debossing tool, also called a debossing tip, is used to press on the materials giving it an everlasting imprint. Instead of a solid end, it has a rollerball which allows the color to slide onto the material rather than dragging on. This feature gives sharp images and opens up new possibilities. It is used in the Cricut Maker. It goes into the Quickswap housing and like any other blade into clamp B.

Linking Cartridges with the Cricut Explore Air

While you cannot use your machine offline, your cartridges will work fine. Here is how to link your cartridge with the Cricut Explore Air.

Using your browser, visit www.cricut.com/design and sign into your account.

After logging in, click on the account button (it is green in color).
Click on "Cartridge Linking" from the drop-down menu.
Fix the cartridge firmly in the cartridge port. Ensure the machine is switched on and connected to the PC.
The cartridge if detected will trigger an alert prompting you to link the cartridge to your account.
Click "Link Cartridge"

Pairing the Cricut machine through Bluetooth to the Computer

To get your Cricut Explore Air 2 paired with your computer or mobile device, you are required to take the following steps: - Make sure your Wireless Bluetooth Adapter is in place and working.
- Have the Cricut Explore Air 2 turned on, and it should be at most 15 feet from your PC.
- Check to be sure your computer is Bluetooth enabled by taking the following sub-steps on your computer.
☐ Go to the "Start button" and right-click on it.
☐ Select the "Device Manager."
☐ If you have the Bluetooth listed in the device manager, definitely it is Bluetooth enabled; otherwise, you will have to get a USB device referred to as Bluetooth Dongle to get your computer interacting with other Bluetooth devices.
- You can now close your Device manager once you have confirmed it is Bluetooth enabled.
- Go to the "Start menu."
- Select "Settings."
- Go to the "Devices" option and open it.
- Make sure the Bluetooth is active and select "Include Bluetooth or another device.
- Click on "Bluetooth," you can then grab a cup of coffee while your PC searches for and pairs with the Cricut Machine.
- Select the Cricut machine once it appears on the list.
- In a case where you are prompted to input in a PIN, type in 0000 and click on "Connect."
- Once you select the Connect option, your Cricut Explore Air 2 machine will now be paired to your computer.

Note: The Cricut Explore Air 2 machine might show up as an Audio on the Bluetooth list. If this happens, its okay, and you can go ahead with pairing.

In a situation where you have multiple Cricut machines, make use of the device code in identifying which one you like to pair. The device code can be found on the serial number tag at the bottom of the machine.

Unpairing or removing the Bluetooth device

The removal or unpairing of your Bluetooth device from the Cricut Explore Air 2 varies based on the version of the operating system in use. You are required to take the following steps in the process of unpairing or removing the Bluetooth device: - Go to the Start menu - Select Settings - Select the Devices option - Choose the device you want to remove and click on the "Remove device."
- You will be prompted to confirm your action.

Resetting the Cricut Explore Air 2 Machine

When some issues arise with your machine, there might be a need to perform a hard reset for such a problem to be resolved. In performing the hard reset, you are required to take the following steps: - Turn off the Cricut Explore Air 2 machine.
- Simultaneously hold down the Magnifying glass, pause as well as the power buttons.
- Hold the three buttons down simultaneously until the machine displays a rainbow screen, and you can release the buttons afterward.
- Promptly follow the on-screen instructions that follow.
- Get the process repeated one more time.

How to Cut Heavyweight and Lightweight Materials

Before delving into this project, I would like to explain a few important tips for this project that will help you accomplish the task accurately. Go over them as much as you can to fully understand each of these tips. It will definitely help you.

Do not eject the mat when you pause the machine to clean or replace a blunt rotary blade. If you remove the mat, it will be difficult to get the correct alignment of the cut and finish your project with accuracy. So, what you can do is pause the machine, remove the rotary blade, clean or replace the rotary blade, put it back in and hit the Cricut button to continue. You will have to do all these without ejecting the mat because if you do eject the mat, you terminate your project and will start all over.

Before you unload your material from the machine, make sure that you check your project and that the cut has been done all the way. If the cut is not all the way, you can restart the cut all over as long as you did not eject or move the mat.

The Design space will also be notifying you of the progress of the cut: how many passes to complete your project, and the amount of time remaining to finish your project. This is amazing as it will help you get the progress of your work any time you check on it. That is, in case, you need to carry out other pressing task at hand.

The materials required for this project includes Cricut machine (Maker or Expression), 3" x 24" Bass wood, rotary blade, and painter's tape.

The first thing, as usual, is to design your text to be cut on Cricut Design space. In case you don't know how to do that, please go to the sections How to Design with Cricut Machine and How to Edit Text in Cricut Design Space.

There is no room for assumptions here because it will save you time and money too. But if you already know that and you have your design ready, it is time to go the task at hand.
1. You have the design in your Cricut design space, so click Continue.
Select the type of material by clicking on Browse All Materials.

Type in Bass wood in the materials and choose the type of Bass wood, preferably 1/16 Basswood.
Click Done. Ensure that you follow the instructions on the cutting window by moving the star wheel to the right of the machine. I believe that you still remember why this is important? Then, the materials should be secured to the Strong Grip mat using tape. Of course, the material should not be more 11" wide.
Insert the rotary blade to the accessory clamp. By the way, the machine will give a warning if the blade is not inserted.
Now, you load the mat into the machine by pressing on the Load/Unload button.
The machine will start cutting when you press the flashing Cricut button. It will make an entire pass of the image the machine is going to cut before cutting the full image. Of course, this will take time because of the thickness of the cut. Therefore, you can do other pressing task at hand.

Unload the mat by pressing the Load/Unload button which will be blinking when the task is complete.
Remove the tape and your material from the mat.
Use the weeding tool to remove your design from the whole material gently.
Working on this project would have stirred your creative mind on many ideas you can accomplish following this approach.

Chapter 3: Cricut Design Space software For Cricut Explore Air 2

How to Upload Images with A Cricut Explore Air 2?

Uploading your images to Design Space is a walk in the park once you get a grip on the basic concepts. As stated earlier, there are two significant categories of image files that can be uploaded to the Design Space.

Vector Images; .dxf and .svg files. They are uploaded in more than one layer in such a way that you can edit varying independent parts in the platform.
 Basic Images; .png, .jp, .gif and .bmp are uploaded in the form of a single-layered image. This implies that what you see in the preview of the image before printing and cutting is exactly what you will get after the whole process is completed.

After your image is ready, which you might have bought on the Cricut platform or designed yourself, the time is now here to upload it. The next logical step to take is to open the Design Space.

Tap on the 'Browse Files" tab and search for the relevant file from your PC.
If the file is a vector image, a preview will come up after the upload is complete. At this point, you can rename the image and save it from this point.

On the other hand, if the file is a basic image, you can carry out any of the following functions: - Select the type of vision; this serves to determine the complexity of the picture. If the image been

uploaded does not contain too much information, you can pick the Simple Image option, and if the details in the image are much, you can select the Moderately or Complex Image Options.
- Tap on the Continue icon.
- Select and Erase; here, you can carry out the editing process on your basic image. This involves erasing and cropping out the unneeded parts by making use of the available tools.

When you are satisfied with the result, tap on the continue button.
- Name and Tag; in this section, you can give your image a name and also decide if it will be a cut image or a print and cut image.
- Save - You will then be taken back to the upload image screen. The image is now prepared and ready to be cut or printed.

Adding Fonts
A lot of folks have the misconceptions that they need to add fonts to Design Space. The truth here is that you do not need to do that. To get your desired fonts, you will have to download them to your PC and then install it. The downloaded fonts will only be available on the system to which you downloaded and installed it on and not on any other system in which you log into your Design Space account on.

Go with the following steps to download and install fonts to the Design Space on your PC
Get a site where you can download the fonts from. Here are some of the websites that you can make use of; esty.com, fornsquirrel.com, fontspace.com, creativemarket.com, datfont.com. Note that some of the fonts are free, while others are not. If your finished product is going to be sold, you should obtain the license or get commercially free fonts. On any of the sites that you choose to get your font from, you can browse through the catalogue available there to pick the one that best suits your current project.

Click on download when you have decided on the font you want to go with. It will download straight to your PC.

Search for the downloaded file on your PC, or better still, go straight to the Downloads Folder, it will most likely be there. The data comes in a zipped folder, unzip it (right-click on your mouse or the touchpad, and select the undo option) to get access to the fonts.

When you are in the file, tap twice in quick succession on the .ttf file. A prompt will come up initiating the installation of the fonts, tap on confirm to begin the process.

Open your Design Space and open a new page, and from there, click on the text tool. Enter a sentence or a word and then move onto the font selection option. You can tap on the system option to have a look at all the fonts that are installed on your PC or simply enter the name of the font that you want.

Despite the vast library of custom images, the Cricut Design Space has, there are files that you may want to cut yourself that may not be available in the system. Since Cricut Design Space supports DIY designs, you can design your own files and upload them to the Design Space for cutting. You can either use Adobe Illustrator or Photoshop to create your own designs.

To upload and use images

Open the Cricut Design Space environment and click, "Upload Image" from the left-hand menu.

Browse through the list of uploaded files and select the image.

Select, "Insert Image".

Select from the type of images Cricut Design Space will ask you.

Another tab will open, select the part of the image you want to cut and the one you do not want to.

Choose whether your image is a regular image or a print-then-cut image.

The file will appear in your work area on the screen. Sometimes, the imported data do not come at the correct dimensions, so you would have to edit. The "edit" menu is on the right of the screen.

Select, "Go" in the top right of the screen and cut your design.

Making a Vinyl Sticker

First of all, you need to have an idea of the vinyl sticker that you want. Get ideas online or from forums. Once you have gotten the picture, make a sketch if it to see how the sticker would look. After you have done this, follow the steps below;

Use an image editing software like Photoshop or Illustrator. Design to your taste and save. Make sure you know the folder it is saved to.
Now, open your Design Space.
Click "New Project".
Scroll to the bottom left-hand side and click "Upload".
Drag and drop the design you created with your photo editing app.
Select your image type. If you want to keep your design simple, select simple.
Select which area of the image that is not part of it.
Before you forge ahead, select the image as cut to have a preview. You can go back if there is a need for adjustments.
Select "Cut".
Weed excess vinyl.
Use a transfer tape on top of the vinyl. This will make the vinyl stay in position.
Go over the tape and ensure all the bibles are nowhere to be found.
Peel away the transfer tape and you have your vinyl sticker.

Best Tools and Software's for Cricut Machine Explore Air 2

Cutting Mat
The Cutting Mat gives a platform on how the materials are going to be laid into the Cricut Machine.

The cutting mat is designed to be sticky on one of the sides to securely hold the material in place during the cutting, scoring, or inking process.

The cutting mat is made up of three types, with each of them used for different kinds of materials. So, the kind of cutting mat you choose to use solely depends on the materials you are working with. Here are the three types of Cutting mats as well as the materials that work with each of them:

- Standard Grip (the one in green color)
- Window clings
- Vinyl
- Regular with Embossed cardstock
- Heat transfer (Iron-on) with regular vinyl
- Firm Grip (the one in purple color)
- Magnetic material
- Foam
- Wood as well as Balsa
- Posterboard
- Backed fabric
- Corrugated Cardboard
- Leather with Suede
- Chipboard
- Light grip (blue color)
- Light cardstock

- Construction paper
- Printer with scrapbook paper
- Vellum

Cutting Mat Covers

The plastic shield is used for covering the cutting mat when purchased. The plastic shield can be pulled off and placed back quickly.

You are always advised to keep and place back the cover of the mat after you are done ever to keep the cloth clean and helps maintain the stickiness.

It is important to always wipe over your cutting mat with some baby wipes. In cleaning your cutting mat, the nonalcoholic baby wipes are recommended to keep your cutting mat from building up with vinyl and cardstock residue after cutting processes.

It also keeps it clean from specks of dust and lint that may be floating about.

Tool Cup

The tool cup is the part that holds scissors, pens, and other Cricut tools in use. The pen is used by getting the accessory clamp A opened and dropping in the pen down into it, after which the clamp is then closed.

Accessory Storage Compartments Apart from the Tool Cup, the Cricut Explore Air 2 machine is made up of two compartments which are also used in holding tools, these are: - Smaller Compartment - Larger Compartment

The smaller compartment is positioned at the left for holding additional blade housings, the accessory adapter as well as the blades. The lower chamber is made up of a magnetic strip for

securely keeping the replacement blades and prevents it from rolling.
The larger compartment is used to store more extended tools and pens.

Accessory Clamp A
The accessory clamp A comes preinstalled as the accessory adapter, and the pen for drawing instead for having to cut can be inserted through this part. It also helps in holding the scoring blades.

The Cricut Scoring Stylus
The Cricut Scoring Stylus is an essential tool, especially for your card projects. So on purchase, it is necessary to check to make sure this tool comes with the Cricut machine.
They are available for free when you purchase the Cricut machine.

Blade Clamp A
Cricut Explore Air Machine has the Blade clamp A already preinstalled in them. The replacement or the removal of bits of vinyl can also be done here.

Smart Set dial
The Cricut Explore Air machine, through its fast mode of operation, enables the user to turn and indicate which material is to be cut with the twice fast style with the use of the Smart Set dial. All you need to do is to rotate the Smart Set dial and choose the material you will be cutting.

Removing and Replacing the Accessory and the Blade clamps of the Cricut Explore Air Machine To remove the accessory clamp or blade, pull open the lever, after which you will then get the metal housing pulled out.

The blade is positioned seated inside; having a tiny plunger on the top, pressing this down will reveal the edge which is held out magnetically.

To get the blade replaced, if the need arises, all you have to do is to get the edge pulled out and drop the new knife in.

Standard Grip Cutting Mat:
The cutting mat is sticky in nature. It is made sticky so that it holds the material being cut in place as it is being cut. Before any operations are carried out, the material to be cut or written on is placed on the Cutting Mat. The mat serves as the work surface for the machine.

Blade and Housing:
This comes preinstalled in the machine. The blade and its housing are attached to one of the two tool holders. You can get other blades and blade holders to cut unique materials

Cricut Cardstock:
In the box, you have some cardstock. This lets you hit the ground running and begin your first project. The cardstock comes in different colors and textures. You could purchase extra material if the cardstock provided in the box proves to be inadequate.

Pen and Accessory Adapter:
The adapter is preinstalled on the second tool holder. It is on this tool holder that the pen or any other accessory is affixed. The adapter holds whatever accessory you wish to use on the secondary tool holder. To use a pen with it, you simply drop a pen into it.

Power Cord:
The Cricut Explore Air 2 runs on electricity. The power cord connects the machine to a power outlet.

USB Cord:
The USB cord connects the device to the computer. It is vital to compare the Cricut Explore Air 2 to the computer with the USB cord when connecting for the first time. This lets the necessary drivers be installed in the networks. After the essential drivers get installed, subsequent connections can be made wirelessly.

Mat Guides:
The Mat Guides are found on the sides of the tray. They keep the Cutting Mat firmly in place and prevent it from moving as the material upon it is being cut. This helps achieve exact and intricate cuts.

Rollers:
The rollers work to push the material being operated under the tool holders so that they can be worked on. The Cutting Mat is placed on the rollers and they roll back and forth to push the cutting mat back and forth. This was the tool holder can reach all parts of the material being worked on to give an exact cut.

How to Cut Vinyl from A Cricut Machine?

First, place the Vinyl liner side down onto the Standard grip mat. Then place it inside the machine after selecting the design. Push the go button to start.
For a smooth placement of the vinyl, you should use vinyl transfer tape. Transfer tape is a kind of pre-mask that transfer vinyl graphics to a substrate after being cut and weeded.
After cutting is done, remove the negatives of the image by a weeder or a tweezer, only leaving the wanted design on the mat. Now remove the Transfer Tape liner. Carefully with the sticky side

down, place it on the mat with the design. Gently press to remove any air bubbles.

Whatever surface you want the design on, it should be clean and dry. Carefully place the vinyl on the surface and gently press it down. Remove the tap by peeling it off at a 45-degree angle. If it is difficult, burnish it by using a scrapper.

How to Cut Basswood by Cricut?

For cutting a word, make sure that it is not thicker than 11 mm. Use a strong grip mat for its cutting. Handle the wood carefully as the wood can be more fragile and easier to break. Use a craft knife and a ruler for this project. Clean the wood or use compressed air to remove all the dust. Mirror the images on Design Space. Brayer can be used to provide adhesion to the mat. Remove the white wheelers to the side of the machine. Check that the wood is not under the rollers; otherwise, it can cause damage. Make sure the design stays inside the edges of the wood — test before cutting the project.

How to design with Cricut machine

I know that you have lot of ideas stuck in your brain and looking for a way to express them. What you need to do is set up your Cricut Explore Air machine, set up the Design Space, and start expressing those ideas immediately.

Working with Fonts in the Design Space
One of the unique features of the Cricut Design Space is the ability to brand your project with distinct fonts and text. Most project with Cricut machines start with the Design Space and you know what?

There is more to it than meet the eye. Let me start with fonts in the Design Space.

How to Add Text to Cricut Design Space
For users of Windows, navigate to the left-hand side of the Canvas and select the *Text* tool. For iOS or Android user, the Text tool is at the bottom-left of the screen.
Select the font size and the font type you wish to use and then type your text in the text box. Do not freak out when you did not choose the font parameters before typing the text, with Cricut Design Space, you can type the text before selecting the font on Windows/Mac computer.
Click or tap on any space outside the text box to close it.

How to Edit Text in Cricut Design Space
To edit the text is super simple. Double click on the text to show available options. Select the action you wish from the list of the options displayed including font style, type, size, letter and line spacing.

How to Edit Fonts
Select the text you wish to edit on the Canvas or you can insert text from design panel, or select a text layer from the Layers Panel.

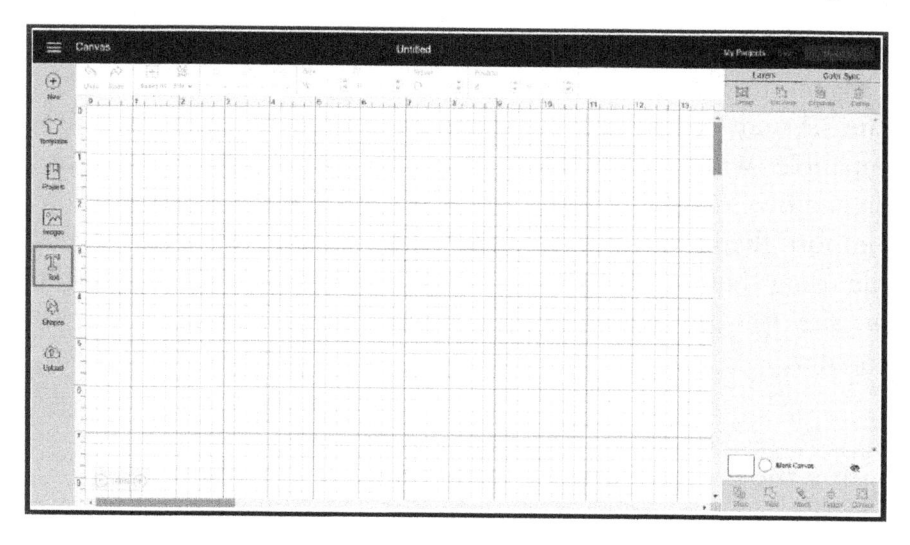

When the Text Edit Bar pops up, you can start changing the font using the available options. These options include Font, Font DropDown, Font Filter, Style, Font Size, Line Space, Alignment, and more.

How to Write Using Fonts

A simple way to write font using Cricut pen with Cricut Explore Air machine is to change the line type of your text from 'Cut' to 'Write'. Next is to choose the font type you wish to use and select the "Writing style" of your choice. Note that the fonts used in the Writing style is similar to the text written by hand but the Cricut machine will write it as if it is tracing the outside of the letters. I believe you know how to use fonts now and what the final form of the fonts will look like. Now, I want to discuss the different types of fonts.

System Fonts

System fonts refer to fonts installed on your computer or mobile device. Every time you sign in, the Cricut Design Space will automatically access your system fonts and allow you to use them for free in the Design Space projects.

Some system fonts have design components that are not compatible with Cricut Design space because they were not designed by Cricut. Do not be surprise when you encounter failure to import them into the Design Space, or they behave unusual while using them in the Design Space. Use the instructions on the font site or app when downloading fonts to your device or computer.

Finding the current firmware version on my machine

It is recommended to have the updated version of the firmware of your device for optimal effective use. This part of the book helps with the latest firmware version that is available for all the Cricut machines.

Finding the current firmware version of the Cricut Explore machines - Make sure you have your Cricut Explore machine connected and powered on.
- Sign in to the Cricut Design Space.
- Go to the upper left corner of the Design space and select the account menu.
- Select the "Update Firmware"
- You will be prompted with a pop-window, select your machine out of the dropdown list and give the software a few moments to detect your machine.
- You will receive a message letting you know if your firmware is up to date or not once your machine has been detected. If your machine is not up to date, you will be notified of any available updates.

Here is the list of the latest firmware versions:
Cricut Explore: 1.091
Cricut Explore Air: 3.091
Cricut Explore Air 2: 5.120
Cricut Explore one: 2.095
Cricut Maker: 4.175

It is to be noted that the Cricut Explore Air or Cricut Maker firmware can also be checked making use of the Design Space on the computer.

Finding the current version of Design Space

To help get the best result with the use of your Cricut Explore Air, it is recommended that you make use of your latest software version. As updates are being released, this actual version changes. To find the current version of the Design Space, you are required to take the following steps: - Go to the taskbar and click on the arrow to display the hidden icons.
- Place your mouse and hover on the Cricut Design space icon.
- Once you hover on the Cricut Design Space, the plugin version should come up.

The Fast Mode of the Cricut Explore Air machine and how it is used

The Cricut Explore Air 2 machine is designed to work in the fast mode, which allows the machine to cut and write up to two times faster than we have in the previous Cricut Explore models. The fast mode is also employed in the Cricut Makers machines as well.
The Fast mode features are made available with the Iron-on, Vinyl, and Cardstock material settings, which are set to Vinyl to Cardstock+ on the Smart Set dial available on the Explore machine.

To make use of the Fast Mode feature of the Cricut Explore Air machine, here are the basic instructions that you will need to follow: - When all is set for writing and cutting your project, simply go to the Cut screen.

- The Fast Mode option will be made available if you have chosen the right material for the mode.

- Toggle the switch to the "ON" position by clicking or tapping the switch to get the Fast Mode activated. It is to be noted that the Cricut Explore Air 2 machines tend to make a louder noise while making use of the fast mode features; this is normal.

Cleaning and Care

Cleaning your Cricut machine involves basically caring for your mat. All other cleanings will have to do with maintenance of your machine.

There are different ways of cleaning Cricut mat based on their types:

For FabricGrip Cricut mat:
Do not use scrapper tool to remove bits of fabric on the Cricut mat unlike other Cricut mats

The oils on your finger can reduce the adhesive on the mat's surface, therefore, avoid touching of the surface with your fingers.

Use only Cricut spatula, tweezers or StronGrip transfer tape to clean this mat.

Cleaning agents including soap and water should not be used on this mat

For Other mats:
Use the tool called scrapper to clear all the leftovers from your Cricut mat

For smaller leftover bits difficult to remove, use a sticky lint roller and roll it over your Cricut mat to remove them.

Wash your Cricut mat with any gentle detergent and water then leave to dry.

Use nonalcoholic cleaning wipe to clan the surface of your Cricut mat.

Cutting Blade

Every single blade you use might get up to fifteen thousand individual cuts before it needs to be replaced. To prolong this number of individual cuts, place the aluminum foil onto the cutting mat and cut out a few designs. This process keeps the blade extra sharp and lengthens the life of the blade. This number of cuts can be greatly based on the types of materials cut by the blade. If you are doing many projects in which thick materials need to be cut the blade will deteriorate quickly; the blade can also deteriorate quickly if you are cutting many materials on high pressure. A good way to know if your blade needs to be replaced is if your cuts' quality starts to decrease greatly. If this happens it's best to replace the cutting blade. When replacing the blade, it is always best to get blades that are Cricut brand. Generic blades are often not the best quality and will cause you to replace your cutting blade constantly. To install the new blade once you've ordered the correct one, you need first to unplug your Cricut Cutter machine. Always unplug the machine before installing anything in your Cricut cutter. Next, you must remove the old, dull cutting blade from your Cricut Cutter machine. The process of how to do this has been mentioned numerous times in this book and the last chapter. Once the cutting blade assembly has been separated it is now time to eject the blade. Find the small silver button above the adjustment knob and press the button down; this will eject the cutting blade. Be very careful when doing this as the blade is extremely sharp and can easily cut through the skin. Keep all blades away from children and pets. To put in the new blade, insert the blade on the end of the blade assembly opposite of the blade release button. The blade will then be pulled up into the assembly. Place the assembly back into the machine by reversing the process previously written about in the last chapter.

Getting the Cricut Cutting Mat cleaned
It is important to always wipe over your cutting mat with some baby wipes. In cleaning your cutting mat, the non-alcoholic baby wipes are recommended to keep your cutting mat from building up with vinyl and cardstock residue after cutting processes.
It also keeps it clean from specks of dust and lint that may be floating about.

The Cutting mat in addition to the cutting blade needs to be taken care of. One cutting mat can have a life of anywhere from twenty-five to forty cuts. The cutting mat's experience can vary from this amount depending on the pressure and speed at which the cuts have been made and the type of materials that have been cut on the mat. To prolong the life of your cutting mat, remove any debris from the mat after a cut and always avoid scraping the mat.

If you scrape the mat, it can push any debris further into the mat. After each craft, it is best to run lukewarm water over the mat and dab it dry with a towel afterward. When a material can not adhere to the cutting mat any longer, it is time to replace it finally. It is recommended to get many cutting mats and rotate between them to prolong all the cutting mats. This extends the mats' life because one cutting mat will not be cut on for many, many projects in a small amount of time. It is also recommended that you keep all of your cutting mats and all of your cartridges and blades in a very organized manner. Throwing the haphazardly components can destroy and deteriorate them so it is best to keep them in a very organized fashion. A benefit of keeping your Cricut Cutter components organized is that you won't lose or damage the very expensive items necessary for several projects.

Cricut Machine

The final thing to keep clean is the actual Cricut Cutter machine. The machine needs to be wiped down with a damp cloth. Only wipe down the external panels of the machine and with the machine unplugged. Always wipe down the machine with a dry cloth after cleaning the outside of the machine. Never clean the Cricut Cutter machine with abrasive cleaners such as acetone, benzene, and all other alcohol-based cleaners. Abrasive cleaning tools should never be used on the Cricut Cutter machine either. Also, never submerge any machine component or the Cricut Cutter machine into the water as it can damage the device.

Always keep the Cricut Cutter machine away from all foods, liquids, pets, and children. Keep the Cricut Cutter machine in a very dry and dust free environment. Finally, do not put the Cricut Cutter machine in excessive heat, excessive cold, sunlight, or any area where the plastic or any other components on the Cricut Cutter machine can melt.

Using or creating custom material settings

The Cricut Explore Air machines are used for cutting different kinds of materials. It is designed with pre-programmed settings on the design space to create flexibility when working on projects using various materials. Apart from these pre-programmed settings, you can create your own as well.

Making use of Custom material settings - Get signed into the Design Space and create a project.
- Turn on your Cricut Explore machine.
- Have your Cricut Explore machine connected to your computer.

- Go to the Project Preview screen and ensure that the Smart Set Dial is appropriately locked to Custom.
- Click on "Browse All Materials."
You can simply search for the material by name or scrolling to browse the list. Note that all the materials having the Cricut logo next to them are the Cricut branded materials.

How to create a new Custom material
This becomes handy in a situation where your choice of material is not available on the materials list. When this happens, you can simply try the settings with the closest match to your material or build a new setting.

It is important to note that new Custom materials cannot be added to the Cricut Design space when using the Android device. Still, any materials that are added from the Computer, iPhone, or iPad will be made available on the Android app.
To create a new material setting, you are required to take the following steps below: - Go to the menu and select the "Manage Custom Materials" or select the "Materials Settings" located at the bottom of the page when browsing materials for projects to gain access to the Custom Materials screen.
- Select the "Add New Material" by scrolling down to the bottom of the list.
- Have the name of the material indicated.
- Click on the "Save" option.
- After saving the material, you will have the chance to make necessary adjustments with the use of the following: ☐ Multi-cut: This helps in directing the machine to cut multiple times in the same image, and it is usually used for thick materials.
☐ Cut pressure: This adjusts the slider or using the +/- buttons.
☐ Blade type: You can select from the deep-point blade or high-grade Fine-Point blade for the Design Space to prompt accordingly.

☐ Select "Save" to get your new custom material saved after configuration.
☐ Close the materials screen with the "X" sign that will be found at the top-right corner.

After this, your new material will be found in the materials list and can be found using the search option. It is to be noted that the star can be used in adding the material to your favorite.

Cut Vinyl with A Cricut Machine

There are different types of vinyl that you can use.
Oracal 651, I would recommend using it for PERMANENT works as the strong adhesive might compromise your surface and leave a lot of residue. It is perfect for outdoors works because it is water resistant. But you can generally choose Oracal 651 for your indoor creation that you know you will make a heavy use with, like mugs, plates, bowls. But this might not be working for everyone, so I recommend you first give a try in one mug or two.
Oracal 631 is generally used for wall decals and other internal works and it is appreciated because it can last a little while but can't stand up to heavy applications. So, it is NOT PERMANENT. However, you can create infinite things with it, like phone cases, interior decorations, stencils, etc…

Heat Transfer Vinyl (More known as HTV)
This is a common and easy to apply method, also for who is starting from scratch. After cutting the vinyl piece, you use your iron to apply the vinyl to a fabric surface. It holds up through the washing machine and looks very professional. You can customize your favorite clothing. As you are reading in this guide, this method is also known as T-Shirt Vinyl or Iron-on Vinyl. There is a variety of brands, but the most often recommended is Scissor Easy Weed. Easy to use, it comes in various styles and colors and it holds up

through the washing machine, it looks perfect. It is ideal for: Socks, T-shirts, and Stuffed animals, Canvas tote bags, Costumes, anything with fabric

Printable Vinyl
Printable Vinyl comes both in Heat Transfer and Adhesive types. All you need to have with this particular material is a normal inkjet printer. The design can be printed out on your vinyl.

Using Snap Mat cutting multiple Colors

Take pieces of vinyl of different colors, cut and put them all on your Cricut Mat, and make it easier to take a picture of it, I suggest laying your mat on the floor. Then from your Cricut App, click categories, then Projects in the Cloud, then select the project you will cut and click customize, then replace and then Make it.

Next click on Snap Mat and you can place the camera over the floor on your Mat and wait for the box to turn green, hold it for a few seconds and take the picture.
Once the picture popped up, select use, and then select continue. You can start your creation with multiple colors in one mat. You can create images and text and swipe from one color to another.

Cricut Scrapbooking

Scrapbooking is the most recent crafty phenomenon. With the introduction of digital electronic cameras, traditional picture albums have gone by the wayside and better method to keep essential photos and the memories attached. There are many tools for avid scrapbookers from various papers, stickers, shapes and scissors; would it not be fantastic to have all these products in one main place and at the touch of a button? Cricut Expression is the answer.

This individual electronic cutter enables you to produce some of the most individualized and beautiful shapes to include flare to even you're the majority of papercraft standards.

Those concerned that a maker might waste paper by not making use of all the areas available, do not worry. The Cricut has been created not only to develop terrific shapes and font styles, however it will do it in such as the manner in it will make the most of the user of the paper, which will help keep the amount of waste to a minimum.

How do you desire to get your words onto your page?

The simplest is to find a writing design you like and practice up until you are more than happy with it. Otherwise it's a trip to your regional scrapbook shop to spend your robust generated income on alphabets - again!

So ... having filled the dishwasher, the cleaning machine and the drier, got the kids to school, made appointments for the hair and the dental professional dresser for everyone, went to the PTA meeting and got the groceries for dinner, you just have time between your lunch date with hubby and gathering the dry cleansing to run to the scrapbook store before it's time to gather the kids from school, offer them a snack, prepare supper so it's prepared when you all get back from soccer practice, then house once again to consume dinner, aid with research, get the kids to bed, and go over some household issues with hubby before you hit the sack yourself ... By the method, when do you have time to scrapbook?

Anyway, when you do make it to the scrapbook store what you will discover there? You need to create humungous choices:

- Alphabet Sticker Labels Rub-Ons
- Die Cuts Stamps

- Word and Expression Decorations

Any of these could make fantastic titles, journaling and beliefs on your designs. Let's have a look at some of them;

Alphabet sticker labels
The disadvantage is they never seem to come with adequate letters, and you can only make a couple of words in the same style. Nevertheless, you can utilize the remaining letters as 'drop capitals' at the beginning of paragraphs in your design.
You can get off with a range of different styles in this method by adding some layouts, that will allow you to mix and match different designs within the title or bullets. It's enjoyable to include casual style characters in the middle of your journaling, too.

Rubon
These were called transfers when I was a child, and only came as letters. They now come as individual letters or words and expressions in black or various colors, and numerous gorgeous designs, too.
As the name recommends, you merely rub them onto your page with the little stick offered. If you lose the stick.), (You can utilize a bone folder or a coin It's an excellent concept to cut around the words you desire to use and position them thoroughly or you may find stray pieces from the word next door that you hadn't meant to transfer.
Rub-on looks good and provides a professional finish.

Alphabet stamps
These are an excellent buy as you can prevent the 'never-have-all-the-letters-I-need' syndrome that occurs with other media - and they are re-useable!
If you choose for clear stamps, it's simple to stamp words with duplicate letters. Simply line up the letters on a clear acrylic block to

form your word, leaving the correct size area for the replicate letters which you add on a 2nd pass.

To conserve the right space, put another stamp in the place where the replicate letter will go, and when you've completed the word remove it and you're entrusted to an area where you mark the missing letter later on. You can stamp the letters accurately since you can see where you are stamping. After use, simply wipe clean, change on the sheet and they're prepared for next time!

Electronic and mechanical systems

The numerous cutting machine systems have some terrific alphabets, but, if you are brand-new to scrapbooking they can seem an expensive way to develop your titles. Suppose you believe you will also use some of the many other shapes readily available. In that case, the results are outstanding and well worth the cost. You will get exceptional usage out of these mainly if you make your own greetings cards, too.

Before you make the trip to your regional scrapbooking store consider utilizing your computer system. You currently have a variety of font styles on it and there are much more available to download devoid of the web.

Your computer is one of the most flexible ways to develop a title or journaling. With the massive selection of typefaces available you will discover one that fits your layout design, but much more beneficial is the versatility when it comes to size. You can have the font as large as you desire for a title, or little sufficient to get all your journaling on a tag.

You will conserve a lot of money with the aid of your computer system.

How do you get titles from your computer to your design?
It's fast and effortless to do.
Select a font style and size it appropriately for your task.
Type your words, and then print using the reverse image setting on your printer alternatives.
Transfer to the incorrect side of your picked pattern or color paper or cardstock,
Cut out and stay with your scrapbook job or card.
If you don't have, or can't find the reverse image setting, then: thoroughly trace around your words - a lightbox will help you here - on the ideal side of the paper, cut out inside your lines.
It's great to have so many ranges of alphabets for our designs. However, do attempt to avoid using one design too typically, as it will be monotonous to make and to view an album filled with the very same styles.
Now you see how simple it is to make excellent titles and journaling, there's nothing stopping you. Have a good time creating your memories - and might you have time to preserve them on lovely scrapbook page designs.

Chapter 4: Solving the most common problem when using Cricut Explore Air 2

Helpful Troubleshooting Techniques

Problems with printing images
The Explore machine will work with various printers, but some printers will jam when using card stock. The best option is to use a printer that feeds the card stock from the rear. The less turns the card stock makes in the printer the less chance of it jamming.
Play it safe and don't use a laser printer for vinyl or sticky material. The heat of the printer will melt the material and could damage the printer.

Design Space has a printable area that is 6.75 by 9.25. This is a lot bigger than past versions.
When you're working with an image, you're going to print select a square from the Shapes tool and place it behind your image. Make the size of the square 6.75 and 9.25. Then you can see while you're working with you image whether or not it is within the printable area. Make the square a light color so you can see it separate from your image.

You can put more than one image in the box. Attach the images so you can move them all at one time. Delete the box before printing. It's easier than ever to create custom designs for multiple uses by changing their Line type instead of redesigning the whole project.

Pens

When you're inserting a pen into your machine, place a piece of scrap paper under the pen. This keeps the pen from marking up your material or your machine when you click it into the clamp.

There are several ways to breathe new life into dried markers sometimes just soaking the tip will work or refilling the pen with 90% alcohol.

Besides the homemade universal pen adapter I mentioned, the tube shaped pencil grips fit some markers making them compatible with the Explore.

Problems with cutting images

Before unloading the mat try to determine if the material has been cut to satisfaction. If not manually hit the cut button on the Explore and cut it again several times.

Use the Custom Material Settings in Design Space to increase or decrease the pressure, add multiple cuts, choose an intricate cut setting, or change materials. Within each category there are several listings for different kinds of paper or card stock for example. Just try selecting another type and see if that helps.

Create your own custom settings for any material by selecting Manage Custom Materials from the main menu. Then just click Add New Material and enter the information.

Some intricate designs won't cut well in Fast Mode so just cut it regularly. Make sure the blade and mat are clean.

If your images are not cutting correctly be sure and wipe the mat and scrape off any access material left from previous projects. If the mat is severely scored or gouged replace it.

Try switching to another mat such as the stickier blue mat. If the mat isn't sticky enough the material can slip and won't cut properly. Or tape the paper to the mat.

Then carefully clean the blade. If there is still a problem, it might be time to replace the blade. Using the new German Carbide blade is your best option for optimal cutting. Believe it or not there can be a slight difference in the cutting edge between one new blade and another.

Make sure the blade fits tightly in the housing. Regularly clean out the blade housing of fibers that accumulate and interfere with the cutting process. Blow into the housing or use a straightened paperclip and carefully loosen and stuck material.

Since the deep cutting blade angle is different, try using it on regular material when experiencing problems.

If you get a message saying image is too large you simply need to resize it to make it smaller. Some people think that since the mat is 12 x 12 they can use 12 x 12 images. But there is a little space left for margins, so the largest image size is 11.5 x 11.5. You can purchase a 12 x 24 mat to make larger cuts of 11.5 x 23.5.

If all else fails, try a different material. Some users find that certain brands of paper or card stock work better than others.

Mats

If your mat is too sticky when it's new place a white T-shirt on it and press lightly or just pat it with your hands. This will reduce some of the stickiness.

When using a brayer and thin paper don't apply a lot of pressure on the mat. This makes it hard to remove without ripping the paper.

Always clean your mat after each use. Use a scraper to remove small bits of lint or paper that have been left behind. These small scraps will cause problems with future projects.
You can wipe the mat with a damp cloth. Then replace the plastic cover between uses to prevent dust and dirt from sticking to the mat.

When the mat has lost its stickiness; tape the material to the mat around the edges or wash it with a little soap and water, rinse, let dry and it's good to go.
Have you seen those food grade flexible cutting mats or boards? Some users are turning them into Cricut mats. Look for the thin plastic ones that are 12 x 12 or 12 x 24.
Use spray adhesive and cover the mat leaving a border so the glue doesn't get on the rollers or just spray the card stock's back to adhere to the makeshift mat.

Load and unload
When you load the mat into the Explore always make sure that it's up against the roller wheels and under the guides. This assures the material will load straight when you press the load button.

When the cut is complete never pull the mat out of the machine as this can damage the wheels. Always hit the unload button and then remove the mat.
To extend the life of the mat turn it around and load it from the bottom edge. Position the images on different parts of the mat instead of always cutting in the upper left corner.

Curling
Here's how to avoid curling material into a useless mess. When working with new mats they tend to hold on for dear life.

When you're pulling a project off the mat, do not remove the paper (or whatever material) up and away from the mat. This will cause it to curl into a mess.

Instead turn the mat over and curl it downward. Pull the rug away from the paper instead of pulling the form up and away from the mat.

It seems like a slight difference, but it will save you from trying to uncurl and flatten a project. Just remember how curled the mat was when you first unboxed it had to wait till it flattened out.

Blades

When cutting adhesive material, glue accumulates on the blades and should be periodically removed. Dip a Q-Tip in nail polish remover to clean any sticky residue build up. Check the cutting edge for nicks and that the tip is still intact.

Note: These blades are incredibly sharp. Always use the utmost care when removing them or replacing them into your Cricut. Never leave them lying within reach of children. Save the tips and cap the blades before trashing them.

For best results use the German Carbide blades. The regular Cricut blades will fit in the Explore blade housing even though they're shaped differently.

At this time there is no German Carbide deep cut blade for the Explore. The blade that comes with the deep cut housing for the Explore is the regular deep cutting blade.

Materials

When you're planning a project with a new material it's good to do a small test first to make sure the material cuts the way you want. This will save you from potential problems and from wasting a large amount of material.

Try one of the in-between settings on the Smart Set Dial. Some card stock is thicker than other types so you may need to adjust settings, use the multi cut settings or re-cut the image manually by hitting the cut button again.

By default, the Smart Set dial for paper, vinyl, iron-on, card stock, fabric, poster board has been set up to work best with Cricut products. Each material has three settings on the dial. If the cuts aren't deep enough, increase the pressure or decrease the pressure if the cuts are too deep. For even more control use the custom settings within Design Space.
Additionally, using a deep cutting blade (with the housing) or adjusting the mat's stickiness may help.

Iron-on Vinyl
Sometimes the iron-on vinyl sticks to the iron. First, be sure your iron is not too hot. Follow the recommendations on the product. Ensure you purchased the type of vinyl that can be applied with an iron not a professional heat press.
Next, try using parchment paper, Teflon sheet or a piece of cotton fabric between the vinyl and the iron. Use a firm heat resistant surface such as a ceramic tile or wooden cutting board to place your project on. Press and hold instead or ironing back and forth.
Always flip the image in Design Space. Put the vinyl shiny side down while cutting and shiny side up when attaching to the material.

Iron-on Glitter Vinyl
When working with glitter vinyl I move the dial one notch passed iron-on vinyl toward light card stock. It seems to cut better using that setting.
After you make the first cut do not remove the mat from the machine. Check to see if it cut through the vinyl, sometimes I have

to run it through one more time for a complete cut. Especially if it's a new brand I haven't worked with.

Stencils
There are many materials you can use to make stencils. Some users suggested plastic file folders that can be found cheaply at a Dollar Store. Another option is sending laminating sheets through a laminating machine and then putting them through your Cricut to cut the stencil. Run it through twice to make sure cuts are complete.

Problems with machine pausing
If your Cricut machine stops while cutting, writing or scoring I've already made several suggestions to correct the problem here's another option.

It maybe the project itself if it always happens try deleting that project and recreating it. Turn off your computer and disconnect from your machine. Turn off your Cricut machine and wait a few moments. Then restart and reconnect.

Problems with Bluetooth wireless
If you're using an Explore Air or Explore Air 2 your Cricut machine is already Bluetooth enabled. But with an Explore or Explore One you will need to buy a Bluetooth adaptor.

When using Bluetooth be sure your machine is within nearby, no more than 15 feet from of the computer.

Make sure to verify your computer is Bluetooth enabled. If not, you'll need to buy a Bluetooth Dongle and place it in an unused USB port.

If you lose the Bluetooth connection, try uninstalling your Cricut under Bluetooth devices and then reinstalling.

Some people find their Design Space software works faster using the USB cord instead of the Bluetooth connection.

Chapter 5: FAQs about the Cricut Explore Air 2

Why does Design Space say my Cricut machine is already in use when it's not?
To resolve this, make sure that you've completed the New Machine Setup for your Cricut. Try Design Space in another browser. The two that work best are Google Chrome and Mozilla Firefox; if it doesn't work in one of those, try the other. If that doesn't clear the error, try a different USB port and USB cable. Disconnect the machine from the computer and turn it off. While it's off, restart your computer. After your computer restarts, reconnect the machine and turn it on. Wait a few moments, then try Design Space again. If you're still having the same problem, contact Cricut Member Care.

Why doesn't my cut match the preview in Design Space?
Test another image and see if the same thing happens. If it's only happening with the one project, create a new project and start over or try a different image. If it happens with a second project, and your machine is connected with Bluetooth, disconnect that and plug it in with a USB cable. Larger projects may sometimes have difficulty communicating the cuts over Bluetooth. If you can't connect with USB or the problem is still occurring, check that your computer matches or exceeds the system requirements for running Design Space. If it doesn't, try the project on a different computer or mobile device that does. If your computer does meet the requirements, open Design Space in a different browser and try again. If the problem continues, try a different USB cable. Finally, if the issue still hasn't resolved, contact Cricut Member Care.

What do I do if I need to install USB drivers for my Cricut machine?
Typically, the Cricut drivers are automatically installed when you connect it with a USB cable. If Design Space doesn't see your machine, you can try this to troubleshoot the driver installation. First, open Device Manager on your computer. You'll need to have administrator rights. For Windows 7, click Start, right-click on Computer, and select Manage. For Windows 8 and up, right-click on the Start icon and click Computer Management. Within Computer Management, click Device Manager on the left-hand side. Find your Cricut machine on the list—it should be listed under Ports. Still, it might be under Other Devices or Universal Serial Bus Controllers. Right-click on it and select Update Driver Software. In the box that pops up, select Browse My Computer. In the box on the next screen, type in %APPDATA% and click Browse. Another box will pop up where you can search through folders. Find AppData and expand it. Click Roaming, then CricutDesignSpace, then Web, then Drivers, then CricutDrivers, and click OK. Click Next to install these drivers. Once it's finished, restart your computer. Once it's on, open Design Space again to see if it recognizes your machine.

Why does my Cricut Maker say the blade is not detected?
Ensure that the tool in Clamp B is the same one Design Space recommends in the Load Tools step of the Project Preview screen. If you don't have that recommended tool, unload your mat and select Edit Tools on the Project Preview screen. Here, you can choose a different device. If the agency and the selection already match, carefully remove the device from Clamp B and clean the reflective band on the housing. Reinstall it in the clamp and press the Go button. If that doesn't resolve the problem, remove the tool

again and clean the machine's sensor. Reinstall the tool and press Go again. If the Maker still doesn't detect the blade, try a simple test using a basic shape with one of the other tools. If that works, there may be something wrong with the drive housing of the original device. If the problem continues with other tools or don't have another tool to test, try uninstalling and reinstalling Design Space and retry your project. If the issue persists, or if you've discovered it's an issue with the tool housing, contact Cricut Member Care.

Is Wireless Bluetooth Adapter required for All Cricut Explore machines?
No. It is only required for Explore and Explore One. Explore Air and Explore Air 2 have in-built Bluetooth and therefore no need for Wireless Bluetooth Adapter.

How do you differentiate between the Cricut Explore machines?
The tool holder is the first difference. Explore One has one tool holder which means it can cut & score in two steps while Explore, Explore Air, and Explore Air 2 come with double tool holder for cut & write or cut & score in one single step.
Explore and Explore One require a Cricut Wireless Bluetooth Adapter to cut wirelessly from your iOS, Android or computer while Explore Air and Explore Air 2 have in-built Bluetooth.

Is carry bag included in Explore series machine package?
No. carry bag is not included in the package, but you can buy it separately.

Is it possible to write & score with my Explore One machine?
Yes, but to do this, you will need to buy Explore One Accessory Adapter. Switch this adapter with the blade housing to write or score with Explore One machine.

Are the weights and dimensions of Explore Series machine similar? What are their dimensions?
Yes, they are similar. The approximate weight is 9.5 kg (21 lbs), length: 56.33cm (22.17"), width: 17.76cm (6.99") and height: 15.16cm (5.97").

Why is my Cricut machine making a grinding noise?
If it's the carriage car making a loud noise after you press the cut button, and it sounds like the carriage might be hitting the side of the machine, record a short video of it and send it to Cricut Member Care. If the noise is coming from a brand-new engine the first time you use it, contact Cricut Member Care. Otherwise, make sure that you're using the original power cord that came with your device. If the machine isn't getting the correct voltage, it may produce a grinding sound. If you are using the machine's power cord, adjust your pressure settings. If it's too high, it might have an unusual sound. Decrease it in increments of 2–4, and do some test cuts. If it's still making the issue even after decreasing the cutting pressure, contact Cricut Member Care.

What if my Cricut is making a different loud noise?
Make sure that you don't have Fast Mode engaged for cutting or writing. If it's not on, take a short video of the problem to send to Cricut Member Care.

Why is my mat going into the machine crooked?
Check the roller bar to see if it's loose, damaged, or uneven. If it is, take a photo or video of it to send to Cricut Member Care. If the

roller bar seems fine, make sure that you're using the right mat size for the machine. Next, make sure the mat is correctly lined up with the guides and that the edge is underneath the roller bar when you prepare to load it. If it's still loading crookedly even when properly lined up with the guides, try applying gentle pressure to the mat to get it under the roller bar once it starts. If none of this works, contact Cricut Member Care.

Why isn't the Smart Set Dial changing the material in Design Space?
Make sure that the USB cable between the computer and the Cricut Explore is appropriately connected. If so, disconnect the Explorer from the computer and turn it off. Restart your computer. Once it's on, turn on the Explore, plug it into the computer, and try the cut again. If it still isn't changing the material, connect the USB cable to a different port on the computer. If it's still not working, try Design Space in multiple web browsers and see if the problem replicates. If it does, try an entirely different USB cable. Check for Firmware Updates for the Explore. If you don't have another USB cable, the Firmware Update doesn't help, or there are no Firmware Updates, contact Cricut Member Care.

What do I do if my Cricut Maker stopped partway through a cut?
If the Knife Blade stops cutting and the Go button is flashing, the Maker has encountered some sort of error. In Design Space, you'll get a notification that the blade is stuck. This might have been caused by the edge running into something like a knot or seam if too much dust or debris built up in the cut area or if the blade got into a gouge in the mat from a previous cut. To resume your project, do not unload the mat. This will lose your place in the project, and it will be impossible to get it lined up again. Check the

cut area for dust or debris, and gently clean it. If there's dust on top of Clamp B, brush it off with a clean, dry paintbrush. Do not remove the blade. Once the debris is gone, press the Go button. The machine will take a moment to sense the Knife Blade again, and then it will resume cutting.

Why is my fabric getting caught under the rollers?
Be sure to cut down any fabric so that it fits on your mat without going past the adhesive. If you have stuck the fabric and realize it's hanging past the adhesive, use a ruler and a sharp blade to trim it. Or, if it's the correct size but slightly askew, unstick it and reposition it.

Why would my Cricut Maker continuously turn off during cuts?
This can happen from a build-up of static electricity while cutting foil and metal sheets. Makers in dry areas are more susceptible to this. Spritzing water in the air will dissipate the build-up. Be careful not to spray any water directly on the Maker. Using a humidifier or vaporizer in the area where you use your Maker can help avoid the static build-ups. If this doesn't seem to be what's causing the issue, contact Cricut Member Care.

What do I do about a failing or incomplete firmware update?
Be sure to use a computer to install the firmware update and that you're connected with a USB cable rather than Bluetooth. Verify that the computer meets the minimum system requirements; if it doesn't, you'll need to use another computer that does. If it does and you're still having problems, disconnect the Cricut from your computer and turn it off. Restart the computer. Once it's back on, open Design Space and try the firmware update again. If it still freezes up or doesn't complete, try the update using a different web browser. The next step is to try another USB cable. If that doesn't

help or don't have another USB cable to try, contact Cricut Member Care.

What do I do if my Cricut machine is having power issues?
If your Cricut Maker, Cricut Explore One, or Cricut Explore Air 2 is having power issues, these are the troubleshooting steps. If the machine doesn't have any control or only has it sometimes, make sure that the plug is completely plugged into the power port on the device, the power adapter, and the wall outlet. The cutting mat can sometimes knock the power cable loose as it goes through the machine. You can avoid this by making sure the excess cord isn't bundled up behind the machine. If everything is securely plugged in, make sure that you're using the genuine Cricut power cable that came with your device and that the green light on the adapter is lit up. If you're not using the Cricut power cable, you can buy one or contact Cricut Member Care. If you are, try using a different wall outlet. If it's still having problems, try another Cricut power cable. If the issues continue even after this, take a short video of the issue happening and forward it to Cricut Member Care.

What do I do if I'm having issues with the machine's door?
If the door won't open or won't stay open, take a short video to forward on to Cricut Member Care. If the door won't close or won't stay closed, make sure there aren't any accessories loaded into the accessory clamp. If there aren't, take a photo or short video to forward to the Cricut Member Care team.

Where Can I Download Software for my Cricut Explore Air Machine?
For iOS users or Android users, you can get Cricut Design Space on the iOS App Store and Google Play, respectively. All you need do is to download it, install it and log in
For uses on a computer, visit design.cricut.com and then sign in with your login details. There will be a prompt to download Cricut

Design Space. Download the plugin and install it and you are good to go.

Does My Cricut Explore Air need a Wireless Bluetooth Adapter?
No. Your machine is Bluetooth enabled. There is no need for a wireless Bluetooth adapter.

Can I link my cartridges to more than one account?
No. You can link your cartridges to only one Cricut account.

Can a cartridge be unlinked after it has been linked?
No. A cartridge once linked to an account cannot be unlinked.

I linked my cartridge to older software; can I still use it in Cricut Design Space?
Once you have linked your cartridges to older software like Cricut Craft Room, there will be no need to relink them on Cricut Design Space because they will be automatically available there.

I have linked my cartridges; how do I access them?
All the cartridges you have linked to your account can be found in your Cricut account. Go to Cricut Design Space and look under "My Image Sets" in the Insert Images window. You will find all the cartridges you have linked to your account.

Can I use physical cartridges without linking them?
No. For you to use any cartridge on your Cricut Explore Air, it must be linked to your account.

What type of materials can I cut with my cricut?
This machine cut more than 80 types of materials, clipboard, soda cans and even more thicker materials?

Can I upload my images?
You can upload your image or any other files that are already formatted and compatible with Cricut design space? The SVGs is one of the best image files because it uses 37 math formulas to create image based on point between lines.

What is the duration of my cutting mat?
You can cut through each cutting mat 20-50 full cut, but it depends on the card stack's nature and the cut size?

Can I make use of other paper size?
Yes, you can? One corner of the paper can just be aligning with the mat before loading your mat. Use the blade navigation button to adjust the cutting blade to the paper upper right side.
After which you tap on set paper size on your keypad, then allow the machine to start cutting on your paper

Can I learn how to create my own customize project with cricut design software without much stress?
yes, you can create and design your custom project any way you wish it to be without much weight.

Chapter 6: Tips for beginners

Want to enjoy your machine? Here are a few tips and tricks that will help you:

De-tack your cutting mat!

Your Cricut Explore Air will arrive with a cutting mat upon which you will put your projects before cutting. When purchased newly the cutting mat is usually very sticky. I would advise that you prime the cutting mat before your first use. Priming makes it less sticky such that your paper projects do not get damaged. You prime the cutting mat by placing a clean dry fabric over the cutting stock over the cutting mat and pulling it out again.

Keep Your Cutting Mat Clean

Use wipes to keep your cutting mat clean. Be careful with alcohol wipes as they could make the carpet lose stickiness. You can also use the plastic cover to store your cutting mat when it is not in use.

Use the Proper Tools

Use the correct Cricut Tools. The best tools are the tools from the Cricut Tool Set. This toolset contains tweezers, scrapers, scissors, spatula, and a weeding tool. These tools make work go very smoothly.

Start Your Cricut Journey with the Sample Project

It is best to start with the sample project and the material provided. The materials you will find in the package will be sufficient for you to start an initial sample project. Start with a simple sample project to have a feel of how the machine works.

Always Test Cuts

When carrying out projects, it is advisable to do a test cut before running the whole project. You can designate a simple cut to test run your settings before cutting material for the project. If the blade is not well set the test cut will reveal it.

Replace Pen Lids after Use

Replace the pen lids when you are done using your pens. This avoids it from drying out. It is a good thing that Design Space sends a notification that reminds you to put the lid back on!

Link Your Old Cricut Cartridges

If you have cartridges you have used with your older machines, you can still hook them up with your new device.

Bend the Cutting Mat to Get Materials off the Cutting Mat

To remove cut materials from the cutting mat (incredibly delicate Vinyl); you can bend the carpet away from the fabric. That way, you can use the spatula to help get the cut material off the cutting mat.

Use the Deep Cut Blade for Thicker Materials

Use the deep cut blade to cut through thick materials. These materials could be leather, cardboard or even chipboard. Get the edge and the blade housing.

Always replace the pen lids after use

You should ensure you avoid forgetting your pen in the machine after you are done with a project. This might result in your cell drying out, so you should always remember to have the lid back on it after you are done.

Linking your old Cricut Cartridges to your Design Space Account

In a situation where you have old cartridges from previous machines, it helps hook this up with your new machine. It is to be noted that cartridges can only be linked once. In a situation where you are buying a second-hand cartridge, you will need to confirm if it has not been linked to a machine before.

Get materials off the Cutting mat

Getting the project peeled from the mat can cause curling; therefore, you can instead just peel the mat from the project. Just have the carpet bent away from the card rather than the other way round.

Get the Deep Cut blade

You are advised to order the deep cut blade. It is useful in cutting through thick cards, chipboard, leather, etc. It works perfectly with the Cricut Explore Air 2.
You should get the blade housing along with the blade.

Always Replace the Blades

It is usual for Cricut blades to wear out after being used for sometimes. The blade will start to be ineffective and will no longer be smooth; at this point, it is necessary to have the blades changed. Some other signs that show that it's time for the blade to be replaced include when it starts lifting or pulling the vinyl off the backing seat, they start to tear the cards or vinyl and incomplete cutting process.

Keep Your Cutting Mat Clean

Use wipes to keep your cutting mat clean. Be careful with alcohol wipes as they could make the carpet lose stickiness. You can also use the plastic cover to store your cutting mat when it is not in use.

Use the Proper Tools

Use the correct Cricut Tools. The best tools are the tools from the Cricut Tool Set. This toolset contains tweezers, scrapers, scissors, spatula, and a weeding tool. These tools make work go very smoothly.

Start Your Cricut Journey with the Sample Project

It is best to start with the sample project and the material provided. The materials you will find in the package will be sufficient for you to create an initial sample project. Start with a simple sample project to have a feel of how the machine works.

Always Test Cuts

When carrying out projects, it is advisable to do a test cut before running the whole project. You can designate a simple amount to test run your settings before cutting material for the project. If the blade is not well set the test cut will reveal it.

Replace Pen Lids after Use

Replace the pen lids when you are done using your pens. This avoids it from drying out. It's a good thing that Design Space sends a notification that reminds you to put the lid back on!

Link Your Old Cricut Cartridges

If you have cartridges you have used with your older machines, you can still hook them up with your new machine.

Bend the Cutting Mat to Get Materials off the Cutting Mat

To remove cut materials from the cutting mat (especially delicate Vinyl); you can bend the mat away from the material. That way, you can use the spatula to help get the cut material off the cutting mat.

Use the Deep Cut Blade for Thicker Materials

Use the deep cut blade to cut through thick materials. These materials could be leather, cardboard or even chipboard. Get the blade and the blade housing.

Use Different Pens Where Necessary

Like you should use different blades for different materials; you should use different pens for different uses. There are different pen adapters available which you can use with your machine.

Make Use of Free Fonts

There are many free fonts you can use. You can make use of these fonts for free instead of purchasing fonts on Cricut Access. When you identify a desired free front, download it and install it on your computer. The font will appear on Cricut Design Space.

Use Different Blades for Different Materials

Do not use one single blade for all the different materials you will cut. For example, you can have one blade for cardboard, another for only leather and one for vinyl. It is best to have different blades for different materials because each material wears differently on the blade. A dedicated blade will be best because it will be tuned to the peculiarities of each material.

Use Weeding Boxes for Intricate Patterns

When cutting delicate or intricate patterns it is important to use weeding boxes in the process. Create a square or rectangle using the square tool in Cricut Design Space and place it such that all your design elements are all in it. Doing this makes weeding easier as all your design elements are grouped within the square or rectangle you have created.

Always Remember to Set the Dial

This sounds like stating the obvious setting the dial to the right material is something you can easily forget. The consequences of forgetting to set the dial to the appropriate material range from damaged cutting mats to shallow cuts on the materials. You can prevent these by always setting the dial before cutting.

Make use of the Free SVG files

Apart from making use of the designs available in the Design Space store, you can have your SVG files created or employ other SVG files available on the internet. This will help you in saving a lot of money.

Other pens compatible with the Cricut Explore Air 2

Apart from the Cricut pens, we have other pens that are compatible with the Cricut Explore Air 2 machine and any other machine that uses the accessory adapter. These pens include American craft pens and Sharpie pens. Nevertheless, the Cricut pens, when compared to these other pens, are of higher quality.

Have the Mat correctly loaded

Before beginning the cutting process, it is crucial to ensure that your mat is successfully loaded. You have to ensure that it slips correctly under the rollers.

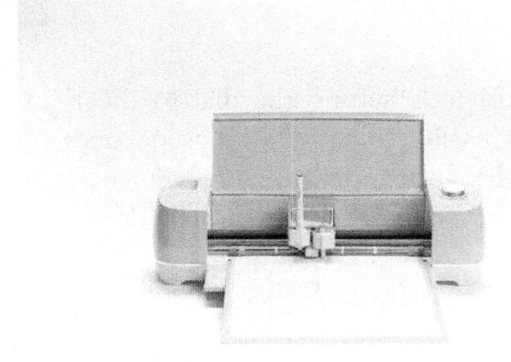

In a situation where the mat is not correctly loaded, the machine may just start cutting before the grid top on the mat or may not cut at all.

Tips on How to Do Iron-On or Heat Transfer Vinyl Project

A heat transfer vinyl has a clear plastic back that allows it to adhere to fabrics when applied to it. Therefore, iron-on vinyl project is a great way to create your customized t-shirts, hats, bags, totes and more. You can use the Cricut Maker to cut the vinyl material and then do the heat transfer vinyl project yourself. This is an amazing way to be classy and creative. Here are tips on how to iron-on a vinyl project:

Prepare the project area and measure it correctly. There is no need for assumptions as this may prove costly later on. So, get a tape to measure the length and width of your vinyl material. Ensure that you use the same tape to measure all your project materials; this is very important.

Adhere strictly to the manufacturer's instructions and recommendations for your iron-on vinyl material. This will save you a lot of time and reduce waste which will result from doing the wrong procedure.

Ensure that you mirror your image before cutting. Mirroring the image refers to flip it so that it can cut backwards. Though, a pop up may remind you to mirror the image if you have not done so. Mirroring the image will make sure that the heat transfer side of the image will appear correctly on the shirt or bag.

Place the iron-on vinyl on the mat with liner side down. The right mat for this project is Cricut Standard Grip Cutting Mat.

Place any thin cotton material between your vinyl project and the pressing iron to avoid melting the vinyl material.

Use heat press to heat transfer vinyl to your project. This method will ensure that the right pressure and temperature is applied to the vinyl for bonding between the it and project. This is the recommended method but if you don't have a heat press, then make sure that your pressing iron does not go higher than is required for the fabric you are using. Then, press the iron firmly on the cotton material covering the vinyl project.

Peel the liner off the vinyl. If some of the vinyl pieces are not firmly attached, put the cotton material back over it and again apply pressure on it with the iron. Do this at short intervals until you meet your aim.

Note that heat transfer should be applied only to fabrics or solids that can withstand the heat from the iron.

These same steps are also applied when you create Christmas tea towels and other customized iron-on vinyl on fabrics. If there are steps you didn't get quite well, do well to go over and read them again. As you grab the content, allow your creative mind to roam and discover ways to beautify this design to come up with your customized design.

There are many designs that you already have, and you are eager to try your hands. Do not be afraid, just get busy and with the above steps to guide you, there is no problem.

Free fonts are available for your project

Many free fonts are available, which can be used for your different projects. You can visit the fontbundles.net to get fonts downloaded. After downloading, install it on your computer. It should then automatically appear on your Cricut Design Space.

Installation of Fonts into the Design Space

You will need to sign out of your Cricut Design space and sign in back into it after you have successfully installed the fonts on your computer to have the new fonts show up in the Design space. In some cases, you may also need to restart your computer to have the font show up.

What to do when the Cutting mat begins to lose its stick the cutting mats always come sticky; it is, therefore, important to always clean the mat to ensure they maintain this stickiness for a longer time.

When the cutting mat has eventually lost their stickiness, and you don't have a new one to get them replaced yet, you can make use of tape in holding down your vinyl or card in place while avoiding areas that will need to be cut.

Recommended for taping down your card or vinyl when the cutting mat loses its stickiness is the medium tack painters' tape.

Making use of different blades for different materials

Having dedicated blades for different materials is a way of keeping the sharpness of the blades intact and doing an excellent cutting job. For example, having a blade to be used on vinyl only while another for cardstock, helps in having your blade around for such a long time simply because different materials will wear differently on your blades. Vinyl is more easily cut on the blade than when cutting through a card.

Always Mirror your image when cutting HTV
It is still advisable to get your image mirrored when cutting the HTV. For example, when cutting heat transfer vinyl using your Cricut, there will be a need to get your designed mirrored.
Once you have selected the "Make it" option, you will be prompted with an opportunity to mirror your design, which will have to be chosen for each mat.
Have your HTV placed on the Cutting Mat the right way in the upward direction You will have to put your vinyl shiny side facing down on the cutting mat to cut the heat transfer vinyl so that that carrier sheet will appear underneath with the dull vinyl side placed on the top.

Always remember to set the dial
It is easy to forget having the material setting changed most times, especially when you are done designing and want to start the cutting process. Though the Cricut Design Space will always let you know what material you have the dial set to as you are about to get a design cut out, this can be overlooked as well. To save yourself any mistake of cutting through immediately after your design is done with, you are always advised to have your dial settings checked.

Use Different Pens Where Necessary
Just like you use should use different blades for different materials; you should use different pens for different uses. There are different pen adapters available which you can use with your machine.

Make Use of Free Fonts
There are many free fonts you can use. You can make use of these fonts for free instead of purchasing fonts on Cricut Access. When you identify a desired free front, download it, and install it on your computer. The font will appear on Cricut Design Space.

Use Different Blades for Different Materials
Do not use one single blade for all the different materials you will cut. For example, you can have one blade for cardboard, another for only leather and one for vinyl. It is best to have different blades for different materials because each material wears differently on the blade. A dedicated blade will be best because it will be tuned to the peculiarities of each material.

Use Weeding Boxes for Intricate Patterns
When cutting delicate or intricate patterns it is important to use weeding boxes in the process. Create a square or rectangle using the square tool in Cricut Design Space and place it such that all your design elements are all in it. Doing this makes weeding easier as all your design elements are grouped within the square or rectangle you have created.

Always Remember to Set the Dial
This sounds like stating the obvious setting the dial to the right material is something you can easily forget. The consequences of forgetting to set the dial to the appropriate material range from damaged cutting mats to shallow cuts on the materials. You can prevent these by always setting the dial before cutting.

Additional tips on Effective Use of Your Cricut Explore Air 2

Always clean your Cricut cutting mat after every project. Roll a lint roller over the Cricut mat to remove tiny leftovers of dirt and lint from the surface of the mat.

To make absolutely sure that you do not regret your action while using any Cricut machine, Cricut Explore Air 2 included, make it a habit of always testing the cutting of your material by using a small piece of the material you wish to cut first before cutting the main material. Watch out these materials: wood, fabric, or felt because present different challenges during the cut process.

When you want to detach your processed material from the cutting mat after unloading it, roll the Cricut mat backwards away from the material instead of peeling the material away from the Cricut mat.

Always organize your blades and knifes in separate compartment or container. This will help you pick the correct blade or knife for a particular project because mixing them up may lead you to use an inappropriate blade for a project which might result to blunting the blades or even outright damage.

Organize your Cricut tools so that they will not be flying everywhere around the project area to avoid messing up with your project or even causing you bodily harm. These tools include scissors, spatula, scoring tools, pic, weeding tools, *etc.*

It is important that you keep your blades sharp every time so that you do not get your materials messed up while cutting and get them replaced when necessary.

Make sure that you dispose of the used ones properly to avoid injury to you and those around you especially moms with little kids. I am sure you do not want your kids to get hurt from the blades.

Use this important resource from the makers of Cricut Explore Air 2; their website Cricut.com where you are granted access to many YouTube videos and project ideas. If you need more help, search for information on Google or Pinterest.

Using features such as fonts and a few projects on Cricut will cost you a few bucks but you can cut this cost by subscribing to Cricut Access. With this, there is worry of cartridges and all purchases will stay in your account.

If the cut edges of the material, you are working on, is rough and uneven then it simply means that the blade you are using is blunt. The solution is to replace the blade with another one.

If the material, on the cutting mat, is moving while being cut, then it means that your mat is not sticky enough. The solution is to replace your mat and the used material or use tape to hold your material firmly to the mat.

Conclusion

I believe that you have gained insight into the possibilities associated with Cricut Explore Air 2 machine, increased your knowledge about it and obtained value for money spent in purchasing this book.

Presently your innovative potential is exponential. Cricut explore air 2 offers the most stretched out scope of tools for cutting, scoring, composing, and including enlivening impacts – all so you can take on any undertaking, you can envision. Besides, with more devices coming, Cricut Maker develops with you as you ace each new craft. Choose a wide assortment of sewing examples and quilt squares, including hundreds from Simplicity. Cricut Maker cuts and denotes every one of your pieces in only a couple of clicks.

This book will sure help your creative ability in the world of craft, and you will be amazed how much people appreciate the good things you will be creating with your Cricut Explore Air 2 machine. Take your place in the world of art after reading and digesting this book to start creating beautiful craft for yourself, family and friends.

CRICUT MAKER FOR BEGINNERS

*The Step-by-Step Guide to Master Your Cutting Machine,
Easy to Follow Even if You Have Never Used it Before.
A Handbook with Simple Tips, Illustration &
Screenshots*

Introduction

Okay, you've bought a Cricut machine, and you are excited. You have thought so much on what you are going to do with it. Now you have it. You really don't know the process. Well, that is why I am here. We would talk extensively about Cricut project ideas.

Whatever you have in mind, maybe you want to become this craftsperson, or you just want to do it for fun in a school or office we have several ideas for you here
You can buy these machines from an online store or at a craft store. And the price would definitely depend upon the model you choose. Furthermore, the prince can range anywhere from $100-$350 (and above), so it is better you narrow down your needs and go for it. Whatever makes your work more comfortable and efficient can be regarded as a significant investment. The Cricut is one of them; it is rewarding and fun to use. Anyone can benefit from it. Because of its efficiency, we have Cricut in places we never envisioned that they would be in previous years.

We have Cricut in offices and workshops. Does that sound strange to you? It shouldn't be because Cricut is never meant to be a home-only tool. It is time-saving and makes your work so professional, and the beautiful thing about it is that there are no limits to it, you can do whatever you can. If you're reading this book, then you have a Cricut machine in your possession, and maybe you don't really know how to use it. Well, I am here to help you with that.

First, we have the Cricut maker which is a machine used with design space. This Cricut maker has a cloud-based online software. And this particular series or design cannot function alone you would need to use the design space on a desktop or a laptop computing, and of course, internet connection is needed.

Another special provision provided with the Cricut maker is that you can make use of the offline feature in the design space app whenever you're using the design app on an IOS device, i.e., an iPad/iPhone or MacBook. This means you can make designs and all without an internet connection. This is just one device, and that is not all because each device has its own peculiarities added to the general feature that we all know. We also have the Cricut Explore Air.

This invention of Robert Workman with the collaboration of fellow investors like Jonathan Johnson, Matt Strong, and Phil Beffrey is also pronounced as cricket. This product has been able to gather so many revenues in sales within a short period of time because of its effectiveness and handiness.

This machine has been in work for years, and it totally blows everyone's mind and any other cutting machine out there. They keep bringing more and more to the table, and they keep adding something new every now and then. The Cricut has been able to dominate that market because of its reliability, performance, durability and its firmware also. This force of paper crafting revolution can also work without being connected or hooked to a computer. There are some designs that are portable and convenient to carry. Are you thinking of creating an endless assortment of shapes, letters, and phrases? Don't think too far, just get a Cricut.

Chapter 1: How to choose the right machine for your needs

On the whole, your choice of model depends on the type of use you will be giving it. This is the main criteria to take into consideration. If you are a casual hobbyist, then you might want to get the basic model. This will allow you to avoid spending more than you'd like while getting all of the benefits from the Cricut Machine. If you are planning on using it for business purposes, then it might be best to consider getting the top of the line model.

With that in mind, let's take a look at the criteria that we can take into consideration when purchasing a Cricut Machine. So, your answer to the following questions will help you make a decision on which model is the most suitable for you.

Criteria for Choosing a Cricut Machine

Here are five questions that you ought to ask yourself when looking to purchase your first Cricut Machine. Be honest as the answers to these questions will reveal the right model for you. That way, you can get the most out of your Cricut Machine without breaking the bank.

What am I going to use it for?
If you are a casual hobbyist and crafter, that is, you don't plan to use the machine heavily, the Explore Air model would suit you just fine. This model offers all of the capabilities that the other models offer though it isn't quite as robust as the others. This is perfect if you don't plan to use it heavily, such as cutting a large number of

items in one go. It's perfect if you are looking to cut one or two items at a time.

On the other hand, if you are looking to make heavy use of the machine, such as in the case of business use, then the Cricut Maker may be the best option for you. While it's the priciest, it's also the fastest and most robust of the lot. Given the fact that it's the most powerful model, you'll be able to cut anything and produce a large number of items in a short time.

How much am I willing to spend on a Cricut Machine?
On the other hand, if you are looking for a more budget-friendly solution, then the Explore Air makes the most sense. As we have stated earlier, if you are looking to avoid spending a great deal of money, then you can even pick up a used one. Since the Cricut Machine is pretty solid, you won't have to worry about it being in bad shape. Of course, it depends on how it was treated by its previous owner. But on the whole, they are usually in pretty good shape, especially if it doesn't have a lot of mileage on it.

If you are looking to purchase it for business purposes, then you might want to consider the Cricut Maker. It offers all of the features you need and will handle any workload you throw its way. While any of the other models will do the trick, the Maker is by far the fastest machine. In the world of business, time is certainly an important consideration. So, it only makes sense to get the fastest machine available to you.

Should I upgrade my Cricut Machine?
Assuming you have already taken the plunge with your first Cricut Machine, you might consider upgrading your current model. This is especially true if the breadth and scope of your projects have outgrown your current machine.

A note of caution though: if you are looking for serious power, then getting the Maker is the best way to go. However, it isn't recommended to get it used, at least not if you're looking to upgrade for serious use. The reason for this is that the Maker is a powerful machine, but it may be put through the wringer. So, getting a brand-new makes sense if you're considering putting some serious mileage on it. Alternatively, the Joy can be a great upgrade, particularly if you something smaller to work with.

What add-ons can I get with the Cricut Machine?
When you get a Cricut Machine, you get access to any number of add-ons and tools which can be used to make any number of creations. These add-ons consist of pens, cartridges, and other tools that can be used to make effects beyond the standard cutting function. Cricut has gone a long way toward making a vast array of tools available. That's something that can't be said about other similar kinds of machines on the market.

It is worth paying close attention to the chapter in which we will discuss the types of tools available to you. That way, you can see for yourself just how many options you have available. In the end, the Cricut Machine offers the best balance in terms of capability and function. You can create plenty of designs while working with several techniques. When you put it all together, the overall capabilities of the Cricut Machine place it at the top of its category.

Quick Overview of the Main Models

The Cricut Machine is one of the most sophisticated tools that can be used in the world of arts and crafts. It allows you to make a myriad of creations by combining its specially designed software and then translate it into a physical form of art.

In essence, the Cricut Machine is a cutting machine. It can cut any number of materials based on predetermined patterns that you develop in the specially designed software. In these creations, you can take a material, and have the Cricut Machine cut out the patterns you want it to.

Now, it should be noted that this device is meant to cut only. It doesn't do any printing. So, that's an important thing to keep in mind. For instance, you can cut out an elaborate design on a piece of leather and then color it to your liking. If you are making a birthday card, you can cut out the design you like and then color it using your technique of choice (pastels, crayons, paints, watercolors, and so on).

That being said, the Cricut Machine is a great tool for any type of project. You can go as elaborate as you like. The important thing is to make sure you have the right idea in mind. Based on that, you can make anything work for you.

Cricut Maker

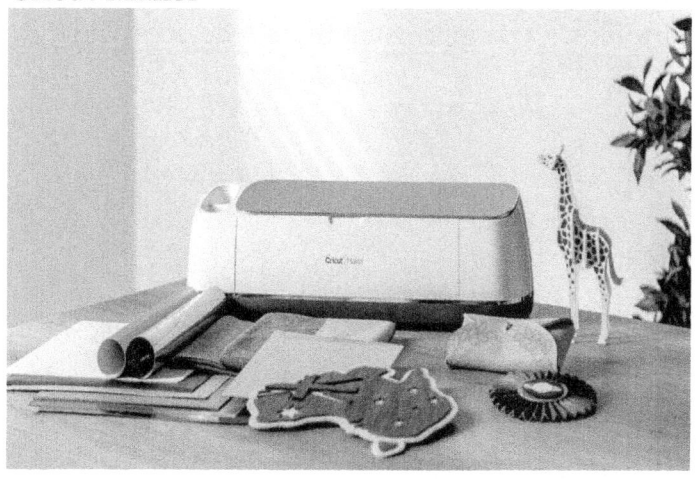

The Cricut Maker is the first and only device from Cricut that can be used with a Rotary blade to cut fabrics directly. It is also equipped with a scoring wheel that can exert varying pressure to allow scoring of thicker papers. It provides the most diverse variety of tools to cut, score, write, and even decorate; so you can truly bring your dream projects to life. Moreover, the company is looking to add even more tools that can be used with Cricut Maker and quickly switched to support your creative growth continually.

With the versatile housing slot, you can just press the "quick release" button on the device to mount any desired tip and kick start your craft project.

Features:
- Fast and precision cut creating a rotary blade.
- Use the knife blade to cut thin as well as thick materials.
- Use 12 x 12 inches cutting mats with fine point pen.
- It offers a number of digital sewing patterns.
- Use your own designs.
- It comes with a device docking slot.
- Equipped with Bluetooth wireless technology.
- A USB port allows charging your mobile devices while in use.

Cricut Joy

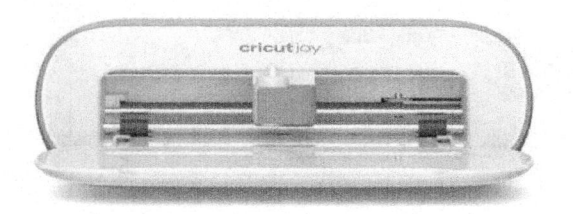

It's the most up to date machine Cricut discharged. It's very small and it can cut, draw a wide assortment of materials. the Cricut Joy can cut and remove vinyl and iron-on without a tangle!

You may have the option to buy them on amazon or utilized. In any case, they are not good with Cricut Design Space and the product they used previously – Cricut Craft Room – has been closed down totally. Composing with your Cricut is so natural and fun. It's an extraordinary method to give an undertaking proficient introduction with an individual and custom made feel.

On the off chance that you sew a great deal it might simply be justified, despite all the trouble to have that rotating shaper. Also, how cool is it to have wood patterns? Words cut in wood are overly popular at this moment. Furthermore, who realizes what number of more apparatuses Cricut will come out with that will just work in the Maker.

Cricut Compare Models

Cricut is exploring one, Cricut Explore Aire, Cricut, and Cricut Explore Air 2 Maker.
With these options, you might be wondering what the differences between them are and what to buy.
I will explore these models and then briefly explain the Cricut machines should be used depending on the depth on the ship.

Cutting force
The machine comes with a carbide blade premium German first category, which can be cut through thick materials and light equally clearly and cleanly form. Even if exploring one is recommended for beginners, it is very professional. The blade is also very durable.
As for the width of cutting, explore one can cut sizes ranging from 23
½ "high and ¼ to ½" 11 wide.

Although the explore one looks excellent, there are some activities that can be done in the design space Cricut if you are using this model.
Cricut Design Space is very user-friendly when used to explore one. It accepts .jpg, .png, and .bmp.

In addition, the Cricut Explore One cannot work wirelessly. To add comfort to it and does not care about the cost, then you can buy a Bluetooth adapter and use it to transfer images or files wirelessly.

Explore Cricut Air
While this is quite similar to the Explore One model, which also comes with some additional features, the main difference between them is the presence of the built-in Bluetooth adapter. If you enjoy

seeing no cables and wires around your workplace, especially with the risk of tripping over them, then this model solves that problem.

Capacity

Explore air is also exploring different ones as it has a double carriage. This means that you can draw, write, or record while mowing because it has two clamps to hold both tools. This saves you money because you do not have to buy an adapter tool.

Materials

Explore air is quite liberating when it comes to materials. It features a dial that can allow you to choose the material you are about to cut. This way, you do not have to guess the depth of the blade and spoil the material.

The machine will know how deeply felt the need to cut and what kind you have to be paper or vinyl. This is especially great for beginners' feature that they are not well versed in the depths of the sheet.

Difference in Models

In general, there is no difference between the three models of Cricut Machine. They are all capable of cutting out the same types of patterns and materials. As such, may casual hobbyists would instead go for the Joy (especially when looking affordability and portability) or the Explore Air (especially when looking for an excellent entry-level product). However, it's the Maker that shines when it comes to using all of the tools available. By using the Maker, you have the opportunity to unlock the power of the Cricut Machine. It can cut through thicker and stricter material while allowing you the versatility of the various tools we outlined in the previous chapter.

If you are seriously considering the Cricut Machine for heavy-duty crafting or business purposes, then the Maker makes the most sense. After all, it will provide you with the best all-around features and value. Sure, the price is the highest, but in the end, the large array of projects you will be able to carry out will may the machine worth the investment.

Additionally, you will find that the size of the materials will vary between the Joy and Explore Air/Maker. Given the fact that the Joy is much smaller, you are only able to cut materials roughly half the size of the other two machines. This is something which you need to keep in mind if you are considering the Joy. Otherwise, any of the three models will provide you with excellent results.

Chapter 2: Cricut Maker

Machine Setup and How to Prepare the Material

First, you'll want to set up the Cricut Joy. To begin, create a space for it. A craft room is the best place for this, but if you're at a loss of where to put it, I suggest setting it up in a dining room if possible. Make sure you have an outlet nearby or a reliable extension cord.

Next, read the instructions. Often, you can jump right in and begin using the equipment, but with Cricut machines, it can be very tedious.

Make sure that you do have ample free space around the machine itself, because you will be loading mats in and out and you'll need that little bit of wiggle room.

The next thing to set up is, of course, the computer where the designs will be created. Make sure that whatever medium you're using has an internet connection, since you'll need to download the Cricut Design Space app. If it's a machine earlier than the Explore Air 2, it will need to be plugged in directly, but if it's a wireless machine like the Air 2, you can simply link this up to your computer, and from there, design what you need to design.

Imputing Cartridges and Keypad

The first cut that you'll be doing does involve keypad input and cartridges, and these are usually done with the "Enjoy Card" project you get right away. So, once everything is set up, choose this project, and from there, you can use the tools and the accessories within the project.

You will need to set the smart dial before you get started making your projects. This is on the right side of the Explore Air 2, and it's basically the way you choose your materials. Turn the dial to whatever type of material you want, since this does help with ensuring you've got the right blade settings. There are even half settings for those in-between projects.
For example, let's say you have some light cardstock. You can choose that setting, or the adjacent half setting. Once this is selected in Design Space, your machine will automatically adjust to the correct location.

You can also choose the fast mode, which is in the "set, load, go" area on the screen, and you can then check the position of the box under the indicator for dial position. Then, press this and make your cut. However, fast mode is incredibly loud, so be careful.
Once it's confirmed, you can go to images, and click the cartridges option to find the ones that you want to make. You can filter the cartridges to figure out what you need, and you can check out your images tab for any other cartridges that are purchased or uploaded.

You can get digital cartridges, which means you buy them online and choose the images directly from your available options. They aren't physical, so there is no linking required.

Cartridge

Cartridges are expensive, they truly are, but they are so easy and fun to use as well. Cartridges contain a huge amount of images and fonts. They are all themed so they can be purchased according to what you need them for. Some cartridges only contain letters, and these have really cool fonts that can be used to write on cards or cut with your machine. Each one of them also has a fair amount of options that will allow you to customize the design as much as you want.

You will need to link the cartridge of the new machines to the Design Space; hence, an internet connection is necessary if you wish to work with them within the application itself. The older machines do not have such a requirement, but the upgraded ones do. So, either way, you will need an internet connection for linking the cartridges or setting up with Design Space.

Loading Your Paper

To load paper into a Cricut machine, you'll want to make sure that the form is at least three inches by three inches. Otherwise, it won't cut very well. You should use regular paper for this.

Now, to make this work, you need to put the paper onto the cutting mat. You should have one of those, so take it right now and remove the attached film. Put a corner of the form to the area where you are directed to align the paper corners. From there, push the form directly onto the cutting mat for proper adherence. Once you do that, you just load it into the machine, following the arrows. You'll want to keep the paper firmly on the mat.

Press the "load paper" key that you see as you do this. If it doesn't take for some reason, press the unload paper key, and try this again until it shows up.

Now, before you do any cutting for your design, you should always have a test cut in place. Some people don't do this, but it's incredibly helpful when learning how to use a Cricut. Otherwise, you won't get the pressure correct in some cases, so get in the habit of doing it for your pieces.

For effective cutting, it is recommended that the paper to be cut should not be lesser than 3" × 3". Cardstock is also recommended in order to achieve the best result. In case you are using the machine for the first time, you can become familiar with the device by practicing with cheaper materials.

In order to cut a paper on the machine, the form should be placed on the cutting mat. It is better to first try it with a form of 6" × 12" if you are not used to the machine. First, remove the protective film of the cutting mat.

You will then ensure that a corner of the paper is aligned. Proceed by pressing the writing unto the cutting mat to make it fit in well. Once this is done, the paper is ready to be cut. In case you want to choose other paper sizes, check the Advanced Operations.

How to Remove Your Cuts from Cutting Mat

The machine will automatically load the mat and the paper after pressing the load paper key. In the rare occurrence that this does not happen, don't hesitate to push the Unload Paper key.

Once you press the Unload Paper key, you will go through the procedure again. It should work unless there is an issue with the machine. A likely problem is the unavailability of up to 1 ft. (30.5 cm) of clear space.

This clear space is needed in the front and back of the Cricut machine for paper movement.

Removing your cut from the mat is easy, but complicated. Personally, I ran into the issue of it being more involved with vinyl projects since they love to just stick around there. But we'll explain how you can create significant cuts and remove them, as well.

The first thing to remember is to make sure that you're using the right mat. The light grip ones are good for very soft material, with the pink one being one of the strongest, and only to be used with the Cricut Maker. Once the design is cut, you'll probably be eager about removing the project directly from the mat, but one of the problems with this is that often, the project will be ruined if you're not careful. Instead of pulling the project from the mat itself, bend the mat within your hand, and push it away from the project, since this will loosen it from the carpet. Bend this both horizontally and vertically, so that the adhesive releases the project.

Use this spatula to lightly pull on the vinyl, until you can grab it from the corner and lift it up. Otherwise, you risk curling it or tearing the mat, which is what we don't want.
You will notice that Cricut mats are incredibly sticky, and if you don't have a Cricut spatula on hand or don't want to spend the

money, metal spatulas will work, too. You can put the paper on a flat surface and then lightly remove it. But always be careful when removing these items.

How to design With Cricut Maker

When you see the finished product from a Cricut machine, you will definitely be blown away. The neatness and appealing look of a typical project done with the Cricut machine will take your breath away. However, only a few people understand the process involved in the creation of such unique designs.

Curious to know how the Cricut machine is able to cut out materials effectively? You are reading the right book. There are three significant steps involved when using the Cricut machine:

<u>Have a Design</u>
If you have a PC, you can access the Cricut Design Space to access the library of designs. If you have a Mac, you can access the same platform to select a vast variety of formats. In case you don't have any of these two but possesses an iPhone or iPad, you can use the Design Space for iOS.

If what you have is an android, you are covered as well. This is because you can take advantage of the Design Space for Android. These are online platforms where you can select any design that best suits your taste.

You can also customize a ready-made design to suit your need. For example, you can resize it or modify the shape. You can also add a text or image as you wish till you have the design just as you want it.

Prepare the Machine
Having selected the design, you intend cutting out with the machine, you are ready for the next step. The device needs to be prepared by turning it on. Once you switch on the device, you actually don't need to do anything.
You don't have to press any button unless you are using the machine for the first time. In that case, the device will give you instructions on what to do. It is that simple.
That is why both beginners and experts can make use of the Cricut machine without issues. Your computer or phone will have to be paired with the device via Bluetooth for the first time. However, this will not be needed subsequently because the machine will remember the pairing.

Hence, once the machine is switched on, the pairing between the phone and the machine becomes automatic. The implication of this is that once the machine is switched on, the machine is ready. The next step is to send the design to the machine.

Send the Design to the Machine
This is the last stage of the process of cutting with the Cricut machine. Once the machine is powered on, at the top right corner of the screen, you will see the Make It button. This button is a big green button on the Cricut Design Space.
The first thing the software does is to preview the various mats you have. A mat represents a sheet of material; hence, having two different colors in your project implies two rugs. There are times that your project can be a combination of a fabric and a paper.
The machine will request that you pick the particular material you want to use for the first mat. Simply choose whether it is paper, vinyl, fabric, leather, or any other material. Once you do this, the machine will automatically adjust pressure, speed, and the brush blade as necessary.

Hence, just ensure you do your part of instructing the machine to do your bidding as desired. You can trust the Cricut machine from that point to do all that is needed for a perfect project. After the machine has adjusted itself to cut, you will put the material into the Cricut cutting mat.

It is obvious that you don't have to be a genius before you are qualified to use the machine. The instructions are simplified such that anyone who can understand basic English language can use it. Therefore, if you have been thinking that you might not be able to operate this machine, you are wrong.

How to Clean The Cricut Maker

With an extended period of use, it is likely that your machine would have collected dirt and grime. So, here are some tips on how you can clean your machine and keep it looking and working as new.

Prior to cleaning the machine, make sure that it has been powered off and disconnected from the power source.
Use a microfiber cloth or a piece of soft clean cloth sprayed with a glass cleaning solution to clean the machine.
In the case of static electricity build-up on the machine due to dust or paper particles, use the same cloth to wipe off the residues and get rid of the static from the machine.
For grease build up on the bar that allows the carriage travels, use a soft cloth or tissue or cotton swab and gently remove the oil from the machine.

Do not use nail polish remover or any other acetone-containing solution to clean the machine, as it may permanently damage the plastic shell of the machine.

To keep the machine running smoothly, you may want to grease it following the instructions below:
Power off your machine and carefully push the "Cut Smart" carriage to the left of the machine.

Use a tissue to wipe the carriage bar (located in front of the belt).
Now, carefully move the bar to the right and clean again with the tissue.
Carefully move the bar to the center and use a cotton swab to lubricate both sides of the carriage by applying a light coating of grease around the bar to form a 1/4-inch ring on each side of the carriage.

In order to evenly distribute the grease on the carriage, slowly move the carriage from one end to another a couple of times and wipe off any excessive oil.
Note – It is recommended to use grease packet supplied by Cricut only, and no other grease from a third party should be used.

Cricut Design Space software For Cricut Maker

For craft enthusiasts and people that love the Cricut die cutting system, it is no longer news that digital die cutting units are incredibly restrictive.
They mostly allow users to cut a small number of fonts and they are not cheap at all.
Thankfully, there are a few programs out there that have managed to open Cricut to enable them to cut designs, True Type fonts created by users and many more.
Below is a list of the best third-party software to use with Cricut.

Make the Cut

This is an excellent third- party Cricut Design software that comes with simple but highly effective design features e.g. it packs quick lattice tools, and it can convert raster images into vectors for cutting. The program has been around for some time. Some of the most outstanding features of the tool include;

It comes with advanced editing tools, and it is quite easy to use (even for a newbie) because the user interface is effortless to learn.

The software works with many file formats and it also uses TrueType fonts

The software comes with Pixel trace tool that allows users to take and convert raster graphics into vector paths for cutting.

Make The Cut is a user-friendly and flexible Cricut related software that adds more utility to the digital die cutting machine that is usually limited in terms of usage and application.

Sure Cuts A Lot

The Sure Cuts A Lot software gives users complete control of their designs without the restrictions of cartridges featured in Cricut DesignStudio.

Users must install a firmware update to their Cricut die cutting machine; however, they can do this for free by downloading the trial version of DesignStudio. It is a straightforward task to perform. Some of the features of the Sure Cuts A lot software include;

It allows users to use the OpenType and TrueType fonts.

It is the one and only Cricut Design tool available that comes with freestyle drawing tools.

It allows users to create unique designs with basic drawing and editing tools.

The program works with Silhouette, Craft ROBO, and Wishblade die cutting machines.

It is specifically designed to open up all of Cricut's cutting features and abilities.

It allows users to edit the individual nodes the make up the path.
It comes with an auto trace feature that converts raster graphics into vector images

Cricut DesignStudio

Cricut DesignStudio, a product of ProvoCraft is a program that allows users to connect Cricut to a personal computer so that they can do much more with Cricut fonts and shapes.
For those that don't know, Provo Craft is the same company that manufactures Cricut die cutting machines. With the aid of various tools, this Cricut software allows users to adjust fonts and shapes.
Some of the best features of the software include;
Users have the option of previewing and creating designs with different images from the Cricut library.
Users will have to purchase a cartridge to cut.
The software comes with a high level of customization to the Cricut library, and the extra features are beneficial
People that use this software are still limited to the same shapes and fonts from the cartridges they own, but bearing in mind the tools that are packed in the program, that is not an issue.
The program remains a perfect option to use alongside your Cricut, and you'll be able to get the best out of its features. To know more about the software, go to their official website.

Making Your First Project Idea

Now that you have everything set to go, it's time to start with your first project. If this is the first time that you are using a Cricut Machine, then do follow the guidelines we will be presenting in this chapter as they will help you avoid some of the most common mistakes.

On the whole, using a Cricut Machine and the Design Space software is pretty straightforward. This means that you don't need any specialized knowledge to make fair use of this software. Of course, if you have used design software in the past, then that experience will certainly come in handy. Nevertheless, you don't need to have any previous experience to make your creations come to life.

So, here are five useful tips that you can put into practice when starting with your very first projects.

<u>Do your homework</u>
When starting out, it's always a good idea to go over sample project ideas before you actually start cutting. In this book, you will find great project ideas which you can put into practice right away. Do, it's a great idea to go over these ideas before you begin designing your creations. In addition, the internet is filled with great design ideas. So, you can poach some of these ideas and use them for your benefit. On the whole, there are really talented and creative designers out there who have come up with sample projects to help new users get the hang of the Cricut Machine.

As you gain more practice and proficiency with the Cricut Machine, it's a good idea to keep perusing project ideas. It could be that you find images which you can later customize to your own liking. This will make it easier for you to get the hang of the types of projects you can come up with. Over time, you will be able to make your ideas from scratch!

<u>Start small</u>
When you don't have much experience with the Cricut Machine and Design Space, it's a good idea to start with small projects. Such projects don't take up a lot of time and are easy to put together. As you gain more experience and proficiency, you can tackle bigger and bigger projects. But when starting out, it's always a good idea to

tackle smaller projects. That way, you won't become overwhelmed by the complexity of a larger project.

Also, it's essential to consider that if things don't go quite as planned, you won't feel frustrated by this. So, you will be able to manage your skills and expectations in such a way that you won't get discouraged early on.

Practice makes perfect

Like anything in life, becoming a pro with the Cricut Machine and Design Space take time and practice. Now, this doesn't mean that you need weeks and weeks of training and study. What it does mean is that the more projects you take on, the easier it will become to use the Cricut Machine and Design Space. So, it definitely helps to take on more and more projects.

Of course, we all have pretty tight schedules nowadays. So, it's not precisely simple to sit down at your computer and work for hours on end on projects. Yet, if you can dedicate a couple of hours a week to your projects, you will find that it will really help you get the most out of the Cricut Machine. In this manner, you will quickly build up your proficiency. Before you know it, you will be coming up with genuinely creative and innovative ideas.

Easy does it

One of the first reactions that newbies to the Cricut Machine get is to be gung-ho about using their brand-new machine. However, enthusiasm tends to wear off. This is why it's a good idea to take on one project at a time. You see, when you get ahead of yourself and take on multiple projects at once, things can get a bit muddled. While there is nothing wrong with being aggressive and trying to make the most out of your new machine, taking on multiple projects early on can be a bit confusing and potentially overwhelming. This might even lead you to feel discouraged. So, the perfect antidote to this point is to take on one project at a time.

The sense of satisfaction that you get from completing your very first projects is indescribable.

Draw out your idea on paper first
Design Space is a fantastic tool. It is the perfect companion that enables you to translate the ideas in your head to practical applications. As such, you can put its instruments to fair use without much complication and with relative ease.

However, one of the most significant setbacks that first-time users run into is not having a clear picture in their minds about what they would like to do. This can lead you to feel dissatisfied with your creations. Also, it can make finalizing a design a bit challenging.

This is why we recommend that you sketch out your idea on a piece of paper first. This will help you to organize your thoughts before hitting Design Space. While the finished product may differ significantly, it certainly helps to have a good idea of what you plan to do. This technique is similar to what writers do with a storyboard. They outline the story before writing. That way, they know where they will begin and where they will end. If they change their mind along the way, that's fine. The main point is to avoid having your ideas go down paths that won't lead anywhere practical.

How to Upload Images with a Cricut Maker

There are many images to choose from in the library, but it also encourages the use of your images. Images are categorized into two types. The first type is Image, and the second is the Pattern.

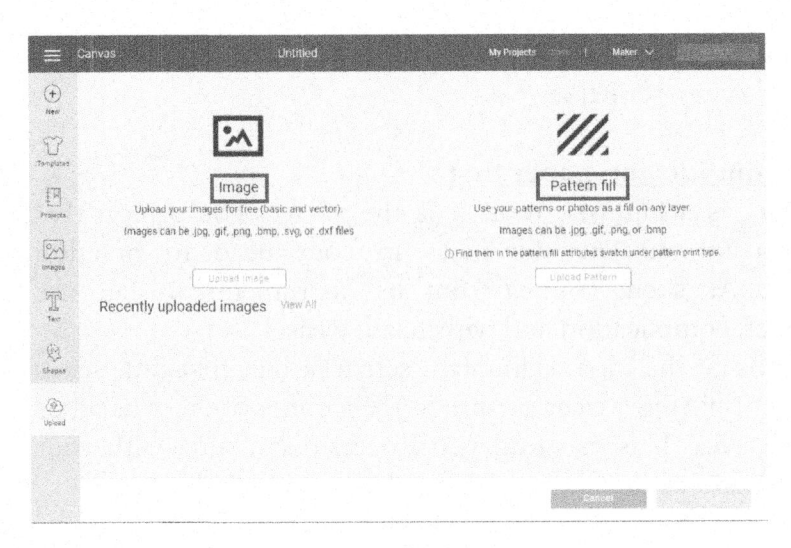

Images:

Images also have two types, Basic and the other one is Vector.

Necessary images like JPG, GIF, PNG, are uploaded as one layer. Uploading the image will require a few steps that the software will guide through. There are two ways to use the picture.

First, by print and cut features, print the image and then calibrate the Cricut to cut around it.

Second, is to cut only the outer edges of the image directly on the machine.

Vector files come in SVG Dxf files, which are not uploaded as a single layer but multiple layers. Other imported images from different software can also be uploaded. You can search the uploaded image by searching its name/tag. Also, all uploaded images can be seen by applying the filter uploaded.

Pattern:

Uploaded patterns can be seen in the Layers Attributes Panel under the Pattern option. Files that can be uploaded are .jpg .png .gif .bmp. When uploading, choose appropriate tags and name for easy searching. You can also access this by clicking uploaded in Patterns filter.

How to upload an image from Photoshop?

Cricut Design Space does not allow you to make changes to the images that you want to use. If changes are to be made to the design, then another software like Adobe Photoshop should be used first. Adobe Photoshop does not save vector files, so if the picture has multiple layers, it will be compressed into one. Images best work in jpg. Files, but others can also be used.

Firstly make the required changes in the image using Photoshop. Then save the file in jpg. Format and name it.

How to select an image?

It is effortless to select an image onto the Canvas. There are four methods for this task:

First, select an image from inside the Canvas. When an image is selected, it will be shown in the Layers Panel in the highlighted form, and a bounding box will appear around the image.

Or, select an image from the Layers Panel. This will also like the print on your Canvas

Another option is to select an image from drawing a box. Then draw a box around the idea that it is entirely inside it. The package will turn blue, and the image will be selected.

If there is one image, select the 'Select All' option. If there is more than one image, then all of them will be chosen.

Working with uploaded photos

Select the option for upload images under the upload page

If it is a photo, then select the option 'Complex Image' under the upload screen. Then click 'Continue.'

For the photo to retain its details, it should be used in print and cut. It is done by default, and it is saved as print and cut image. Now click save.

Back on your upload screen, click on the photo and then click insert. The image is now ready to use.

This photo can be manipulated using different tools such as slip tool, or flatten tool. The slip tool can be used to cut the picture or cut images out of the photo. The flatten tool can insert different pictures on the photo.

Patterns

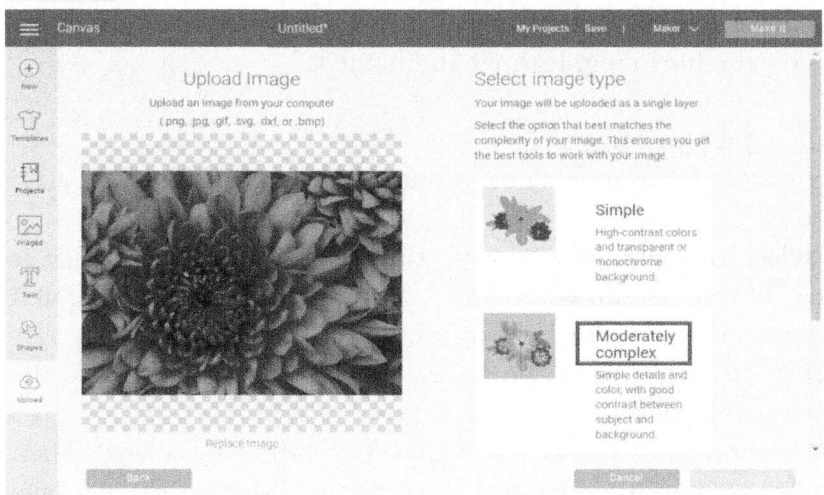

Select the option for upload pattern under the upload screen.
Browse the photo using its name and selected.
Name and add appropriate tags to your photo to make searching easy.
A shape can be used to cut the image to make a pattern. First, insert a form in the Canvas. Open the 'Layers Attributes Panel' under the 'Image Layers' option. Now select 'Line Types' and then 'Patterns.' Different patterns will open along with the photo. Select the desired photo and fill the shape.
Use different editing tools to your likings, like rotate, scale, pan, and mirror.

Cut Vinyl with A Cricut Maker

First, place the Vinyl liner side down onto the Standard grip mat. Then put it inside the machine after selecting the design. Push the go button to start.

For a smooth placement of the vinyl, you should use vinyl transfer tape. Transfer tape is a kind of pre-mask that transfer vinyl graphics to a substrate after being cut and weeded.

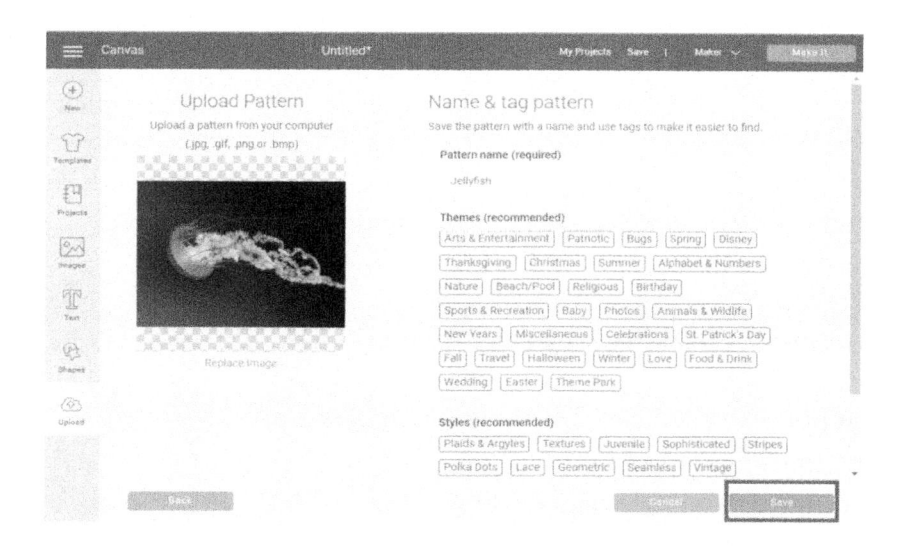

After cutting is done, remove the negatives of the image by a weeder or a tweezer, only leaving the wanted design on the mat. Now remove the Transfer Tape liner. Carefully with the sticky side down, place it on the mat with the system. Gently press to remove any air bubbles.

Whatever surface you want the design on, it should be clean and dry. Carefully place the vinyl on the body and gently press it down.

Remove the tap by peeling it off at a 45-degree angle. If it is difficult, burnish it by using a scrapper.

How to Make Stickers

There are a lot of designs and decors one can use the Cricut machine to create. Some of the stickers one can use the machine to create and cut are as follows:
- Cupcake stickers
- Sticky labels
- Planner stickers
- Safari animal sticker
- Vinyl sticker for car windows amid any other types of sticker your heart so desires

Now let us explore individual designs that can be effected with the machine.

Procedure for Making Cupcake Stickers

The supplies needed for this brand of stickers are:
- the Cricut machine,
- printable sticker paper,
- an inkjet printer.

The following are the steps to follow in creating cupcake stickers:
- Log in to the Cricut design spaces.
- Start a new project and click on the Images icon on the left side of the screen.
- Select the cupcake image(s) you want.
- Highlight the whole image and use the Flatten button to solidify the image as one whole piece.

- Resize the image to the appropriate size you need. You realize this by clicking on the image then dragging the right side of the box to the size you desire.
- Click Save at the top left to save your project. Save it to be a Print and Cut image, after which you click the Make It button at the right hand of the screen.
- Examine the end result and click Continue if it's what you expected. This will lead you to print the design onto the paper.
- Adjust the dial on the Cricut machine to the required settings.
- Place the sticker paper on the cutting mat.
- Load the cutting mat into the machine, and push it against the rollers.
- Press the Load/Unload button and then the Go button to cut the stickers.
- Sit back and relax while you watch the Cricut machine cut your designed stickers for you.

Procedures for Making Sticky Labels

Supplies needed are as follows:
- Cricut machine
- Printable sticker paper
- Inkjet printer

Take the next few steps to bring this sticker to life:
- Log in to the Cricut design space.
- Start a new project.
- Click on the Text icon and input your text.

- Select the font of your desire from the available font package.
- Highlight the texts and change the color by using the available colors on the color tray.
- Click on the Print option to change the file to a print file from a cut file.
- Click on the Ungroup icon to adjust the spacing of the text.

After adjusting the spaces, highlight all and use the Group icon to make them one whole piece again.

- Click on the Shape icon and insert a shape.
- If it's a rectangle you need, insert a square, unlock the shape, and drag it to a rectangle.
- Change the shape's color using the color tray.
- Highlight the text and use the Align drop-down box.
- Make use of the Move to Front icon to move the text to front.
- Highlight the design and click on Group.
- Duplicate the label as much as you want.
- Highlight the whole design and use the Flatten icon to keep it together during printing.
- Highlight the design and right-click then select Attach.
- Click on the Go button and print the design on the printable sticker paper.
- Adjust the dial on the Cricut machine to the required settings.
- Place the sticker paper on the cutting mat.
- Load the cutting mat into the machine, and push it against the rollers.
- Press the Load/Unload button and then the Go button to cut the stickers.

Your sticky label is ready for use.

Working With Images/Edit Panel

The blank Edit Bar is shown in the picture below. All the functions that can be seen on the Edit Bar are explained right after, so we can get you started on creating your first craft project on Design Space.

Undo/Redo – You can use the "Undo" button to revert to your previous state and use the "Redo" button to perform the step that was undone.

Linetype – All the way, the machine can interact with the design base material on the mat, namely, Cut, Draw, Score, Engrave, Deboss, Perf, and Wavy are called as "Linetype."

Linetype Swatch – If you would like to choose additional layer attributes for your design, you can select the "Linetype swatch." The alternatives available will be updated on the basis of the "Linetype" you selected. When the "Cut" option is chosen, you will notice a solid line next to the "Linetype" icon, an outline if the "Draw" is determined, and when the "Score" is chosen, a "/" will be visible. Here are some details on the features that will be available for your selected "Linetype."

Cut Attributes

Material colors – You can select the desired color on the "Material colors palette" to instantly match the colors of your project. A checkmark will be displayed in the "color swatch" for the design layer that you are working on.

Primary colors – You will also be able to select a color from the "basic color palette."

Advanced – You can move the slider to choose a color from the "custom color picker," or if you know precisely the "hex" numbers for your desired color, simply plug those numbers in, and you will get that color for your design.

Draw Attributes – If you have selected the "Draw" Linetype, you will be given the option to "Choose a Cricut pen type" from the drop-down. The colors available for your selected "pen type" will be displayed in the list accordingly.

Print - You can select this option for accessing "Print Then Cut" color and pattern choices.

Fill Swatch – If you would like to choose from other Fill attributes for a layer, click on the

Original Artwork – If you are not excited about the fill of the design and want to restore to the original image, you can do this by selecting "Original artwork."

Color - You can choose your desired color from the current material colors, a primary colors palette, the custom color picker, or by entering a hex color code.

Pattern - You could also fill an image or text layer with a design. If you filter the pattern selection by color, it will be easier to find the right way, which you can further modify using the "Edit Pattern" tools.

Size – If you need to alter the height or width of an object, then you can simply type in the exact dimensions in the given boxes or click on the "stepper" to increase or decreases the size while looking at the changes on your design. Remember to first lock the image aspect ratio by clicking on the "Lock" icon to ensure that, as you modify one dimension, the whole image will be changed in the same proportion.

Rotate – You will be able to modify the angle of the selected item using the stepper, or you can type in the exact degree by which you want to alter the image.

More – If your screen resolution doesn't allow the complete Edit Bar to be visible, then you would see a "More" drop-down containing the features that do not appear on your screen.

Position – You can use this option to change the status of your selected item using the stepper, or you can type in the exact distance by which you want to move the image from the top-left corner of the Canvas.

Editing Fonts

If you decided to add text to your design or select a "text object" on the Canvas or select a "text layer" in the Layers Panel, the "Text Edit Bar" will be displayed directly below the image "Edit Bar" on your screen. All the functions that can be seen on the "Text Edit Bar" are shown in the picture and explained below.

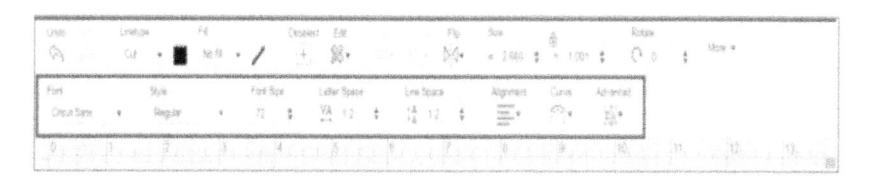

Font – This will provide you a list of Cricut fonts along with all the fonts available on your computer.

Font Drop-Down – You will be able to view all the fonts available to you or may choose to view just the Cricut fonts, or only fonts installed on your system, or all the fonts at the same time, using the "Font Drop-Down." Font filters may also be searched and applied. Just browse the font list and choose your desired font to be applied to the selected text.

Font Filter – You can use this feature for filtering the fonts by category and alter the fonts that are displayed in the "Font Type" menu.

All Fonts – To view all available fonts that can be used for your project.

System Fonts – To view only the fonts installed on your system.
Cricut Fonts – To view just the fonts from the Cricut library.
Single Layer Fonts – To view fonts containing only a single layer.
Writing Style Fonts - To view fonts that are designed particularly to be written by hand. These fonts are characterized by letters with a single stroke that makes them appear like handwritten letters.

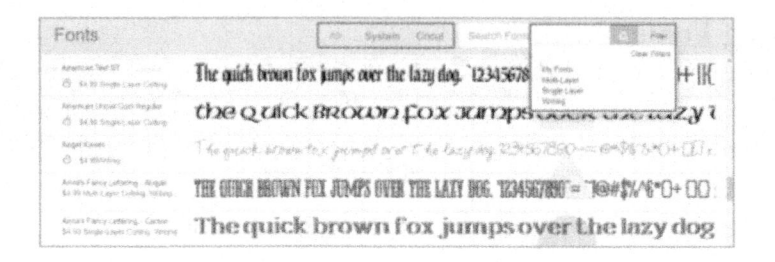

Style – This feature will allow you to select the type of your font, such as regular, bold, italic, and bold italic. You may also see the option of "writing" when the appropriate font has been selected. Remember, the style of Cricut fonts may differ from your system fonts.

Font Size – You can adjust the size of the fonts by typing in the desired point size or using the stepper to change the font size by 1 point gradually.

Cricut Scrapbooking

Scrapbooking can verge on a fixation for us. We're continually attempting to make that ideal page design or locate that perfect little touch that will make our scrapbooks that significantly improved. You can utilize the Cricut machine to make kick the bucket cuts of scrapbook page formats and afterward rapidly offer them to other fans such as yourself. On the off chance that it is your obsession, at that point it will be no issue thinking of some amazing plans!

Solving the most common problem when using Cricut Maker

Fixing Cricut Design Space Issues
When you put everything into consideration, it is safe to say that the Design Space software is excellent.

No system is perfect, and there's always room for improvements, but on the whole, the software works excellently for several projects. However, there are a couple of related issues that are predominant with the software, including; freezing, slow loading, crashing and not opening at all. When you're faced with these issues, there are several things you can do to fix them, including;

Slow Internet Connection
You must understand that a slow internet connection is one of the leading causes of Design Space problems without saying much. Poor internet connection translates into problems for the software because it requires consistent download and upload speeds to function optimally.

Several websites only require good download speeds e.g. YouTube, thus users on these sites can do away with slow upload speeds. However, unlike those sites, Cricut Design Space requires good upload and download speeds to function optimally because users are always sending and receiving information as they progress with their designs.

Note: If you're using a modem, you're likely to have a more stable connection if you move closer to it.

Run a speed test
You can use a service like Ookla to run an internet speed test.
For Design Space to run optimally, Cricut specifies the following;
- Broadband connection
- Minimum 1 – 2 Mbps Upload

- Minimum 2 – 3 Mbps Download

After running the speed test, if the results are not good, and you are convinced that the connection is affecting to your Design space issues, you should wait until the connection improves or you call your service providers. There is also the option of switching to a new internet service provider with a proper internet connection.

Background Programs
If you're running too many background programs while using Design Space, it might also be a problem.

Some multi-tasking crafters are fond of engaging in different activities while designing on Design Space. For example, some simultaneously chat on Facebook, while downloading movies, watching videos on YouTube, and designing on Design Space. These activities will affect your app and make it malfunction badly, thus it is important to shut down other projects and focus solely on Design Space.

While it is important to close other apps and shut down other activities, there are other things should also do;
- Run a malware check
- If you're using windows, you should upgrade you drivers
- Clear your history and cache
- Defragment your hard drive
- Check your anti-virus software and update if needed

If you execute these tests, it might speed up the system, or even solve all related problems.

Your Browser
Your Design Space software might be having issues due to your system browser.

For you to access Design Space, Cricut recommends using the latest version of the browser you use. Be it Edge, Chrome, Firefox or Mozilla; just make sure that it is up to date. If it refuses to work on a particular browser, open it in another browser to see if it works. Although the reasons are unknown, sometimes its works and even works perfectly.

Contact Cricut

If you've tried all possible options and nothing works, you may have to call Cricut customer care to look into the issues you're faced with.

Chapter 3: Cricut Joy

Machine Setup and How to Prepare the Material

One way or another, you found yourself in possession of a Cricut joy machine and you have been worried about setting it up correctly? Well, there are lots of people like you on this table. Setting up your machine could look somehow complicated or tedious. However, this section is majorly written to guide you through it; the unboxing process and the setting up. So, relax and bring that Cricut machine out wherever you've stashed it. It takes approximately 1 hour to finish setting up a Cricut machine. With this guide, you should be done in less than an hour. Let's get right on it, shall we?

Opening the box
To make sure that we are together all the way through, we will go through even the most trivial step; opening the box.

You should be having a number of boxes right now in front of you if you went for the whole Cricut bundle. And there should be a big box among those boxes which contains the Cricut joy machine itself. If you open that big box, the first thing you should find is a Welcome packet, most of the tools will be in that packet. You should find a welcome book, rotary blade and cover, a USB cable, a fine-point pen, a packet that contains your first die-cutting project. The USB cable is sometimes the last thing you'll see in this packet, it's hidden under every other stuff. Underneath this welcome packet is your Cricut joy machine.

Unwrapping your cricut joy machine and supplies

We are getting to the exciting part. Let's unwrap your machine and find out what's inside.

When trying to unwrap your machine, you'll find it covered in a protective wrapper that looks filmy and also with a cellophane layer. Try to carefully unwrap the top foam layer so you can see the machine. After that, remove the remaining part of the Styrofoam that protects the inner machine housing.

When you unbox the whole casing, you should expect to find the following tools;

- Cricut Machine
- USB and Power Cables
- Rotatory blade with housing.
- Fine point blade with housing
- Fine point pen.
- Light-Grip and Fabric-Grip Mats (12 x 12)

Setting up your cricut joy machine

Once they are all connected, open your computer browser to continue the setup. Visit the **Cricut Sign-in Page** and click on the "Sign in" icon. You will have to either sign in with your account details or create a new account for yourself if you don't already have one. This is necessary so as to be able to access the Cricut Design Space.

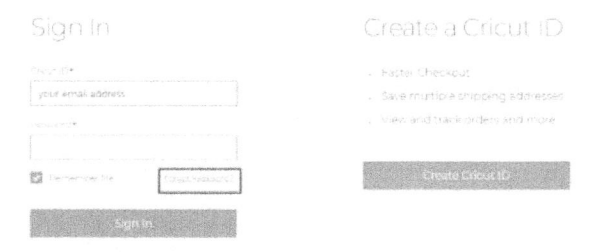

Create a Cricut ID

Your Cricut ID is your golden ticket to all things Cricut

First Name

Last Name

Country
Please select

☐ I accept the Cricut Terms of Use
☑ Send me free inspiration & exclusive offers

Email / Cricut ID

Retype Email / Cricut ID

Password

Already have a Cricut ID?

Sign In

If you do not have an active account yet, don't bother to fill any information on the sign-in fields. Click on the "Create Cricut ID" in the green box and then fill out every field with the required information and click on "Submit."

Now, it's time to link your machine to your account. It takes some people a lot of time to finish this part successfully. To make it easier, follow the procedures below.
After signing in, go to the upper left corner of the page and click on the drop-down menu icon (with three lines) beside "Home."

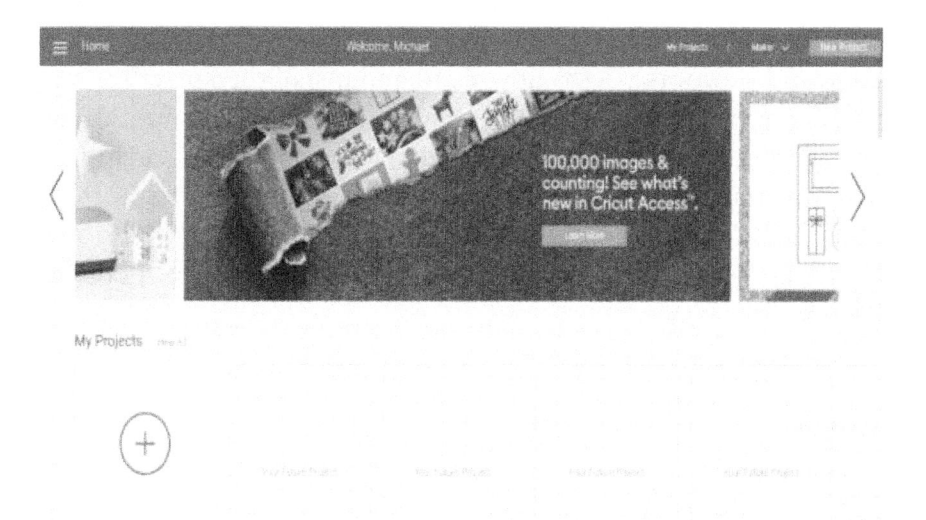

When the drop-down menu appears, select the "New Machine Setup."
On the next screen that pops up, click on your Cricut machine model.

Another webpage will appear with instructions on how to connect

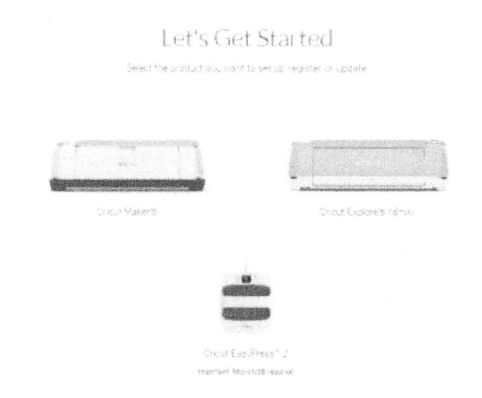

your machine. Follow the instruction accordingly.

When you follow the instructions, it automatically detects your machine and prompts you to download and install the software.

The site is user-friendly, so you'll be directed on how to go about the installation. And if you already have an account, you may still need to download it again. Cricut updates their design space often, there could be some new tools in the latest version that you don't have access to. It only takes about five minutes to get the installation done.

Cartridge

Designs are produced using parts put away on cartridges. Every cartridge accompanies a console overlay and guidance booklet. The plastic console overlay demonstrates key determinations for that cartridge as it were. Anyway, as of late Provo Craft has discharged an "All-inclusive Overlay" perfect with all cartridges discharged after August 1, 2013. The motivation behind the all-inclusive overlay is to simplify the way toward slicing by just learning one console overlay instead of learning the overlay for every individual cartridge. Designs can be removed on a PC with the Cricut Design Studio programming, on a USB associated Gypsy machine, or can be legitimately inputted on the Cricut machine utilizing the console overlay. There are two kinds of cartridges shape and textual style. Every cartridge has an assortment of imaginative highlights that can consider several different cuts from only one cartridge.

More than 275 cartridges are accessible (independently from the machine), containing textual styles and shapes, with new ones included monthly. While a few cartridges are conventional in substance, Cricut has to permit Disney, Pixar, Nickelodeon, Sesame Street, DC Comics and Hello Kitty. The Cricut line has a scope of costs. The cartridges are compatible, even though not all alternatives on a cartridge might be accessible with the little machines. All cartridges work just with Cricut programming. They must be enrolled to a solitary client for use and can't be sold or given away. A cartridge obtained for a suspended machine will probably wind up futile at the point the machine is ended. Cricut maintains whatever authority is needed to suspend support for certain product renditions whenever, which can make a few cartridges quickly out of date.

The Cricut joy Craft Room programming empowers clients to join pictures from different cartridges, consolidate pictures, and stretch/turn pictures; it doesn't take into account the formation of discretionary designs. It additionally empowers the client to see the pictures showed on-screen before starting the cutting procedure so that the final product can be seen in advance.

Loading Your Paper

To load paper into a Cricut machine, you'll want to make sure that the paper is at least three inches by three inches. Otherwise, it won't cut very well. You should use regular paper for this.

Now, to make this work, you need to put the paper onto the cutting mat. You should have one of those, so take it right now and remove the attached film. Put a corner of the paper to the area where you are directed to align the paper corners. From there, push the paper directly onto the cutting mat for proper adherence. Once you do that, you just load it into the machine, following the arrows. You'll want to keep the paper firmly on the mat.

Press the "load paper" key that you see as you do this. If it doesn't take for some reason, press the unload paper key, and try this again until it shows up.

Before you do any cutting for your design, you should always have a test cut in place. Some people don't do this, but it's incredibly helpful when learning how to use a Cricut. Otherwise, you won't get the pressure correct in some cases, so get in the habit of doing it for your pieces.

Selecting Shapes, Letters, and Phrases
When you're creating your Design Space design, you usually begin by using letters, shapes, numbers, or different fonts. These are the basics, and they're incredibly easy.

To make text, you just press the text tool on the left-hand side and type out your text. For example, write the word hello, or joy, or whatever you want to use.

You can choose different Cricut or system fonts, too. Cricut ones will be in green, and if you have Cricut Access, this is a great way to begin using this. You can sort these, too, so you don't end up accidentally paying for a font.

The Cricut ones are supposed to be made for Cricut, so you know they'll look good. Design Space also lets you put them closer together so they can be cut with a singular cut. You can change this by going to line spacing and adjusting as needed.

Adding shapes is pretty easy, as well. In Design Space, choose the shapes option. Once you click it, the window will then pop out, and you'll have a wonderful array of different shapes that you can use with just one click. Choose your shape, and from there, put it in the space. Drag the corners in order to make this bigger or smaller.

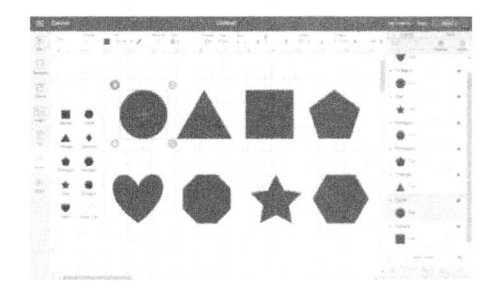

There is also the score line, which creates a folding line for you to use. Personally, if you're thinking of trying to make a card at first, I suggest using this.

Once you've chosen the design, it's time for you to start cutting.

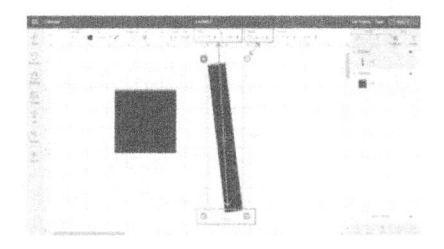

How to Remove Your Cuts from Cutting Mat

For placing your material to cut it on the mat, it's essential to know the placement. First, the mat's cover should be removed and placed elsewhere. The Cricut maker comes with a blue Light Grip mat, which is used for cutting paper mainly. The match will be slightly sticky for the suitable placement of the material. When loading, the material should be placed in the top left corner of the mat. Be sure to press down gently so that the material could be evened out. Place the top of the mat in the guides of the machine. Gently press on the rollers and press the load/to unload the button on top of the Cricut. Once loaded up, the software will tell you the next step. After the project has been finished, the material needs to be unloaded. Press on the load/unload button and take out the mat from the machine. The right way to remove the material from the mat is to be placed on a level surface, and the mat should be peeled off. A scrapper or a tweezer can peel off the remaining scraps.

How to design With Cricut Joy

When you break it down to its most basic operation, the Cricut joy does two things. It cuts, and it draws. However, these two functions have over a million uses and can be used on hundreds of materials, making it a truly versatile crafting powerhouse. Breaking it down to these two features seems almost like an injustice to the adaptability and versatility that this machine truly has.

There are more than 50 crafts you can do using your Cricut joy machine. Here, I will discuss in simple terms these amazing items:
Cut fabrics: the rotary blade was designed to cut seamlessly through any fabric including silk, denim, chiffon, and heavy canvass. Coupled with the mat, hundreds of fabrics can be cut without any backing. This is amazing!

Vinyl Decals and stickers: Is cutting vinyl decals and stickers your hobby, then you need Cricut Maker machine as your companion. Get the design inputted in the Design Space Software and instruct the machine to cut. As easy as that. The delivery will be wonderful. So what are you waiting for? Get to work!
Greeting Cards: The power and precision of the Cricut Maker makes cutting of paper and makes greeting cards craft less tedious and saves ample time. Your Christmas cards, birthday cards,

success cards and other greeting cards will be delivered with accurate, unique and amazing style.

How to Clean The Cricut Joy

If you want your Cricut machine to last for a long time, you must keep a routine basis. This means appropriately cleaning and maintaining cutting mats and blades.

Cricut machine maintenance
When the Cricut machine is used, eventually, paper particles will inevitably lead to reverse charging, dust, and debris. Also, the fat in the device will begin to stick to the track carriage.

If you want your machine to last long, then you should be cleaned regularly, or otherwise, be damaged prematurely. Here are some cleaning tips to help clean out the engine.
Before cleaning the device, disconnect it from the electrical outlet. This will prevent electrocution or any other accidents that may damage the device or damage.
Apply a small layer of fat on both sides of the carriage smart cut around the bar so that they form a ring is a quarter inch on both sides.
To make fat even become the car, push the smart carriage cut on both sides slowly and repeatedly.

Clean any grease that stained the bar while I was oiling the machine.
You can buy a pack of pasta Cricut. This works better than using a third-party package paste for the machine.
It will not get damaged. This is especially true if the Cricut machine makes a squeaking sound after using another product grease.

This process is almost the same as lubricating the machine maker Cricut too.

Maintaining the Cricut cutting mat

You also have to clean and maintain your Cricut cutting mat because cutting is carried out.

If the cutting is not clean, it can stain the machine. Also, if your cutting mat has left grip, you can spoil your designs and creations.

When your carpet is no longer sticky because of debris and dirt, cleaning and making it sticky again bring back life.

I will mention the solutions that are not ideal for rose-cut mats, just for green, blue, and purple.

There are many ways to clean your cutting mat.

The use of wet wipes for babies:

Make use of baby unscented bleach-free wipes without alcohol to clean your carpet. Must use wipes lighter babies can be found so that no lotions, corn starch, solvent or oil is added to the cutting base. If not, you could affect the adhesion and adhesive carpet. Also, after cleaning, let it dry completely before using it.

Using a sticky lint roller

You can also use a roll of tape if not find a sticky lint roller. Run the roll through the mat to get rid of hair, fibers, dust particles, and paper particles.

Using hot soapy water

You can also clean the carpet with soap and warm water. You must use the flattest possible soap also to not mess with the mat. Use a clean
Cloth, sponge, soft brush, or Magic Eraser. Also, rinse thoroughly and do not use until completely dry.

The use of an adhesive remover
For heavy-duty cleaning, you must use a reliable adhesive remover to clean appropriately. A to use an adhesive remover, read the instructions properly before you start.
Then spray a small amount on the mat and spread with a scraper or anything that can act as a scraper record.

How to make your sticky mat Cut Again
After washing or cleaning, the cutting mat must again make them sticky.
The most advisable way to do their sticky mat is again by adding glue to it. Obtain a solid stick glue-like Zig Pen 2-Way and apply it on the inside of the rug. Then, cerebrovascular accident glues around the mat and make sure there is no residue of glue on the edges of the carpet.

After about 30 minutes, the glue will become clear. If the cutting mat turns out to be too sticky after applying the glue, you can be used a piece of fabric to reduce the adhesive pressing the material into parts of the mat that are very sticky.
You can also use sticky adhesives or spray adhesives that are ideal for cutting mats.

General maintenance
When the carpet is not in use, it is covered with a transparent cover film so that the dust and hair are not accumulated on the surface of the rug.
Carefully manage their mats. If you want to make sure that the adhesive is not damaged, do not touch the sticky surface with your hands.
Always make sure that your carpet to dry completely before using or concealment. Do not use heat when the mat to dry but can be

placed in front of a fan. Also, make sure that is drying hang both sides will dry up.

Maintaining the Cricut cutting blade
You can use your Cricut beautiful tip sheet over a year if maintained properly! The same goes for other types of cutting blades. When securing the Cricut cutting blade, you have to keep it sharp all the time, so they do not wear out.

Keep your sharp blade essential because it can damage your materials and waste caused if it is not. Also, if you do not keep your knives, you will have to replace them frequently.

Keeping your blade sharp cut
Extending a portion of an aluminum foil in a cutting mat. Without removing the blade from the casing, cut a simple design on the foil. This sharpening the edge and remove paper particles or stuck on the sheet vinyl. This can be used for any type of cutting blade.

For heavy-duty cleaning, should be squeezed a sheet of foil on a ball. It is necessary to remove the blade housing of the machine to use this method. Then press the

Plunger, making the sheet and paste into the aluminum foil ball repeatedly. You can do this 50 times. This will make it sharper and also remove particles vinyl or paper sheet.

How to save your blade
The best way to store the cutting blade is left in the compartment Cricut. It can be placed in the drop-down door that is in front of the machine. This compartment is intended for storing the sheet.

The blade's case can be placed in the plastic points raised in the back of the machine. There are magnets on the front of the computer where you can paste loose sheets.

When you put your sheets on the Cricut machine, never loses its blades.

Cricut Design Space software For Cricut Joy

Moving on to Creating Your Project Template
On the home page, select "New Project", followed by a page with a blank canvas that looks like the grid on your Cricut mats. The words "empty canvas" is a nightmare in itself to any artist, so please just bear with me since we will fill that bad boy up in a second. But first, let's go through the menu options.

New, Templates, Projects, Images, Text, Shapes, and Upload. These are the things that you will see on your left-hand side when you have the canvas open on the screen.

New
New means that you will start a new project and clicking the tab will redirect you to a blank canvas. Be sure to save all changes on your current project before you go to the new canvas. Otherwise, you will lose all of the progress you have already made on that design.

Templates
Clicking on Templates will allow you to set a template to help you visualize and work with sizing. It is very handy for someone who is not familiar with Cricut joy Design Space and doesn't know what sizes to set. If you are cutting out wearable items on fabric, you can change the template's size to fit whoever will be wearing it. I'm sure you can agree that this feature is especially beneficial for the seamstresses out there.

Projects
Meanwhile, projects will lead you to the ready-to-make projects so that you can start cutting right away. Some of the projects are not customizable, but others are when you open the template, which is

pretty cool. Many of these are not free either, which irks me to a new extent. You can choose the "Free for Cricut (whatever machine you have)", and the projects that will turn up won't have to be paid for.

Text
The Text goes without saying. When you select this option, you can type whatever you want and scale it onto your canvas. You may select any font saved in your computer too; that's why collecting those has never been more useful! There is also an option called "multi-layered font", which gives your text a shadow layer. If you are cutting out the letters and shadow layers, the Cricut will do them separately and combine the two later if you wish to. It can create very cool effects so make sure you try that option out. Furthermore, remember that when you are being paid to do a job, the font you are using might require a license to use.

Shapes
Shapes lets you add basic forms to your canvas, which you can tweak to fit your own needs. The shapes include circle, square, rectangle, triangle, et cetera.

Cricut Basic
This is a program or software designed to help the new user get an easy start designing new crafts and DIY projects. This system will help you with image selection to cutting with the least amount of time spent in the design stages. You can locate your image, pre-set projector font, and immediately print, cut, score, and align with tools found within the program. You can use this program on the iOS 7.1.2 or later systems and iPad and several of the iPhones from the Mini to the 5th generation iPod touch. Since it is also a cloud-based service, you can start in one device and finish from another.

Cricut Sync

You just connect your system to the computer and run the synced program to install updates on the features that come with your machine. This is also used to troubleshoot many issues that could arise from the hardware.

Play Around and Practice

You can combine your shapes and images, add some text, and create patterns. The possibilities are endless. The best thing to do is familiarize yourself with the software before you attempt on cutting expensive materials. Start small and cheap - printer paper will be an ideal choice - and cut away. See what works well for you and stick with it. There are many options concerning the Cricut Design Space. The only way to learn all of this is to experiment and click on every tab you see and try different combinations of options when playing around on the software.

Making Your First Project Idea

According to the instruction, there will be directions on your screen that you must follow to create your first project after setting up your Cricut joy machine. You will still be using the link you found on the paper when you were setting up your machine. If you have not yet received your machine and are interested in knowing how it works, or you are looking for extra clarifications, here's what it will say.

First Step

First off, load a pen into the accessories clamp. You can pick whichever color you think will go best with the paper you have received. Next, you want to turn the knob so that the indicator is pointed to "cardstock," considering that is what you will be working with. Have you had a proper look at your mats yet? The blue mat is what you will want to use for this project. You should remove the plastic cover - keep it, don't throw it away as you will need to recover your mat when you're done to avoid dust accumulation - and lay down the paper on the mat with the top left corners of the material and the grid aligned.

Second Step
Make sure that the paper is pressed flat before you push it between the rollers firmly. The mat has to rest on the bottom roller. When it is in place, press the "Load" button to load your mat between the rollers. Press the "go" button, which will be flashing at this stage, and wait for the machine to work its magic on your project. Once everything is done, the light will flash, and you can press the "Load" button again to unload the mat. Your paper will still be sticking to the mat when you remove it.

Third Step
Be careful when removing the material from the mat. Don't be too hasty; take your time so that it doesn't tear. Pull the mat away from the cardstock instead of doing it the other way around. After completing that step, you can now fold the cardstock in half, insert the liners into the corner slots of the card, and it's done!

You have just made your first ever Cricut project in a matter of minutes from start to finish! Congratulations! What are you waiting for? Do more projects! There are a ton of templates you can play around with—practice, practice, practice.

Always keep in mind when starting a new project that you must first have all of the materials necessary to complete the project. It is always helpful to check your stock of tools and materials before getting started. The worst feeling is when you sit down and begin working on a problematic project only to realize you are out of a specific material needed to finish the job. It will save you a lot of time in the long run if you spend a few minutes at the beginning taking stock of your inventory! Working with materials you already have on hand is also a great way to keep your crafting costs low. It will always feel good to know that you made a custom piece of work without spending a ton of extra money just to complete it!

How to Upload Images with A Cricut Joy

For this method to operate, you will need to upload a picture from your desktop. Click complicated once you upload it, and the next window is where the magic takes place.
At the left corner of the top. Look at the wand? Click on it and press on the hair. Click on the continuation button and name the picture. Click the save button.

It's gone, and it's been so simple. Now, let's look after her flesh.
First press back on the magic wand to remove the face, arms, body, and any hard-to-reach pieces. Once you've finished that, take the eraser to wash the remainder of your flesh until it's gone.

Click Continue, identify your picture, and then press Save when the image is to your liking.

Insert both pictures into the surface of your Cricut Design Space. You can bring them back together once you've got them there. One reason I'm excited about this process is that sometimes, like the hair color, I want to change things. I couldn't change the hair color if I left the picture like it was. But I can do that now.
Would you like to know how to edit images in Cricut Design Space as thrilled as I am? I pray so.
Now, go out and do some crafting!

Cut Vinyl with a Cricut Joy

Before cutting, ensure that your Circuit joy machine is set to the right setting to cut vinyl. You can select a thin vinyl setting or set the cut to a thicker level, just to ensure that the Cricut joy machine cuts through the vinyl on the first go-round. You will want to back to stay intact, however (this will make weeding a lot easier when you get to this in the next stop) so don't overdo the cut pressure once you are secure in your vinyl placement on the mat, as well as your machine setting, you are ready to go! Once the mat is loaded and the cut button on your Cricut joy Machine is blinking, you are

ready to hit the button and begin cutting. Design Space will give you a percentage as to how far into the project it has cut.
How to Make Stickers

How to Make Safari Animal Sticker
Supplies needed are as follows:
- Cricut machine
- Printable sticker paper
- Inkjet prints

Follow the next few steps to create this sticker:
- Load your Cricut design space page and start a new project.
- Click on Upload Images and upload the images of the animal you want. This is an image gotten online.
- Highlight the whole image and use the Flatten button to solidify the image as a whole.
- Resize the image to the appropriate size you desire. You do the residence by clicking on the image, then drag the right side of the box to the size you desire.
- Click Save at the top left to save your project. Save it to be a print and cut image, after which you click the Make It button at the right hand of the screen.
- Examine the end result and make necessary adjustment where you deem it fit. Click Continue after the adjustment. This will lead you to print the design onto the sticker paper.
- Adjust the dial settings on the Cricut machine to the required settings.
- Set the sticker paper on the cutting mat.
- Load the cutting mat into the machine, and push it against the rollers.
- Press the Load/Unload button and then the Go button to cut the stickers.

How to Make Vinyl Sticker Car Window
Supplies needed are as follows:
- Cricut machine
- Premium outdoor glossy vinyl
- Transfer tape
- Scraper tool

Follow these steps to create:
- Get and save the image you want to use online.
- Log in to the Cricut design space and start a new project.
- Click on the Upload icon and upload the saved image.
- Click on the image and drag to the next page, then select image type.
- Select the parts of the image you do not want as part of the final cut.
- Select the image as a cute image. You will get to preview the image as a cut image.
- Approve the cut image. You would be redirected to the first upload screen.
- Click on your just finished cut file, then highlight it and insert the image.
- The image is added to your design space for size readjusting. The image is ready to cut.
- Cut the image, and remove excessive vinyl after the image is cut.
- Apply a layer of transfer tape to the top of the cut vinyl.
- Clean the car window really well with rubbing alcohol to remove all dirt.
- Carefully peel away the paperback of the vinyl.

- Apply the cut vinyl on the window. Start at one end and roll it down.
- Go over the applied vinyl with a scraper tool to remove air bubble underneath the vinyl.
- Slowly peel away the transfer tape from the window.

Steps for Making Ice-Cream Stickers

The supplies needed for this are as follows:
- Cricut machine
- Printable sticker paper
- Inkjet printer

Steps to making an ice-cream sticker:
- Log in to the Cricut design spaces.
- Start a new project and click on the Images at the screen's left side. Select the ice-cream image(s) you want.
- Highlight the whole image and use the Flatten button to solidify the image as one whole piece.
- Resize the image to the appropriate size you need. You realize this by clicking on the image then dragging the right side of the box to the size you desire.
- Click Save at the top left to save your project. Save it to be a print and cut image, after which you click the Make It button at the right hand of the screen.
- Examine the result and click Continue if it's what you expected. This will lead you to print the design onto the paper.
- Adjust the dial on the Cricut machine to the required settings.
- Place the sticker paper on the cutting mat.

- Load the cutting mat into the machine, and push it against the rollers.
- Press the Load/Unload button and then the Go button to cut the stickers.
- Sit back and let the machine print out your designed sticker.

Working With Images/Edit Panel

Have you tried to find out how to edit pictures in the layout room of Cricut? Also me. Usually

<u>Editing Images In Cricut joy Using The Slice Tool</u>
To assist me in editing pictures in the Cricut Design Space, I used the Slice device. I'm likely still going to use that method for photos

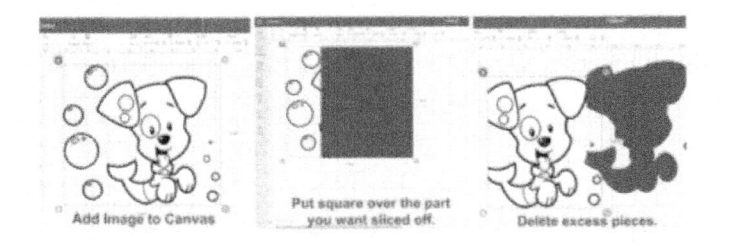

I've already uploaded to Cricut Design Space. Let me explain how to edit images using the Slice tool.

Click on the picture and then click Insert Images to add your attached picture to your Cricut joy canvas. You can add more than one image to your canvas at a time.
Make your picture a lot larger so you can work on it by pressing and pulling it down a little bit on the right upper corner. Just far enough to be able to see it better.

Unlock the table by pressing below the square on the left upper panel. Do you see the icon of the lock? Click on that. Now, using the right top corner, you can transfer the square in any form you want. I placed the circle over the portion that I was about to wipe out, the dog.

Clicking or highlighting the circle, click and hold the change key on your keyboard. Click the picture of the bubble with your mouse, well, bubble for me. This emphasizes both of them.
Click the Slice device at the right upper corner with both the circle and the picture outlined.
Start taking back your slice's parts. There ought to be three parts. They can be deleted.
Continue this method until the manner you want your picture to be printed.

Cricut Scrapbooking

Scrapbooking is a technique of preserving memories that has existed for quite a while and has developed a lot. In past times, the development of one scrapbook was a monumentally outrageous job.

However, with the creation of products like the Cricut cutting machine, things are a lot easier. If you are looking into developing a scrapbook, this poor boy will be the tool for you. You will find lots of great Cricut suggestions in this book that you can make the most of.

Scrapbooks are simply several of the numerous Cricut suggestions. This tool, in case you know the way to maximize it can enable you to make things go beyond scrapbooking like calendars.
If you purchase a Cricut cartridge, you will find a load of designs uploaded in each one. These pre-created themes are usually utilized

for a wide range of items like hangings for walls, picture frames, and greeting cards for those seasons.

Just your imagination is going to limit your progress with a Cricut piece of equipment. With calendars, you can design every month to reflect special events, the mood, and the weather which are associated with it.

The Cricut device can handle that. But in the event that an individual cartridge doesn't keep design which needs, you can constantly go and purchase. It is that simple!

Cricut devices could be a bit costly with the price beginning at 1dolar1 299. That is hefty for anyone to begin with. Be a sensible customer. You can often turn to the web to search for deals that are great on Cricut machines.

Everything now appears to be extremely convenient. Should you look for labor now, the majority has become machine intensive instead of labor-intensive. It doesn't mean suggesting that today, leave the machines and allow them to perform the work.

They nevertheless need the working prowess of individuals. I never wish it involves that time where devices are self - operating.

The art of scrapbook making is but one facet of human civilization, which has become a lot easier due to engineering merchandise, especially the Cricut cutting machine. It is at this time which Cricut scrapbooking takes the center stage.

In case you are considering of putting in the Cricut scrapbooking world, this device is a must-have. You cannot say no and just claim that I can do it by hand because doing this will drive you to the cliff and into the jaws of insanity.

Utilizing Shape Cartridge helps you develop shapes like animals, tags, boxes, dolls, and hearts amongst others. Pick these cutout

symbols to embellish your scrapbook for a fascinating remembrance on your own or a present for someone very special.
Solving the most common problem when using Cricut Joy

Does the Cricut Maker cut fabric patterns such as clothes, pants, shirts, skirts, blouses etc.?
Absolutely Yes, the Cricut Machine can cut through fabric patterns the Cricut Maker comes with 25 patters for sewing to assist you to get started. In addition the Cricut Maker comes with hundreds of design patterns in collaboration with Simplicity.

Does the Cricut Maker etch through glass?
Yes, the Cricut maker can etch glass but not directly. To do this you need to create and cut your own design patterns using the Design space and applying an etching cream onto the glass surface.

Do I lose my projects, uploaded images and cartridges when upgrading the Cricut Maker?
No. Your projects, cartridges and uploaded images remain intact the reason being because you typically use a Cricut ID in the Cricut cloud and not machines with the same Cricut ID and not the machine itself. So you can be sure all you content will be accessible with the Cricut Maker.

Does the Cricut Maker engrave metallic materials such as jewellery or Pet ID tags?
Yes, but to technically achieve this you need a special etching tool for it to go through a third party. This is because the deep engraving functionality may fail on some metallic objects. Among such tools you may need is an etching tool by "Chomas creation" which fits into the Cricut Maker as other tools. With the tool, you can engrave or etch material such as leather, metal clay, silver, aluminum, bronze, copper, plastic, and acrylic

Do I need a printer? What printer should I use?

Absolutely No, Cricut joy machines are not dependent upon printers.

As far as what printer to get, you just need something that prints color! Some of the most versatile Hp machine is the HP Envy, but there are many great printers out there in the market that are not limited to Hp.

Does there exist any difference in the power Cords of the Cricut joy Machine?

No, there is a physical difference in the Power cords of the Cricut joy Machines. However, there is a difference in the output current with the Cricut joy cord upgraded to supply 3A with its predecessors—Cricut Explore having a 2.5A output current supply. This adaption also allows you to charge your mobile phone via its charging port on the right-hand side while multitasking the cutting/writing functionalities.

However if you using the Cricut Explore you can still charge the mobile phone device. Still, the difference is that because of its low current capacity it will either slow, stutter or even shut off (in extreme cases) because the device will need a current supply and the cutting operation —which needs more current supply especially as it requires more cutting pressure.

What materials can I cut using the Cricut joy?

The Cricut engineering team is in the process of experimenting more materials, cutting pressures and guidelines. However the following are some of the materials it cuts; fabric, papers—crepe and tissue, vinyl, cardstock, cork, leather, duct tape, faux leather, chipboard, felt, adhesive foil, among others.

How does the Rotary cutter differ with the fabric blade?
The Cricut Maker can use both, the rotary blade, and the bonded fabric blade. However the difference is that the rotary blade can cut through delicate materials without a backing material. In contrast, the rotary blade will need to use the Adaptive tool system to perform the precision cutting experience.

What is the Pink Mat and how can I use it?
The Pink Mat is useful for cutting fabrics as well as other delicate materials. It is highly durable therefore strong which means it can withstand pressure when cutting thin materials. You may be asking how it needs a strong material whereas the material under cut is thin. It takes a lot of pressure when cutting delicate materials meaning it needs to stay flat on the mat to resist the need to shift.

Are blades and tools of the Cricut joy and other predecessors interchangeable?
Yes and No. The tools of the Cricut joy cannot be used in the Cricut Explore machines however the blades of the Cricut Maker can be used by the Cricut Explore machines. Simply the reason being the Cricut joy came after the Cricut Explore therefore the functionalities of the Cricut Explore differ with that the Cricut joy with the latter being more advanced compared to the Explore. It does not have the drive gears that control the rotary blade and knife, for starters, and the pressure required to operate these tools are simply not present in the Explore.

How does the Cricut joy differ with its predecessors in terms of the software?
Both are similar in terms of software because they use the Cricut Design space. This means that all the Explore projects can be cut by the Cricut joy whereas some project by Cricut Maker can be also

be cut by the Cricut Explore as long as it does not concern the rotary and knife blades.

Chapter 4: FAQs about the Cricut Maker & Joy

Why does Design Space say my Cricut machine is already in use when it's not?
To resolve this, make sure that you've completed the New Machine Setup for your Cricut. Try Design Space in another browser. The two that work best are Google Chrome and Mozilla Firefox; if it doesn't work in one of those, try the other. If that doesn't clear the error, try a different USB port and USB cable. Disconnect the machine from the computer and turn it off. While it's off, restart your computer. After your computer restarts, reconnect the machine and turn it on. Wait a few moments, and then try Design Space again. If you're still having the same problem, contact Cricut Member Care.

Why doesn't my cut match the preview in Design Space?
Test another image and see if the same thing happens. If it's only happening with the one project, create a new project and start over or try a different image. If it happens with a second project, and your machine is connected with Bluetooth, disconnect that and plug it in with a USB cable. Larger projects may sometimes have difficulty communicating the cuts over Bluetooth. If you can't connect with USB or the problem is still occurring, check that your computer matches or exceeds the running Design Space system requirements. If it doesn't, try the project on a different computer or mobile device that does. If your computer does meet the requirements, open Design Space in a different browser and try again. If the problem continues, try a different USB cable. Finally, if the issue still hasn't resolved, contact Cricut Member Care.

What do I do if I need to install USB drivers for my Cricut machine?
Typically, the Cricut drivers are automatically installed when you connect it with a USB cable. If Design Space doesn't see your machine, you can try this to troubleshoot the driver installation. First, open Device Manager on your computer. You'll need to have administrator rights. For Windows 7, click Start, right-click on Computer, and select Manage.

Why does my Cricut Maker say the blade is not detected?
Make sure that the tool in Clamp B is the same one Design Space recommends in the Load Tools step of the Project Preview screen. If you don't have that recommended tool, unload your mat and select Edit Tools on the Project Preview screen. Here, you can select a different tool. If the tool and the selection already match, carefully remove the tool from Clamp B and clean the reflective band on the housing. Reinstall it in the clamp and press the Go button. If that doesn't resolve the problem, remove the tool again and clean the machine's sensor. Reinstall the tool and press Go again.

Why is my Cricut machine making a grinding noise?
If it's the carriage car making a loud noise after you press the cut button, and it sounds like the carriage might be hitting the side of the machine, record a short video of it and send it to Cricut Member Care. If the noise comes from a brand-new machine the first time you use it, contact Cricut Member Care. Otherwise, make sure that you're using the original power cord that came with your machine. If the machine isn't getting the correct voltage, it may produce a grinding sound. If you are using the machine's power cord, adjust your pressure settings. If it's too high, it might produce an unusual sound. Decrease it in increments of 2–4, and do some

test cuts. If it's still making the issue even after decreasing the cutting pressure, contact Cricut Member Care.

Why is my mat going into the machine crooked?
Check the roller bar to see if it's loose, damaged, or uneven. If it is, take a photo or video of it to send to Cricut Member Care. If the roller bar seems fine, make sure that you're using the right mat size for the machine. Make sure the mat is correctly lined up with the guides and that the edge is underneath the roller bar when you prepare to load it. If it's still loading crookedly even when properly lined up with the guides, try applying gentle pressure to the mat to get it under the roller bar once it starts. If none of this works, contact Cricut Member Care.

Why isn't the Smart Set Dial changing the material in Design Space?
Make sure that the USB cable between the computer and the Cricut Explore is properly connected. If so, disconnect the Explorer from the computer and turn it off. Restart your computer. Once it's on, turn on the Explore, plug it into the computer, and try the cut again. If it still isn't changing the material, connect the USB cable to a different port on the computer. If it's still not working, try Design Space in multiple web browsers and see if the problem replicates. If it does, try an entirely different USB cable. Check for Firmware Updates for the Explore. If you don't have another USB cable, the Firmware Update doesn't help, or there are no Firmware Updates, contact Cricut Member Care.

What do I do if my Cricut Maker stopped partway through a cut?
If the Knife Blade stops cutting and the Go button are flashing, the Maker has encountered some error. In Design Space, you'll get a notification that the blade is stuck. This might have been caused by the blade running into something like a knot or seam if too much

dust or debris built up in the cut area or if the blade got into a gouge in the mat from a previous cut. To resume your project, do not unload the mat. This will lose your place in the project, and it will be impossible to get it lined up again. Check the cut area for dust or debris, and gently clean it.

Why is my fabric getting caught under the rollers?
Be sure to cut down any fabric so that it fits on your mat without going past the adhesive. If you have stuck the fabric and realize it's hanging past the adhesive, use a ruler and a sharp blade to trim it. Or, if it's the correct size but slightly askew, unstick it and reposition it.

Why would my Cricut Maker continuously turn off during cuts?
This can happen from a build-up of static electricity while cutting foil and metal sheets. Makers in dry areas are more susceptible to this. Spritzing water in the air will dissipate the build-up. Be careful not to spray any water directly on the Maker. Using a humidifier or vaporizer in the area where you use your Maker can help avoid the static build-ups. If this doesn't seem to be what's causing the issue, contact Cricut Member Care.

Chapter 5: Tips that might Assist You To Begin

If you can you can subscribe to the access for about ten dollars a month to gain access to over twenty thousand different images and over a thousand different projects. You even get over three hundred fonts.

You will also need to keep the plastic sheets that come with the mats to protect them between your uses.
Clean your cutting mats with baby wipes that are water-based to keep them sticky and clean longer.
Use one blade for your cardstock and a separate one for vinyl because this will let them both last longer.

Make sure that you have a deep cut blade.

This is for people who have had the cartridges for an older machine or older cartridge. You can hook these up to your new account. It is a simple thing to do but you should know that you could only link them once so be sure that if you are buying a machine second hand, nothing has been linked yet.

The right tools are important here so you should make sure that you have the toolset. It will contain vital tools that you need, and they can especially help with vinyl.

Know your glue

Many people are huge fans of what is called tacky glue. It gives your projects a little bit of wiggle room when you're trying to position them. The problem is that it can take longer to dry. If this is something that bothers you, you might want to try a quicker one. Zip dry paper glue it's extremely sticky and much faster.

A tip that will go along with the tip above is that you want them to be a layer to pop out from another layer. You can make this happen by using products like pop dots or Zots. They are self-adhesive foam mounts. You can also make little circles using craft foam or cardboard and then glue it between the layers.

Think about a Coach

Business mentors are extremely popular nowadays. Consider going through some cash with a Scrapbooking business mentor who comprehends the business as well as genuinely comprehends the specific brand of energy scrapbook sweethearts share. A mentor can help share business abilities however can go about as an extraordinary coach in managing you to your objectives.

Exhibit Your True Talent with a Business Card for Artists

The financial downturn has left huge numbers of us feeling the squeeze. Numerous individuals are searching for approaches to set aside cash in each part of life. Be that as it may, there are times when a buy must be made, and cautious research regularly structures some portion of the basic leadership the procedure.

Give the Quality of Your Work a chance to radiate through

A business card for specialists is your window to the world, and it should say a great deal regarding your aesthetic edge and abilities. Make it state every little thing about you and what you can offer. Plan a motivating logo that can join the substance of what you can do with an incredible structure. This astute connecting can put you on top of things by helping individuals to recollect who and what you are.

Consider Other Ways You Can Display Your Skills to the World

A business card for specialists is only one of numerous limited time apparatuses you can use to enhance your presentation. It bodes well. The production of a notice is a magnificent method to demonstrate the best of what you do. Try not to place a lot into your sign; that will go about as an obstacle and prevent individuals from getting a vibe of your actual abilities. Consider the area where you can show your blurb. Vital arranging of the setting of your sign can help augment its effect. It will expand the intrigue of your work and open up more potential outcomes.

Remember to tell individuals how to connect!

A business card for specialists needs not exclusively to demonstrate the embodiment of your innovativeness; it likewise fills a need. It needs to tell potential clients how to connect with you. Incorporate all the distinctive contact techniques you have, email, site, telephone numbers, and any online networking you are an individual from. Remember the intensity of internet based life and bookmarking destinations; they can enable feature to considerably a greater amount of your work.

Be Adaptable

Consider chipping away at zones that you hadn't imagined, however will be something inside your abilities. This will enable you to set up notoriety. Another viable method to advance your aptitudes notwithstanding utilizing a business card for specialists is to engage in network ventures where you offer your administrations for nothing. Make something stunning that individuals will see every day; this is an incredible advert for your aptitudes. This will place your work into thousands of individuals' lives and drive more clients to you.

Conclusion

In this book, we have given you the tools to make your Cricut work at its best all day every day. When you can do this, you will be able to make anything that you want because these machines can cut amazingly well and they have so many functions that it could make your head spin. This book has been able to help you see the difference between the different machines and how and why the prices are different. Each machine has something that it does best and the Maker is the best of the four as it can cut more than any other machine. This means that you get to work with new materials that you will not use with the other machines because they can't cut it. They call the Maker the ultimate machine because it can do what others can't.

When you choose the machine that will work best with you, you will find that the website from the company itself is much cheaper than the other retailers that you can find online. The benefit from buying from the company itself is that you do not have to deal with a third party. Instead, you get coupons, bundles and discounts that you are looking for, and there is no problem with the machine. In addition to that, when you buy from a third party retailer, they do not let you bundle at all so you will be paying an extra per item you want. This can get very expensive very quickly.

We also give you great advice on projects that you can do with your particular machine. There are somethings that individual devices can cut and others can't cut very much. If you are doing heavy-duty projects, you will need a machine that can do this. This is why we have compiled the best information for you.

Thank you for downloading this book

CRICUT PROJECT IDEAS

*Power Your Imagination and Creativity with Lots of Unique Cricut Ideas.
A Complete Guide with Illustrations, Tips, and Tricks Suitable for Beginners and Advanced*

Introduction

Are you out of ideas and you don't have enough creativity to create your own design, image, or project? Don't worry! Just find a project you like, grab your supplies, and go for it. If you want to view all Ready-to-Make projects, you will need to access the Projects page of Cricut Design Space and scroll down to see as many projects as you wish. If you are using a desktop computer, or a laptop you can select a Project Category from the drop-down menu located on the upper side of the screen, or if you know what you want, you can type what you need in the search bar.

The view is a bit different if you are using the Mobile App of Design Space. From the Home view, you will see the Categories drop-down, you can tap on it to see different categories, or the Search bar to find what you need.

There are plenty of decorations you can make using these machines, whether it's for Christmas, Halloween, or other seasonal-themed decorations. Perhaps you are looking for something more permanent, like unique hanging planters. For this one, you will need any Cricut Explore Air or Maker, a deep cut blade, a standard grip mat, chipboard, foam brushes, a glue gun, DecoArt Acrylic paint, grey sky and sea glass, light masking tape and leather cording. Plus, you will need a plant (artificial one is better in this case), and a wire (but this is optional). If you choose the live plant, you will need a plastic recipient for soil and some small white gravel.

Enjoy

Chapter 1: project ideas for beginners

1. **A Simple Birthday Card**

Materials

- White and navy cardstock
- Glue or spray adhesive

Where to Find Materials

- Cricut.com
- Swing design
- Cricut.com
- Vinyl
- Iron-on
- Paper
- Infusible ink

- Maker materials
- Amazon.com.

Illustration

- ✓ In Design Space, create a square and adjust the size to 5" x 7".
- ✓ Next, upload the image you want to use. In this example, it is a motorcycle. When the image is on the canvas, separate the layers and delete the ones you do not want to use. This should leave you with an outline of the image you want.
- ✓ Duplicate the rectangle you created and scale it down slightly to fit inside the first rectangle. Consider sizing it 3" x 5". Slide the smaller rectangle on the top of the larger one and then select both rectangles. Select "Align" and then "Center Vertically" and then "Center Horizontally."
- ✓ To remove the unnecessary rectangles, highlight both the rectangles and then select "slice." This allows you to delete the overlapping center rectangles you do not want. This creates a frame for your image and words.
- ✓ Drag your motorcycle image into the frame. Make sure the image touches on the right and left sides of the frame. When you are satisfied with the placement, select "weld" to create a single piece.
- ✓ To add text to your images, select "text" and write the message you want, such as "Happy Birthday" and "Kevin." The font used is "Stencil" because it is best for cutting. It does not leave any remaining pieces in the process. You can play around with whatever font you want but keep that in mind.
- ✓ When the pieces are cut, weed out any remaining parts that you do not want. Attach the background color to the front image and message. Write your message on the back if you want. You can also create this as a folded card by making

the back colorful rectangle as 11" x 15" and adding a score line in the center.

Tips and Tricks

Now, you'll then want to add the text. You can choose the font you want to use, and from there, write out the message on the card, such as "Merry Christmas." At this point, instead of choosing to cut, you want to select the right option – the make it option. You don't have to mirror this, but check that your design fits appropriately on the cardstock itself. When choosing material for writing, make sure you select the cardstock.

From there, insert your cardstock into the machine, and then, when ready, you can press go and the Cricut machine will design your card. This may take a minute, but once it's done, you'll have an excellent card in place. It's super easy to use.

Cricut cards are a great personalized way to express yourself, creating a one-of-a-kind, sentimental piece for you to gift to friends and family.

2. **Welcome to Our Happy Home" Sign**

Materials

- A square wooden board (the size you want your sign to be)
- Baby blue paint, with a matte or chalk finish; paint the wood before making the sign
- Permanent outdoor vinyl; black
- Green StandardGrip cutting mat
- Cricut Fine-Point Blade
- Pair of scissors for cutting the material to size
- Weeder tool
- Spatula
- Brayer for smoothing out the material

Where to Find Materials

- Craft stores
- Superstores
- Vinyl/Heat Transfer Vinyl
- Amazon.com
- ExpressionsVinyl.com
- MyVinylDirect.com
- Craft stores
- Amazon.com
- PaperAndMore.com
- Craft stores

Illustration

- ✓ Take the measurement of your board the width and length.
- ✓ In Design Space, select *'Shapes'* from the left-hand menu, and choose a square.
- ✓ Resize the square by typing in the dimensions of your board.
- ✓ You will need to zoom the shape in, to be able to see it on the screen.
- ✓ You can have the background of the shape in any color. If your text is going to be white, you may want to consider making the box black.
- ✓ You will need to choose a font for the writing on your sign.
- ✓ Click on the *'Text'* option on the right-hand side menu bar.
- ✓ Position the text onto the box frame on the screen, mimicking where you are going to position the writing on your signboard.
- ✓ For this project, choose *'Aaron Script Single-Layer'* cutting font. It is a nice curly font for a sign.

- ✓ Choose the color you want the writing for your sign to be. For the sake of this exercise, we are going to make the font black.
- ✓ Drag the corner of the text box to size the font to how big you want to make it. It must fit comfortably, on your signboard.
- ✓ Remove your template box as you no longer need it, and it is not going to be cut.
- ✓ Now is also a good time to *'Save'* your project and give it a name you will recognize for future similar projects.
- ✓ Make sure you have the correct size cutting board.
- ✓ Cut the vinyl to the size you need. If you have made your fonts fit completely across your sign, make sure the piece is big enough to fit your signboard.
- ✓ Place the vinyl on the Cricut cutting mat. Here is a tip for you: If your mat is losing its stickiness, you need a bit of tape to anchor it firmly to the mat.
- ✓ In Design Space, click *'Make It'* in the top right-hand corner of the screen.
- ✓ Set the material to *'Vinyl'*.
- ✓ You do not need a pen or accessory in the first holder, but you will need to use the second holder's fine-point blade.
- ✓ Load the cutting board with the vinyl and press the *'Load\Unload'* button.
- ✓ When the light flashes, the Cricut is loaded and ready to press *'Go'*.
- ✓ Gently peel back the vinyl. You may need to use the spatula to help peel the back vinyl off.
- ✓ Use the Weeder tool to hook away any vinyl from the middle of the words, for instance, the V-indent on top of the M. Try not to let any vinyl you have hooked, fall back down as it may

- ✓ Once the letters are positioned and stuck down with the top part of the transfer tape, give them a rub to ensure they are stuck down.
- ✓ Gently pull the top of the transfer tape off the wording and your sign is ready.

Tips and Tricks

Due to the strong adhesive that underlines the Cricut Premium Vinyl, once the design has been positioned on the base material, it is hard to reposition the design without causing any damage.

To remove the vinyl sheet from the cutting mat, instead of lifting the vinyl from the mat, peel the mat away for a smoother release of the design with no damage.

If you are not using the "kiss-cut" and cutting through both the vinyl and the liner, then you can just peel away the liner from the vinyl and apply it to the desired surface with your hands and without the transfer tape.

It is recommended to peel the liner at a 45-degree angle, and if the vinyl does not separate from the liner, then just burnish the transfer tape on top of the vinyl and peel away again.

2. Personalized Paper Bookmark

Materials

- Flora Craft ® Make It: Fun Foam Wreath 12 "
- White Ribbon: 1.5" broad and at least 8 yards Colored Cardstock
- Cricut Explore (or hand-cut with scissors)
- Glue Gun

Where to Find Materials

- Handmade paper
- Craft stores –
- Wal-Mart
- Joann Fabrics
- Spoonflower.com

- FabricDirect.com
- Amazon.com

Illustration

- ✓ Foam wreaths can get reasonably chaotic, so I like wrapping the wreath's shape with a ribbon to assist in preventing the foam flakes from getting anywhere. Start by pinning or adding hot glue to the ribbon end and attach to the wreath.
- ✓ Then tightly wrap the ribbon around the wreath, overlapping the ribbon until the entire shape is covered. If you run out of ribbon, don't worry-just pin or glue the end in location, begin a new roll where you left off.
- ✓ If you have no Cricut, you can readily cut these by hand. Cut a spiral, add a scalloped, fringed, or triangular edge to get distinct flower designs. It may take a little longer, and it's a little more work, but your wreath would still look incredible.
- ✓ Assembling the flowers is relatively easy, but time-consuming: start rolling the flower end. If you keep dropping the flower and it slips, add glue drops as required.
- ✓ Turn your flower, spread the petals, and create your flower look more like a flower.
- ✓ Repeat this process until all your flowers are assembled. Throw them into a stack and get some chocolate. You deserve that.
- ✓ Arrange the flowers on your wreath to have an idea of how things fit and see if you need to cut more flowers to fill in vacant places. Once you want it, warm up your glue gun and glue it in location.

Tips and Tricks

You can also upload images, too, if you want to create a huge picture on the pillow itself.

From here, you want to press the attach button for each box, so that they work together and both are figured when centered, as well.

Let the machine work its magic with cutting and from there, you can press the weeding tool to get the middle areas out.

Set your temperature on the easy press for the right settings, and then push it onto the material, ironing it on and letting it sit for 10 to 15 seconds. Let it cool, and then take the transfer sheet off.

3. Fancy Leather Bookmark

Materials

- ✓ Cricut metallic leather
- ✓ Cricut holographic iron-on
- ✓ Purple StrongGrip mat
- ✓ Cricut Fine-Point Blade
- ✓ Weeding tool
- ✓ Pair of scissors for cutting the material to size

- ✓ Brayer, or scraping tool
- ✓ Cricut Knife Blade
- ✓ Thin gold string, or ribbon

Where to Find Materials

- ✓ Express vinyl
- ✓ Craft stash
- ✓ Happy crafter
- ✓ amazon
- ✓ Esty
- ✓ Cricut.com
- ✓ Swing design

Illustration

- ✓ Cut the leather to the size you want it to be.
- ✓ Each leather holder is approximately 2' wide by 6' high.
- ✓ Cut the holographic paper to the size you want it to be; this will depend on the font size and wording you choose for the bookmark.
- ✓ Create a new project in Design Space.
- ✓ Select 'Shapes' from the left-hand menu.
- ✓ Choose the square, unlock it, and set the width to 2' with a height of 6'.
- ✓ Choose a triangle from the 'Shapes' menu, and set the width to 1.982' and the height to 1.931'.
- ✓ Position the triangle in the rectangle at the bottom. Make sure it is positioned evenly, as this is going to create a swallowtail for the bookmark.
- ✓ Select the circle from the shapes menu and unlock the shape. Set the width and height to 0.181'.
- ✓ Duplicate the circle shape.

- ✓ Move the one circle to the top right-hand corner of the bookmark, and the other to the left. These will be the holes to put a piece of ribbon or fancy string through.
- ✓ Align the holes and distribute them evenly by using the 'Align' function from the top menu, with both circles selected.
- ✓ Select the top left hole with the top of the rectangle and click 'Slice' in the bottom right menu.
- ✓ Select the circle and 'Remove' it, then 'Delete' it.
- ✓ Select the top right circle with the top of the rectangle and click 'Slice' from the bottom right menu.
- ✓ Select the circle and remove it.
- ✓ Select the bookmark and move it over, until you see the other two circles.
- ✓ Select the two circles and delete them.
- ✓ Select the triangle and the bottom of the rectangle, then click 'Slice' from the bottom right-hand menu.
- ✓ Place the leather on the cutting mat and use the brayer tool, or scraper tool to flatten it and stick it properly to the cutting mat.
- ✓ Position the little rollers on the feeding bar to the left and right, so they do not run over the leather.
- ✓ Load the knife blade into the second Cricut chamber.
- ✓ In Design Space, click on 'Make It'.
- ✓ Set the material to Cricut metallic leather.
- ✓ Load the cutting board and leather into the Cricut, and hit 'Go' when the Cricut is ready to cut.
- ✓ Unload the cutting board when the Cricut is finished printing, and use the spatula to cut the leather bookmark form out.
- ✓ Use the weeding tool to remove any shapes that should not be on the bookmark.

- ✓ Place the holographic paper on the cutting mat, and put the wheels on the loading bar back into their position.
- ✓ Create a 'New Project' in Design Space and choose a nice fancy font. Do not make it any bigger than 1.5' wide and 3' high.
- ✓ 'Save' the project.
- ✓ Click on 'Make It', and choose the correct material.
- ✓ Use the same iron-on method as the method in the 'Queen B' T-shirt project above.
- ✓ Your bookmark is now ready to use or give as a personalized gift.

Tips and Tricks

This machine is easy to move but it is still fragile so you will need to be sure when you are moving it, if you have trouble alone be sure to get some help.

Do not dig a corner of the scraper into the mat because it will remove the glue.

If your worried about losing the cover to the mat, write on it with a marker so you can see it better. This will make it easier to find if you do lose it. Place the clean side down so the ink does not end up on your mat

5. Personalized Envelopes

Materials

- Envelope 5.5' by 4.25'
- Cricut pens in the color of your choice
- Green StandardGrip mat
- Spatula

Where to Find Materials

- amazon
- Esty

- Cricut.com
- Swing design

Illustration

- ✓ Create a 'New Project' in Design Space.
- ✓ Choose the square from the 'Shapes' menu.
- ✓ Unlock the square, set the width to 5.5' and the height to 4.25'.
- ✓ Choose 'Text' from the right-hand menu.
- ✓ This will be the name and address, the envelope will be addressed to.
- ✓ Choose a font and size it, to fit comfortably in the middle of the envelope.
- ✓ You can choose a different color for the font.
- ✓ Move the text box to the middle of the envelope.
- ✓ When you move the card around the screen, the address text will move with the envelope.
- ✓ Load the envelope onto the cutting board and load it into the Cricut.
- ✓ In Design Space, click 'Make It'.
- ✓ Choose the material like paper.
- ✓ When the project is ready, press 'Go' and let it print.
- ✓ Flip the card over and stick it onto the mat.
- ✓ Use a piece of tape to stick the envelope flap down.
- ✓ Load it into the Cricut.
- ✓ Change the text on the envelope to a return address, or 'Regards From'.
- ✓ Change the color of the pen if you want the writing in another color.
- ✓ When you are ready, click on 'Make It'.
- ✓ Make sure the material is set to the correct setting.
- ✓ When you are ready, press 'Go'.

✓ Once it has finished cutting, you will have a personalized envelope.

Tips and Tricks

Do not leave paper cuts on your mat. Avoid gouging the mat with the scraper as well.

Do not dig a corner of the scraper into the mat because it will remove the glue.

If your worried about losing the cover to the mat, write on it with a marker so you can see it better. This will make it easier to find if you do lose it. Place the clean side down so the ink does not end up on your mat.

Never attempt to clean your machines while they are on. Turn the machine off and unplug it before using a soft cloth to wipe it down.

6. **Clear Personalized Labels**

Materials

- Cricut clear sticker paper
- High-gloss printer paper for the Inkjet printer
- Inkjet printer (check the ink cartridges)
- Spatula tool

Where To Find Materials

- Express vinyl
- Craft stash
- Happy crafter
- Cricut.com

- Swing design

Illustration

- ✓ Create a *'New Project'* in Design Space.
- ✓ Choose the heart shape, from the left-hand side, *'Shapes'* menu.
- ✓ Select an image from the *'Images'* menu, on the left-hand side menu.
- ✓ Choose a picture of a flower or search for *'M1525E'*.
- ✓ Unlock the flower image, position it in the top left corner of the heart. Make sure it fits without any overhang.
- ✓ Select the heart and the flower, then click on *'Weld'* from the bottom right-hand menu. This ensures that the label is printed together as a unit, and not in layers.
- ✓ Select the heart and flowers once again, then click on *'Flatten'* to ensure that only the heart's outline shape is cut out.
- ✓ Choose *'Text'* from the left-hand menu, choose a font, and type the text for your label. You can choose a color for your text.
- ✓ *'Unlock'* and move the text into position in the middle of the label.
- ✓ Adjust the size to fit comfortably.
- ✓ Select the heart shape and the font, then click on *'Flatten'* to ensure the label is cut as a whole, and not layered.
- ✓ To not waste sticker paper, you will want to print as many labels as you can per sheet.
- ✓ Choose the square shape from the *'Shapes'* menu.
- ✓ Position it on the screen, unlock the shape, and set the measurements to a width of 6' and a 9' height.
- ✓ Select the label and *'Duplicate It'*.

- ✓ Move the second label next to the first one. Give the labels a bit of room between each other and the edges.
- ✓ Fit as many as you can on the sheet, then *'Save'* your work.
- ✓ Fill in each of the labels with the text you want.
- ✓ If you have space left over when your labels are positioned, you can create smaller ones.
- ✓ You can actually create all different sizes of labels, patterns, and designs.
- ✓ Make sure that all the labels are for print and are flattened.
- ✓ Select all the labels, and then click *'Attach'* from the bottom right-hand menu.
- ✓ Click *'Make It'* and check that the design and wordings are correct before clicking *'Continue.'*
- ✓ Choose the high-gloss paper option, and set it to the best quality.
- ✓ Load the sticker paper into the Inkjet printer and press *'Send to Printer.'*
- ✓ Choose *'Sticker Paper'* for the Cricut materials.
- ✓ Load the *'Stickers'* into the Cricut, and press *'Go'* when ready to cut.
- ✓ The Cricut will cut out the stickers, so you can peel them off the backing sheet, as and when you need them.

Tips and Tricks

If you want to store your supplies easier, you can purchase a Cricut rolling craft tote. This has a side section that is great for vinyl. A plus for this is that it is a very big size and great for storage.

If you need new mats, a way to save some money is to buy a mat that is 12 by 24 because the vinyl that some people purchase is 12 by 15 or higher.

A long mat is a great option because most people get a lot more use out of it, and it lasts a while. Others cut it in half, and then they have two. The price of the bigger one is usually lower as well.
Wax paper is going for stenciling as well.

7. **Stenciled Welcome Mat**

Materials

- Plain doormat
- Black and green outdoor paint
- Paintbrushes
- Stencil vinyl
- Spray adhesive

Where to find Materials

- MyVinylDirect.com
- Craft stores
- Amazon.com

- PaperAndMore.com
- Craft stores

Illustration

- ✓ Open Design Space and create your message and images you want to have on your welcome mat. Make sure to scale them to fit your project size. When you have your design created, send the file to cut out of your stencil vinyl.
- ✓ Take your stencil from your mat and spray it with spray adhesive. Press the stencil down on your mat where you want the design to appear. Lay a piece of freezer paper over your stencil and place a few heavy books or weights over the stencil. Let it sit with this pressure for at least one hour to make sure the stencil is well attached.
- ✓ Begin painting your stencil when it is done attaching. Use a brush with stiff bristles and stipple it into the fibers of the mat. Try to get the color down deep into the mat. Rub the colors in on top to get a saturated top layer.
- ✓ Once it is done drying, place it on your front porch and welcome your guests with style!

Tips and Tricks

A new mat with a strong stick is the best when working with glitter vinyl.

When using felt on your fabric grip mat do not touch the adhesive area with your hands. Our hands have oils in the skin and it will reduce the adhesive on the mat and its effectiveness.

Make sure that your fabric is smooth so that you can avoid bubbles and lumps.

If you are using a fabric pen, put your fabric pattern side down. This will make it a lot easier on YouTube able to see the fabric pen markings that you need to see.

8. Momma Bear on Board Keep Your Distance Car

Materials

- Outdoor glossy vinyl (clear or white)
- Green StandardGrip mat
- Cricut measuring tape
- Inkjet printer
- Transfer tape
- Rubbing alcohol
- Cricut Fine-Point Blade
- Weeding tool
- Spatula
- Brayer, or a scraping tool

- Pair of scissors, for cutting the material to size

Where to Find Materials

- Express vinyl
- Craft stash
- Happy crafter
- amazon
- Esty
- Cricut.com
- Swing design

Illustration

- ✓ Measure how big you are going to want the decal to be.
- ✓ Open a new Design Space project.
- ✓ Select *'Images'* from the left-hand menu.
- ✓ Type in *'Bear'* in the search bar and choose the black bear (Image #MF7274E7).
- ✓ Position it on the screen and scale it to the desired size.
- ✓ Change the color of the bear to brown.
- ✓ Select *'Text'* from the left-hand menu, and reset the font to *'Bernard MT Condensed'*. It is a nice clear font with a bit of character.
- ✓ Type *'Momma Bear on Board'* on the one line.
- ✓ Hit enter and type *'Keep Your Distance'* on the next line.
- ✓ Center the text and change the color to white.
- ✓ Unlock the text and scale it to size, then position it in the center of the bear.
- ✓ Make sure none of the letters hang over the side of the bear image.

- ✓ Select both the bear image and text, then click *'Flatten'* from the bottom right-hand menu. You can also right-click and choose *'Flatten'*.
- ✓ Load your outdoor glossy vinyl sheet into your Inkjet printer. When you are ready, click *'Send to Printer'*.
- ✓ Press *'Print'* if you are happy with the print setup.
- ✓ Once the printer has finished printing the decal, unload the vinyl sheet from the Inkjet printer.
- ✓ Stick the printed decal onto the cutting mat.
- ✓ Load the cutting mat into the Cricut, and when it is ready, press *'Go'*.
- ✓ When it is done, use the spatula, if necessary, to pull off the backing sheet of the vinyl.
- ✓ Use the weeding tool to weed off any pieces that should not be there.
- ✓ Cut some transfer paper to the size of the decal.
- ✓ Place it over the decal. It is easier to work with it if it is stuck to the cutting mat.
- ✓ Use the brayer, or a scraping tool to smooth the transfer tape over the image, and get all the bubbles out.
- ✓ Take the rubbing alcohol and clean the car window portion that you want to place the decal on.
- ✓ Gently pull the back of the vinyl off, and position the decal on the cleaned window.
- ✓ Once it is on the window, use the brayer or scraping tool to smooth it out and
- ✓ Gently pull off the transfer tape and your decal is on your window.

Tips and Tricks

This machine is easy to move but it is still fragile so you will need to be sure when you are driving it, if you have trouble alone be sure to get some help.

Do not leave paper cuts on your mat. Avoid gouging the mat with the scraper as well.

Do not dig a corner of the scraper into the mat because it will remove the glue.

If your worried about losing the cover to the mat, write on it with a marker so you can see it better. This will make it easier to find if you do lose it. Place the clean side down so the ink does not end up on your mat.

9. Window Stickers

Materials

- Cricut Explore Air (used is a good solution if you want to save some money)
- 2 Premium Outdoor Glossy Vinyl
- Transfer Tape
- Scraper Tool

Where to Find Materials

- Express vinyl
- Craft stash
- Happy crafter
- amazon
- Esty
- Cricut.com
- Swing design

Illustration

- ✓ You can use Premium Outdoor Glossy Vinyl to transform any cut picture into a window decal. If you want, you can select a photo from Cricut Design Space, but I'll explain how to upload an image and generate your cut file. To find the ideal picture, simply google search. There are loads of images to choose from, but the simpler the model, the faster it transfers to a cut file
- ✓ When you discover your picture, right-click to save it to your laptop. Go to Cricut Design Space, click New Project.
- ✓ Click the Upload button situated at the bottom left.
- ✓ Click Upload Image to drag or drop the picture to the next page.
- ✓ Click the Cricut Design Space Upload button to pick your picture type. You can go simple or have fun with the colors; there are a lot of possibilities to choose from.
- ✓ Simply click when selecting the picture type in the Cricut design room and choose now which picture regions are not part of the final cut.
- ✓ Select the picture area to cut the Cricut machine to generate the window decal, the select the picture you have chosen.

- ✓ This also provides you a preview of how the cut picture looks.
- ✓ There is a back button that you can press to adjust to the image before moving forward.
- ✓ After approving, you are taken back to the initial upload screen, but this time you can see your latest cut file among the pictures.
- ✓ Cut your Cricut Machine Vinyl Decal Click the picture to highlight, then select Insert Image.
- ✓ To create your vehicle decals, select the picture to put it into the canvas. That brings the picture to your design region, where you can adjust the image's size or direction. Now you're
- ✓ Apply carefully vinyl transfer paper decal to the window where you want to put the sticker. Then go over again with rubbing alcohol to remove surplus grease or fingerprint smudges.
- ✓ Carefully peel back the vinyl's paperback to allow all elements of the picture release from the sheet.
- ✓ Remove the paper backing from the car window decal to apply the vinyl, begin at one end or corner and roll the plastic down.

Tips and Tricks

Double tipped markers are something to try too. You can find them for about three dollars. You could also keep your roll of vinyl attached and trim what you do not need.

Joining groups on Facebook will let you make friends and get new ideas for projects.

Some courses and classes are taught at crafting stores for people who still need a little extra help.

Make the Cut is a third party Cricut software that offers several more design features and may be worth checking out if you're looking for some new ones.

10. Car Keys, Wood Keyring

Materials

- Wooden tags
- 1 medium-sized jump ring hoop (gold)
- 1 keyring hoop (gold)
- 14" to 5" gold link chain
- Green StandardGrip mat
- Cricut adhesive vinyl (color of your choice)
- Cricut transfer tape
- Cricut Fine-Point Blade
- Weeding tool
- Spatula
- Brayer, or a scraping tool

- Pair of scissors, for cutting the material to size

Where to Find Materials

- Express vinyl
- Craft stash
- Happy crafter
- amazon
- Esty
- Cricut.com
- Swing design

Illustration

- ✓ Open a new project in Design Space.
- ✓ Choose *'Square'* from the *'Shapes'* menu.
- ✓ Unlock the shape, and size it to the length and width of the wooden key tag.
- ✓ Position the rectangle at the top corner of the screen, leaving some bleeding room for the Cricut.
- ✓ Find a cute picture of a car, or search for one after choosing *'Images'* from the left-hand window.
- ✓ Choose *'Text'* from the left-hand menu and type *'Car Keys'*.
- ✓ Select the font that you like, and set it to the same color as the image.
- ✓ Unlock the font, position it where you want it to sit on the key ring; then resize it to fit perfectly.
- ✓ You might want to rotate the text, so it runs long ways on the key ring.
- ✓ Select the rectangle and delete it.
- ✓ Select the image and the text, then click *'Attach'* from the bottom right-hand menu (or right-click).

- ✓ As you should not waste any vinyl pieces, you can do a few of these key ring signs at a time.
- ✓ From the *'Shapes'* menu, select the *'Square'* and unlock the shape.
- ✓ Set the shape size to 12" by 12" and set the *'Fill'* color, to a light grey.
- ✓ Click on the *'Arrange'* top menu item, and send the grey box to the back.
- ✓ *Duplicate'* the design as many times as you need to. You can fit approximately 10 signs across, and 3 signs down. If you do not want to leave any space, shrink the last row of key ring designs down, to fit it to make 4 rows of 10.
- ✓ In order to edit each design's text, select each individually, hit *'Detach'*, and double click on
- ✓ You will need to *'Flatten'* each of the designs so that the text, and car are cut out together.
- ✓ When you have all the key ring signs laid out, select the grey backing square and delete it.
- ✓ Select all the designs and *'Attach'* to ensure they are printed on the same sheet of vinyl.
- ✓ Stick the vinyl onto the cutting board using the brayer, or cutting tool to smooth it out.
- ✓ Load the cutting board into the Cricut.
- ✓ In Design Space, click *'Make it'*.
- ✓ Select the correct material, and ensure the correct blade is loaded.
- ✓ When the Cricut is ready, press *'Go'*.
- ✓ When the labels have been cut, use a pair of scissors to cut the vinyl sheet's design.
- ✓ Pull the top sheet off the design carefully, and use the spatula if necessary.
- ✓ Use the weeding tool to neaten up the design.

- ✓ Place the transfer tape over the design, pull off the backing tape, and place it onto the wooden tag.
- ✓ Use the scraping tool, or your finger to make sure the vinyl has been stuck down properly onto the tag.
- ✓ Gently pull off the transfer tape.
- ✓ Connect the gold link chain to the jump ring on one end and the other's key ring loop.
- ✓ Connect the jump ring to the tag.

Tips and Tricks

Ensure that your projects are carried out using a sealer so that the wood does not get damaged unexpectedly.

Consider using a stamping effect for your paper design, when using wood and paper designs to produce a rustic feel for your project.

When choosing a stain color for the wooden plaque, make sure that your project color aligns with that color and other projects that you already have in your house.

Don't be scared to combine different wood stain colors and use your own customized stain!

For easy and effective application of wood glue, it is recommended to wet the wood with a damp cloth first. After the wood glue has been applied to the plaque, clamp it, and allow it to set for at least 24 hours.

If you are planning to use pallet wood, make sure to clean the pallet plaque using a wire brush.

11. Planner sticker

Materials

- Cricut printable sticker paper
- Cricut Explore Air machine or Cricut Maker
- Cricut standard cutting mat grip
- Printer with ink

Where To Find Materials

- Express vinyl
- Craft stash
- Happy crafter
- amazon
- Esty
- Cricut.com
- Swing design

Illustration

- ✓ Choose the sticker designs. You can choose from the Design shop or upload your own.
- ✓ Start by opening the Design Space program and click on the image option. Then head to the search function and locate the planner stickers. Locate which one you want to use.
- ✓ Place the choices on the canvas and arrange them in the order that you would like them to be.
- ✓ Click the Make It option and the Design Space will direct you to begin printing the image. Follow the directions to print the images.
- ✓ And to proceed, place the stickers in the Cricut to cut the stickers out.

Tips and Tricks

Contact paper is great for cutting out stencils as well and you can find it cheaply in many different places.

Take the felt (the inside felt) and the ink of a child's marker and then you can use the shell to hold any pen that you have like a gel pen and it may fit inside better for your machine.

If you ever forget which mat is used for what, you can write it on the mat not to forget.

12. Nama and Kiss Clitter Tumbler

Materials

- Painters tape
- Mod podge and paint brush
- Epoxy
- Glitter
- Stainless steel tumbler
- Sandpaper wet/dry
- Gloves
- Plastic cup
- Measuring cup
- Rubbing alcohol

Where to Find Materials

- Express vinyl
- Craft stash
- Happy crafter
- Cricut.com
- Swing design

Illustration

- ✓ Tape off the top, and bottom of the tumbler.
- ✓ Make sure to seal them well enough that paint will not get on either side.
- ✓ Spray paint twelve inches away from your tumbler, in an area that is well ventilated.
- ✓ Make sure that the items you used are approved, and will not make you sick.
- ✓ Once your tumbler is dry from the paint you have used, you can add the glitter.
- ✓ This will make a mess, so have something under it to catch the glitter.
- ✓ Put the mod podge in a small container.
- ✓ Use a flat paintbrush to put it on.
- ✓ Take the lid off, and rotate the cup adding glitter gradually.
- ✓ Make sure it is completely covered.
- ✓ Make sure that an excess glitter will come off before removing the tape, and letting it dry.
- ✓ When dry, take a flat brush that is clean, and stroke down the glitter to get any additional pieces not glued down.
- ✓ Add a piece of tape above glitter line.
- ✓ Do the same to the bottom.
- ✓ Get a plastic cup and gloves.

- ✓ Use the epoxy, and measure equal parts of solution A and B into measuring cups.
- ✓ Pour them both in a cup, and scrape down the sides using a wooden stick.
- ✓ Stir for three minutes and pop all bubbles.
- ✓ Your gloves should be on, but if not; put them on now.
- ✓ Add the glitter to the epoxy and stir.
- ✓ Add the mixture to the tumbler, and turn it often while you are doing this. Having a roller or something to turn it on, will help and make sure it is in the air so nothing is touching it.
- ✓ Spin the tumbler for five hours; it should be dry, if not, leave it on a foam roller overnight.
- ✓ Sand the tumbler gently with wet sandpaper.
- ✓ When it is all smooth from sanding, clean it with rubbing alcohol.
- ✓ Then open Cricut design space, and cut out your glitter vinyl.
- ✓ Weed the design.
- ✓ Add a strong grip transfer tape.
- ✓ Transfer the decal to the tumbler.

Tips and Tricks

You can also wear a headlamp for weeding. You can get cheap ones in many different places.

If you use sketch pens to outline your HTV it can help with your weeding.

Placing ruler marks on the edge of your cutting table will help ensure that your cutting correctly and not need a ruler or tape.

Making extra dots for the tops of your J's and I's will help as well as they like to disappear.

When you modify a font, you will not see what the name is inside the Silhouette software.

13. Sleep Eye Mask with Eves

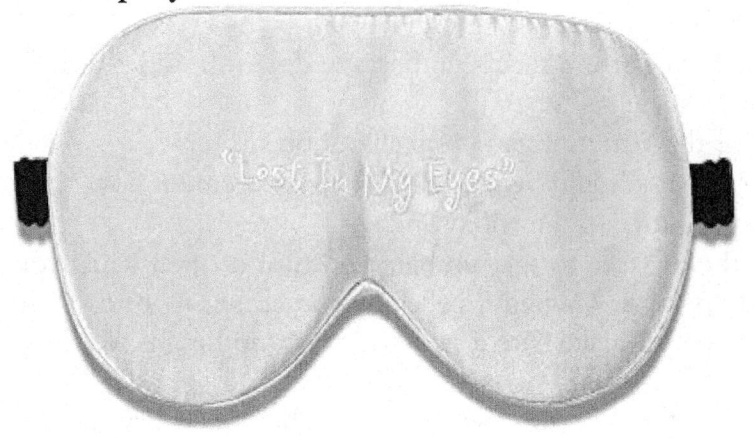

Materials

- Printed or solid top fabric, such as cotton quilting fabric
- Silky or Minky fabric for the underside of the mask that sits over your eyes
- 13 inches of wide, good-quality elastic
- iron-on vinyl in corresponding color, like black
- Sewing materials: scissors, rotary cutter, clear quilting ruler, pins, fray check, fabric marking pen

Where to Find Materials

- Craft stores
- Superstores
- Vinyl/Heat Transfer Vinyl
- Amazon.com
- ExpressionsVinyl.com
- MyVinylDirect.com
- Craft stores
- Amazon.com
- PaperAndMore.com

- Craft stores

Illustration

- ✓ To begin, start with the vinyl image you want on the outside of your eye mask. This can be a word or a graphic. Design the image on Design Space, making sure that the image will fit on an eye mask. In general, you do not want an image longer than four inches or higher than two inches. Once you have your design laid out, send the file to be cut from your vinyl. When the image is done cutting, weed it if necessary and prepare it to be transferred to the eye mask.
- ✓ Lay the bottom, minky or silky fabric on the cutting table with the fashion side or right side of the fabric facing you. Pin one end of the elastic to one side of the material in the center of the eye mask and then bring the other end to the opposite side of the mask, pinning that end in place, too. Pin it so the end is facing out of your fabric. Let about one inch of elastic hang over the edge on each side.
- ✓ Once the elastic is secured, place your top fabric with the vinyl design on top of the minky or silky fabric, placing the design down away from you. Use more pins to attach the two pieces of fabric and prepare the project for sewing. If you are not sewing your project, skip directly to the alternative step.
- ✓ When you are sewed, turn your project right side out by pressing it through the open space you left open. Your mask should look almost complete, but with a two-inch gap still visible. Press the edges of the opening inside the mask and use a needle and thread to close the mask's hole.

Tips and Tricks

For those that do not want to sew the project, you can press the raw edges in on the minky and fashion fabric with your iron.
Use a piece of fusible interfacing cut out in the eye mask's shape but trimmed by ½ inch around the edges. Lay that on the wrong side of your minky or silky fabric and place your fashion fabric on top, with the design facing you. Set your iron on the fabric, with a pressing cloth in between. Add extra interfacing to where you inserted the elastic to add more stability. Make sure the interfacing fully adheres the layers together and that the elastic is secured in place.

14. Coloring Gift Wrap

Materials

- White kraft paper or a big sheet of white paper
- Cricut Explore or Maker
- Cricut Pens
- 1224 mat

Where To Find Materials

- Express vinyl
- Craft stash
- Happy crafter
- amazon
- Esty
- Cricut.com
- Swing design

Illustration

- ✓ Open Design Space and pick your design to begin with. I searched for "draw Christmas" and chosen these adorable woodland creatures, ideal for drawing with pens.
- ✓ After duplicating the images for multiple times, I rotated and resized some of them to create the desired design. I then added the holly design (from my fantastic pal Jen Goode) to fill some larger animal rooms. (Delete the colored layers and use the doodled holly.)
- ✓ Check your readings before sending the design to your device. If 23.5" is larger than 11.5", resize to the maximum dimensions.

Tip and tricks

You can also wear a headlamp for weeding. You can get cheap ones in many different places.

Placing ruler marks on the edge of your cutting table will help ensure that your cutting correctly and not need a ruler or tape.

Making extra dots for the tops of your J's and I's will help as well as they like to disappear.

When you modify a font, you will not see what the name is inside the Silhouette software.

15. Art journal

Materials

- Supplies:
- Glue
- Colored thread
- Large needle
- Paper piercer or something to poke holes in your paper
- Various cardstock in interesting prints
- Various paper in interesting colors and prints

Where to Find Materials

- Express vinyl
- Craft stash
- Happy crafter
- amazon
- Esty
- Cricut.com
- Swing design

Illustration

- ✓ In Design Space, create a square on your canvas. Round the corners. You may want to ungroup the layers and delete the bottom layer. Also, adjust the size of your square to the size of your final notebook. For example, in this example, the notebooks are 5" x 7". This means your square will need to measure 10" x 7".
- ✓ Add your score line to the middle of the square or rectangle shape. You will find this line under "lines." Adjust the size to fit your project and then select "Align" and "Center."

This should automatically adjust the line so it is directly in the middle of your project.
- ✓ Next, add notches to your center score line to tell you where to pierce your paper. You can place another score line at 90 degrees from the centerline and scale it down so it is small. Alternatively, you can place a very small circle over the place you want to pierce your paper and have the machine cut the little spot out for you. Measure down about one inch from the top and bottom to place your holes or notches.
- ✓ If you want to add any custom cut-outs or stickers to the front cover, you can now design those as you desire. Otherwise, you can use shapes and stickers you already have on hand. You can always create these later as well.
- ✓ If you moved the notches or hole marks, you can always group the markings from the cover and copy and paste them for as many pages of the book you are creating. Then move, do not resize, these markings, and place them over the centerline of each page.
- ✓ When you are done designing your pages, send your file to print, cut, and score your cover and pages. Follow the prompts to load your paper and tools into your machine.
- ✓ Thread your needle with the colored thread. Pass your needle through the holes and tie a slip knot. Tighten your knot as tight as possible and then tie off with a regular knot. You can tie on the outside of the journal or the inside. Trim the threads as short as you want.

Tips and Tricks

You can also use your system fonts in your projects. You can go to sites that offer fonts to find a lot of amazing ones for free and then you can use them for your machine.

If you have a smaller or more intricate design you can use a weeding box. This is especially helpful if your cutting multiple designs on one mat.

Load your mat correctly. Both sides of the mat need to be able to slide under the rollers or the mat will not cut in the correct manner.

16. Felt Roses

Materials

- SVG files with 3D flower design
- Felt Sheets
- Fabric Grip Mat
- Glue Gun

Where to Find Materials

- Express vinyl
- Craft stash
- Happy crafter
- amazon
- Esty
- Cricut.com
- Swing design

Illustration

- ✓ First of all, upload your Flower SVG Graphics into the Cricut design space as explained in the "Tips" section. ("How to import images into Cricut Design Space)
- ✓ Having placed the image in the project, select it, right-click and click "Ungroup". This allows you to resize each flower independent of the others. Since you are using felt, it is recommended that each of the flowers are at least 6 inches in size.
- ✓ Create several copies of the flowers, as many as you wish, selecting the colors you want in the Color Sync Panel (by dragging and dropping the images on to the color you want them to be cut on). Immediately you're through with that, click on "Make it" on the Cricut design space.
- ✓ Click on "Continue". After your Cricut Maker is connected and registered, under the "materials" options, select "Felt".
- ✓ After they are cut, begin to roll the cut flowers one by one. Do this from the outside in. Make sure that you do not roll them too tight. Use the picture as a guide.
- ✓ Apply Hot Glue on the circle right in the middle and press the felt flowers that you rolled up on the glue. Hold this in place and do not let it go until the glue binds it.

✓ Wait for the glue to dry, and your roses are ready for use.

Tips and Tricks

Washi tape can hold the paper still if it is moving on your mat.
Contact paper is also good for stencils and it is cheaper than wasting vinyl.
If you have smaller monograms or designs you can reverse weed them.
When you are doing a heat transfer vinyl you can sharpie the guideline to be more visible.
You can use parchment paper for ironing over the heat transfer.
To get a chalkboard appearance look on black paper you can use white gel pens.
If you do not have a lightbox put the design you are trying to weed on a coffee table made of glass, turn a flashlight on and set it on the floor under your table.

Chapter 2: Project ideas for intermediate

17. Custom Coasters

Materials

- The Maker
- Rotary cut and mat or a pair of scissors
- A sewing machine
- An iron
- Cotton fabric and a coordinating thread
- Fusible fleece

Where to Find Materials

- Express vinyl
- Craft stash

- Happy crafter
- amazon
- Esty
- Cricut.com
- Swing design

Illustration

- ✓ Cut your fabric to 12 inches to fit on your cutting mat.
- ✓ Open Design Space and hit the button that says new project.
- ✓ Click on shapes and then insert a heart shape. You will do this from the pop-up window.
- ✓ Resize your heart to 5.5 inches. Click Make It.
- ✓ Change the project copies to four (left corner at the top). Then, click Apply.
- ✓ Click Continue (bottom right).
- ✓ Set your material to medium fabrics like cotton.
- ✓ Load your mat with the fabric attached.
- ✓ Repeat all steps, but this time, you will place the fusible fleece on the cutting mat.
- ✓ Change the heart shape to 5.375.
- ✓ When you select the material, click View More and then type in fusible fleece.
- ✓ Cut out two fleece hearts.
- ✓ Attach a fleece heart to the back of a fabric heart. You will use a hot iron to do this (be
- ✓ Repeat with the second heart.
- ✓ With the right sides together, sew two heart shapes together. Make sure the fleece is attached. Leave a gap in the stitches for turning.
- ✓ Turn heart right side out, then press with the iron.
- ✓ Fold in the edges of the opening and then press once more.

✓ Stitch around the heart a quarter inch from the edge.

Tips and Tricks

Fabric coasters with a Cricut maker are great, and they need only a few supplies. These include the maker itself, cotton fabric, fusible fleece, a rotary cutting mat or some scissors, a sewing machine, and an iron.

Cut the fabric to about 12 inches to fit the cutting mat – if it's longer, you can hang it off, just be careful.

Sew the two shapes together, leaving a gap for stitching and the turning. Clip the curves, turn it inside out, and then fold in the edges and stitch it.

There you go – a fusible fleece heart coaster. It's a little bit more complicated, but it's worth trying out

18. Customized Doormat

Materials

- Cricut Machine
- Scrap cardstock (The color does not matter)
- Coir mat (18" x 30")
- Outdoor acrylic paint
- Vinyl stencil
- Transfer tape
- Flat round paintbrush
- Cutting mat (12" x 24")

Where to Find Materials

- Express vinyl
- Craft stash
- Happy crafter
- Cricut.com

Illustration

- ✓ Create your design in Cricut Design Space. You can also download an SVG design of your choice and import into Cricut Design Space. Make sure that your design is the right size; resize it to ensure that this is so.
- ✓ Next, you are to cut the stencil. You do this by clicking "Make it" in Cricut Design Space when you are done with the design. After this, you select "Cardstock" as the material. Then, you press the "Cut" button on the Cricut machine.
- ✓ When this is done, remove the stencil from the machine and weed.

- ✓ The next step is to mask the parts of the doormat which you do not want to paint on. You can do this using painters' plastic.
- ✓ Now, it's time to spray-paint your stencil on the doormat. Keeping the paint can about 5 inches away from the doormat, spray up and down, keeping the can pointed straight through the stencil. If it is at an angle, the paint will get under the stencil and ruin your design. Spray the entire stencil 2-3 times to make sure that you do not miss any part and that the paint is even.
- ✓ You're just about done! Now, remove the masking plastic and the stencil and leave the doormat for about one hour to get dry.

Tips and Tricks

Vinyl stencils are a good thing to create, too, but they can be hard. Big vinyl stencils make for an excellent Cricut project, and you can use them in various places, including bedrooms for kids.

You only need the explore Air 2, the vinyl that works for it, a pallet, sander and, of course, paint and brushes. The first step is preparing the pallet for painting, or whatever surface you plan on using this for.

And there you have it! Bigger stencils can be a bit of a project since it involves trying to use multiple designs all at once. Still, with the right care and the right designs, you'll be able to create whatever it is you need to in Design Space so you can get the results you're looking for.

19. 3d Paper flowers

Materials

- Cricut Machine
- Cricut mat
- Colored scrapbook paper
- Hot glue gun and glue sticks

Where To Find Materials

- Express vinyl
- Craft stash
- Happy crafter
- amazon
- Esty
- Cricut.com
- Swing design

Illustration

- ✓ To make flowers, you need an appropriate shape for the petals. To make such a shape, you can combine three ovals of equal size. To create an oval, select the circle tool, then create a circle. Then click the unlock button at the bottom of the shape. Once this is done, you can reshape the circle to form an oval.
- ✓ Duplicate this oval twice and rotate each duplicate a little, keeping the bottom at the same point, as shown in the picture.
- ✓ Select all three ovals and weld them together to get your custom petal shape. For each large flower, you need 12 petals – each one about 3 inches long, while for each small flower, you need 8 petals – each one about 2 inches long. For each flower, you also need a circle shape for the base of about the same width as each petal. Arrange the petals and base circle shape in Cricut Design Studio.
- ✓ After you cut out the petals, remove them and cut a slit about half an inch long in the bottom of each one. Place a bit of glue on the left side and glue the right side over the glue for each petal.
- ✓ The next thing to do is to place the petals on the circle base. For large flowers, you need three circles of four petals each. For small flowers, you need five circles on the outside and three on the inside. Put a bit of hot glue on the petal and add to the circle as described above.
- ✓ For the center of the flowers, search Cricut Access for "flower" and chose shapes with several small petals. Cut these out using a different color of cardstock and glue to the center of the flowers.

Tip and tricks

If you do not have a spatula or the scrappers to get things off your mat, you can use a two-inch putty knife to get things off your mat. Painter's tape can be used as a transfer tape on the fly and it has sixty yards in some cases.
If you have smaller transfers scotch tape works in a pinch as well.
Double-sided tape can help keep the corners down on your mat that has lost stick in spots. Scotch brand makes a removable one that is small and sturdy.

20. Luminaries

Materials

- Luminary Graphic (From a Cricut Project)
- Sugar Skull (SVG File)
- Cricut Explore Air or Cricut Maker
- Cardstock Sampler
- Scoring Stylus
- Glue Stick
- Battery-Operated Tea Light

Where to Find Materials

- Express vinyl
- Craft stash
- Happy crafter
- Esty
- Cricut.com
- Swing design

Illustration

✓ The first step is to open your Luminary graphic on the Design Space.
✓ Then go ahead to upload the SVG file of your Sugar Skull and adjust its size to around 3.25" high. After doing that, move the Sugar Skull to the bigger part of the Luminary graphic (in the middle of the two score lines) and center-align it.
✓ Select the Sugar Skull and the Luminary Graphic and then go ahead and click on "Weld".
✓ Try selecting every graphic on the design space and click on "Attach." Then copy and paste the selected graphics on the same page (duplication).

- ✓ Select "Light Cardstock" under the "Materials" menu, and then start loading the Mat and Cut. Also ensure that your Scoring Stylus is in Clamp A. This will automatically change your machine settings from scoring to cutting.
- ✓ When the cut-out is done, fold it along the Score lines. Then start gluing the small Flap to the interior part of the lantern's back.
- ✓ Switch on the Battery-Operated Tea Light, and then place your lantern on top of it.

Tips and Tricks

Having spare scissors can help as well because you will need them for your projects and scissors are one thing that tends to go missing in a craft room. This is another thing that should be kept on a high shelf and away from children.

Another tool you might need is the true control knife. This is something that can easily cut through thin materials or delicate materials.

Do not unload your mat until you know that your cut has made it through the material.

You can also keep your mat clean by running it under lukewarm water and then letting it air dry. Make sure there are no pets or little ones within reach.

If you can, using a lightbox for weeding is going to be able to make the lines so much easier to see.

21. Shamrock Earrings

Materials

- Cricut Maker
- Earring (from a Cricut Project)
- Rotary Wheel
- Knife Blade
- Cricut Leather
- Scraper Tool
- Adhesive
- Pebbled-Faux Leather
- Earring Hooks

Where to Find Materials

- Express vinyl

- Craft stash
- Happy crafter
- amazon
- Esty
- Cricut.com
- Swing design

Illustration

- ✓ First, open the Cricut Project (Earring). You can now either click on *'Make It'*, or *'Customize'* to edit it.
- ✓ Once you have selected one, click on *'Continue'*.
- ✓ Immediately the Cut page pops up, select your material and wait for the *'Load'* tools and Mat to appear.
- ✓ Make your Knife blade your cutting tool in clamp B. This will be used on the Leather.
- ✓ On the StrongGrip Mat, place the Leather and make sure it is facing down. Then load the Mat into the machine and tap the *'Cut'* flashing button.
- ✓ When the scoring has been done, go back to the cutting tool and change it to Rotary Wheel so that you can use it on the Faux Leather.
- ✓ Similarly, place your Faux leather on your FabricGrip Mat, facing down. Then load the Mat into the machine and tap the *'Cut'* flashing button.
- ✓ Take away all the items on the Mat with your Scraper tool. Be careful with the small fringes though.
- ✓ Make a hole on the top circle by making use of the Weeder tool. Make sure the hole is large enough to make the Earring hooks fit in.
- ✓ If necessary, you may have to twist the hook's end with the pliers to fit them in.

- ✓ Close them up after you have looped it inside the hole that was made inside the Earring.
- ✓ Wait for it to dry before using.

Tips and Tricks

If you are looking for cheaper supplies for gifts you can get oven mitts and potholders for a dollar as well and you can personalize them really easily.

Be sure to have a pair of tweezers on hand as well to get little debris off your mats.

22. Valentine's Day Classroom Cards

Materials

- Cricut Maker
- Card Designs (Write Stuff Coloring)
- Cricut Design Space
- Dual Scoring Wheel
- Pens
- Cardstock
- Crayons
- Shimmer Paper

Where to Find Materials

- Express vinyl

- Craft stash
- Happy crafter
- amazon
- Esty
- Cricut.com
- Swing design

Illustration

- ✓ Open the Card Designs (Write Stuff Coloring) on the Design Space, and then click on "Make it" or "Customize" to make edits.
- ✓ When all the changes have been done, Cricut will request you to select a material. Select Cardstock for the Cards and Shimmer Paper for the Envelopes.
- ✓ Cricut will send you a notification when you need to change the pen colors while creating the Card. Then it will start carving the Card out automatically.
- ✓ You will be prompted later on to change the blade because of the Double Scoring Wheel. It is advisable to use the Double Scoring Wheel with Shimmer Paper; they both work best together.
- ✓ When the scoring has been finished, replace the Scoring Wheel with the previous blade.
- ✓ After that, fold the flaps at the Score lines in the direction of the paper's white side, and then attach the Side Tabs to the Bottom Tab's exterior by gluing them together.
- ✓ You may now write "From:" and "To:" before placing the Crayons into the Slots.
- ✓ Place the Cards inside the Envelopes and tag it with a sharp object.

Tips and Tricks

You can also charge your electronics from the USB port that is on the side of the machine.

A brayer might be a good idea for you to invest in because it can make sure your fabric is laying flat and smooth upon your cutting mat.

Keeping your blades separate and organized will help too. Having separate blades for vinyl or fabric will help the blades stay sharp and the way you need them to longer. Keeping the blades separate is also going to help you be more organized.

If you want, you can use a permanent marker on each of the blades so that you know what blade is for what particular material you want to cut with them. It is like owning a pair of fabric scissors. You would not use fabric scissors to cut paper, so instead, keep your blades sharp by keeping them separate.

You can make a small mark which blades are for what material. If you do not want to use the marker on them, you can make a chart. Just remember to replace the cap so that they are not getting mixed up.

23. Glitter and Felt Hair Bow Supplies

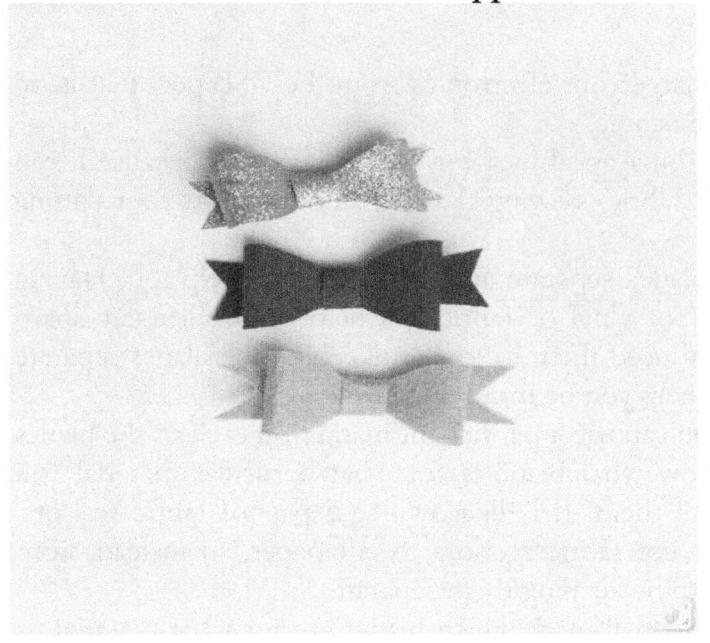

Materials

- Hair bow project file in Cricut Design Space
- Cricut Felt
- Glitter Iron-on Vinyl
- Hair Clips (large and small)
- Cricut Mat
- Glue Gun
- Scissors and Weeding tools

Where to Find Materials

- Happy crafter
- Amazon
- Esty

- Cricut.com
- Swing design

Illustration

- ✓ To start, in Cricut Design Space, open the design (hair bow); then, click "Make it now". If you would like to make any modifications to the design, click "Customize".
- ✓ Insert a regular blade into the Cricut machine. Then place the materials and the appropriate board on the Cricut mat.
- ✓ Send the document to the Cricut machine and cut it out.
- ✓ After the Cricut machine has cut out the felt and the iron-on, remove the excess vinyl, then cut around each of the bows using scissors.
- ✓ Heat your EasyPress. For the appropriate settings, check the EasyPress Guide.
- ✓ Place the vinyl on the cut out felt, sticky side down, then heat with the EasyPress for 10 seconds. For larger pieces, do this for each section one at a time, after which you should smooth the EasyPress over the entire design.
- ✓ Remove the transfer paper and repeat this for all the other bows.
- ✓ Use the glue to stick one side of the bigger bow piece (the piece without the sharp edges) to the other side. This will form a circle.
- ✓ Apply glue on the inside and on the middle of that bow piece. After this, fold the piece so that it forms a bow.
- ✓ Stick the bow to its back piece.
- ✓ Fold the small bow piece to the middle of the bow. Fold it in the back and glue it also.
- ✓ Glue the bow to the bigger or smaller bow clips to have your bow.

Tips and Tricks

You can also spray paint your vinyl if you need a color and you do not have it just make sure that it is Rust oleum metallics spray and give it a quick spray. Make sure that the vinyl is uncut and that you dry it before you cut it.

Make sure that you do a trial run of your materials that you will use for your project first. This will help ensure that you have the proper cutting techniques and have the proper settings in place. This also ensures that you are not wasting materials, time or money.

24. Halloween T-Shirt

Materials

- T-shirt Blanks
- Glam Halloween SVG Files
- Cardstock
- Transfer Sheets (Black and Pink)

- Butcher Paper (comes with Infusible Ink rolls)
- LightGrip Mat
- EasyPress (12" x 10" size recommended)
- EasyPress Mat
- Lint Roller

Where to Find Materials

- Express vinyl
- Craft stash
- Happy crafter
- amazon
- Esty
- Cricut.com

Illustration

- ✓ Import the SVG files into Cricut Design Space and arrange them as you want them on the T-shirt.
- ✓ Change the sizes of the designs so as to get them to fit on the T-shirt.
- ✓ Using the slice tool, slice the pink band away from the hat's bowler part (the largest piece). Make a copy of this band, and then slice it from the lower part of the hat. With these done, you with have three pieces that fit together.
- ✓ You can change the designs' colors as you would like them. When you are done with the preparation, click "Make It".
- ✓ Ensure that you invert your image using the "Mirror" toggle. This is even more important if there is text on your design, as infusible ink designs should be done in inverse. This is because the part with the ink is to go right on the destination material.
- ✓ Click on "Continue"

- ✓ For the material. Select Infusible ink. After this, cut the design out using your Cricut Machine.
- ✓ With the designs cut out, weed the transfer sheet.
- ✓ Cut around the designs such that the transfer tape does not cover any part of the infusible ink sheet. Ensure that this is done well as any part of the infusible ink that is not in contact with the fabric will not be transferred.
- ✓ Preheat your EasyPress to 385 degrees, and set your EasyPress mat.
- ✓ Prepare your T-shirt by placing it on the EasyPress mat, then using a lint roller to remove any lint from the front.
- ✓ Insert the Cardstock in the t-shirt, between the front and back, just where the design will be. This will protect the other side of the T-shirt from having the Infusible Ink on it.
- ✓ If necessary, use the lint roller on the T-shirt again, after which you should heat your shirt with the EasyPress. Do this at 385 degrees for 15 seconds.
- ✓ Turn the part where the design faces on the T-shirt. Place the butcher paper on the design, ensuring that the backing does not overlap the design.
- ✓ Place the EasyPress over the design, and hold it in place for 40 seconds. Do not move the EasyPress around so that your design does not end up looking smudged.
- ✓ Remove the EasyPress from the shirt and remove the transfer sheet.
- ✓ To layer colors, ensure that your cutting around the transfer sheet is done as close as possible, then repeat the previous three steps for each color. This will prevent the transfer sheet from removing part of the color on the previously transferred design.

Tips and Tricks

Many card projects require that you have a stylus. If the machine you bought is part of a bundle it can have the stylus inside it already, but some may not. This is something to ask the person at the store when you are buying one because the stylus can really help.

Make sure that you do a practice project before a real one as well because this will let you get adjusted to your machine and make sure that you do not waste materials on your first project. When you buy your machine, there should be a practice project already in place.

Make sure that your blade is placed correctly. If it is placed too high, it may only cut part of

25. Hand Lettered Cake Topper

Materials to Use

- Glitter Card Stock
- Gold Paper Straw
- Cutting Mat
- Hot Glue Gun

Where to Find Materials

- Express vinyl
- Happy crafter
- amazon
- Esty
- Cricut.com
- Swing design

Illustration

- ✓ Create your design in Cricut Design Space, or download your desired design and import it into Cricut Design Space using the "Tips" section's instructions.
- ✓ Resize the design as required.
- ✓ Click the "Make it" button.
- ✓ Select Glitter card stock as your material in Design Space and set the dial on your Cricut machine to "Custom".
- ✓ Place the glitter card stock on your Cutting Mat and load it into the Cricut machine.
- ✓ When this is done, press the "Cut" button on your Cricut machine.
- ✓ After the machine is done with cutting the design, remove it from the mat. This can be done much more quickly using the Cricut Spatula tool.

- ✓ Finally, using hot glue, stick cut out design to the Gold Paper Straw and stick it in the cake as shown in the picture.

Tips and Tricks

Cricut cake toppers have a little bit of added difficulty because they require some precise scoring. The Cricut maker is probably the best piece of equipment for the job, and here, we'll tell you how to do it. The scoring tool is your best bet since this will make different shapes even easier, as well. You will want to make sure you have cardstock and the cutting mat, along with a fine-point blade for cutting. The tape is also handy for these.

Many people forget that the pen is in their machine after finishing a project, which can be a big no-no. This is because if the lid is not on it, it will dry out and the pens can get very expensive. So be sure to put the pen cap back on and make sure it is all the way on.

Keeping some supplies on demand is a good idea as well, particularly if you're going to be working with vinyl and cardstock. Since most projects use vinyl, you could have some of that on hand along with a pack of cardstock and things of that nature.

Know which machine has which options on it. The machines are different and can come with different settings as well.

26. Unicorn Free Printable

Materials

- Printables
- White Card Stock
- Cricut Mat
- Crepe Paper Streamers (varied colors)
- Gold Straws
- Glue Stick
- Hot Glue Gun
- Scissors

Where to Find Materials

- Craft stash
- Happy crafter
- amazon
- Esty
- Cricut.com
- Swing design

Illustration

- ✓ Import the printable image into Cricut Design Space, following the instructions under the "Tips" section of this book.
- ✓ Resize the PNG image and make it 5" wide.
- ✓ With your Cricut machine, cut the unicorn head using the white cardstock. Also, print and cut out the "stickers."
- ✓ After cutting out the pieces, stick the horn and the other elements using the glue stick.
- ✓ In each color, cut out strips of crepe paper, about 2" wide; then, cut each strip into thirds.
- ✓ On the reverse side of the unicorn head, glue the strips on the back edge (of the head), then glue on the top by the horn. Ensure that only half the length of each strip is on this side, as you will glue the other half on the other side of the unicorn head.
- ✓ Turn the unicorn head back over and glue the crepe streamers in place.
- ✓ Turn the head over yet again and use hot glue to stick the gold paper straw onto the unicorn head reverse side to use as party props.

Tips and Tricks

Printable stickers are the next project. This is super simple and fun for parents and kids. The Explore Air 2 machine works best.

From here, choose the image and flatten it, since this will make it into one piece rather than just a separate file for each. Resize as needed to make sure that they fit where you're putting them.

You can copy/paste each element until you're done. Once ready, press saves, and then choose this as a print then cut image. Click the big button at the bottom that says make it. Make sure everything is good, then press continue, and from there, you can load the sticker paper into the machine. Make sure to adjust this to the right setting, which for sticker paper is the vinyl set. Put the paper into there and load them in, and when ready, the press goes – it will then cut the stickers as needed.

27. Custom Back To School Supplies

Materials

- Vinyl
- Standard Grip Mat
- White Paper
- Markers (including black)
- Pencil Case
- 3 Ring Binder
- IPad Pro (optional)
- Apple Pencil
- Cricut Design Space App

- Drawing app (e.g. ProCreate)
- ProCreate Brushes

Where to Find Materials

- Express vinyl
- Craft stash
- Happy crafter
- amazon
- Esty
- Cricut.com
- Swing design

Illustration

- ✓ The first thing to do is convert your kid's drawing into an SVG file that Cricut Design Space recognizes. This will be done by tracing it in the ProCreate app.
- ✓ Get your child's design – it should not be too complex, to minimize weeding.
- ✓ Open the Procreate app on your iPad.
- ✓ Create a new canvas on ProCreate. Click on the wrench icon and select "IMAGE".
- ✓ Next, click "TAKE A PHOTO". Take a picture of the design. When you are satisfied with the image, click "Use it".
- ✓ On the Layer Panel (the two squares icon), add a new layer by clicking the plus sign.
- ✓ In the layers panel, select the layer containing the picture and click the N. Also, reduce the layer's opacity so that you can easily see your draw lines.
- ✓ Click on the wrench icon, click "Share", then "PNG".
- ✓ Next, save the image to your device.

- ✓ Alternatively, use your black marker, trace the drawing on a blank piece of paper, then take a picture of it using your iPad or phone.
- ✓ The next stage is to cut the design out in Cricut Design Space
- ✓ Open up the Cricut Design Space app on your iPad.
- ✓ Create a new project.
- ✓ Select "Upload" (located at the screen's bottom). Select "Select from Camera Roll" and select the PNG image you created in ProCreate or the image you traced out.
- ✓ Follow the next steps.
- ✓ Save the design as a cut file and insert it into the canvas. Here, you can resize the design or add other designs.
- ✓ Next, click "Make It" to send it to your Cricut.
- ✓ Choose "Vinyl" as the material.
- ✓ Place the vinyl on the mat and use the Cricut to cut it.
- ✓ Now, you can place the vinyl cutouts on the back to school supplies to make your child stand out!

Tips and Tricks

To start, you'll want to cut the main fabric, and you should use straps, the loops, a handle, some gussets for a zipper, and the bottom and side gussets.

The lining should be done, too, and you should make sure you have the interfacing. You can use fusible flex foam, too, to help make it a little bit bulkier.

You can trim this, too. The interfacing should be one on the backside, and then add the flex foam to the main fabric. The adhesive side of this will be on the right-hand side of the interfacing. Add these inner pieces to the outer ear, and then stitch these together.

Choose vinyl, and then insert the material onto the cutting mat. From there, cut it and remove the iron-on slowly.

You will need to do this in pieces, which is fine because it allows you to use different colors. Remember to insert the right color for each cut. At this point, add the zipper, and there you go!

28. Leather Keychain

Materials To Use

- Cricut Iron-on Foil in rose gold
- Cricut EasyPress 2 Small
- Cricut EasyPress Mat
- Cricut True Control Knife
- Keychain Lanyards
- Cricut Normal and Strong Grip Cutting
- Cricut Self-Healing
- Criciut EasyPress

Where To Find Materials

- Express vinyl
- Craft stash
- Happy crafter
- amazon
- Esty
- Cricut.com
- Swing design

Illustration

- ✓ Start by opening up Cricut Design Space
- ✓ Design Space comes complete with many font, pictures and characteristics so that it can be used immediately after you plug into it. You can easily upload your own images, but the project today will only use a Cricut fountain.
- ✓ Create and open a textbox to a new canvas. Specify your name, and in the drop-down list, select the ZOO DAY font. The all-cap fonts are perfect for this. It works great. When the name has been written down, the letter space is decreased so that the letters start to touch each other. Touch them before and after each letter.
- ✓ You can check out my project here, but your own custom names must be created.
- ✓ Make it visible to both layers.
- ✓ Changing the iron-on vinyl color from the top layer to the color... or closing.
- ✓ Double every name now.
- ✓ The background of one version must be visible, the other the front.

- ✓ Select and solder every single name. All letters will be merged into one solid piece.
- ✓ After soldering, the background is solid and each name is solid. Choose and sweat or join all the blue names. Repeat the yellow names soldering.
- ✓ Click on the button to make it.
- ✓ On two separate mats you will bring up the sold or attached words.
- ✓ Mirror the front-end mat picture. Then, with a glittering side, place the iron-on vinyl on your mat. Set the Iron-on Foil configuration of the machine.
- ✓ Click on the "C" button and insert it into the Cricut Maker. It will cut the picture with the fine dot blade beautifully.
- ✓ Remove the vinyl iron and trim the edges once cut. Set it above your Bright Pad Cricut and see where you should weed. It has a breeze. To remove excess vinyl, use the weeding tool.
- ✓ Get the leather ready for the second mat. Leather cutting was never so easy with the Blade and the Builder Knife.
- ✓ To help protect your cutting mat against leather, use the contact paper. Remove the leather packaging and turn it roughly onto it.
- ✓ Place the paper and securely paste it on clear contact paper. Cut the leather in plastic.
- ✓ Slide onto the machine and put the chrome blade in the machine to the right.
- ✓ Make certain you have calibrated the blade beforehand.
- ✓ Put the leather-covered contact paper right on the strong grip mat.
- ✓ Place the blade in the Cricut Maker and have a chrome blade easily cut the leather.

Tips and Tricks

If your mat is not sticky anymore this is a great tip for you. Grab spray adhesive and some painters tape. Tape off your edges and spray on a light coat of the spray. Let it dry overnight.

A light dusting of baby powder on cut vinyl can make darker colored designs show up easier as well as making weeding easier as well.

A plain white paper can be used to create print then cut Cricut projects as well.

Wax paper can also be used for many different projects as well and can cost as little as a dollar or less.

If you want cheaper fabric you can also check out Walmart. They have sections of fabric that are

29. Tassels

Materials

- 12" x 18" fabric rectangles
- Fabric mat
- Glue gun

Where to Find Materials

- Express vinyl
- Craft stash
- Happy crafter
- amazon
- Esty
- Cricut.com
- Swing design

Illustration

- ✓ Open Cricut Design Space and create a new project.
- ✓ Select the "Image" button in the lower left-hand corner and search "tassel."
- ✓ Select the image of a rectangle with lines on each side and click "Insert."
- ✓ Place the fabric on the cutting mat.
- ✓ Send the design to the Cricut.
- ✓ Remove the fabric from the mat, saving the extra square.
- ✓ Place the fabric face down and begin rolling tightly, starting on the uncut side. Untangle the fringe as needed.
- ✓ Use some of the scrap fabric and a hot glue gun to secure the tassel at the top.
- ✓ Decorate whatever you want with your new tassels!

Tips and Tricks

Place your machine on a flat surface. The surface should be long as well.

Follow the directions that your smartphone offers as well.

Glad press N seal can work as a substitute for transfer paper and it is very cheap.

A tennis ball will help vinyl stick to walls that are textured.

Wrap your hand with painters' tape to remove scraps while weeding. This trick is simple but very effective.

Mark your cutting mat to make sure that when you load it, that it is being loaded correctly.

If you want to sharpen your Cricut blade, you should grab a piece of aluminum foil and roll it into a ball and poke your blade in and out. Be VERY careful when doing this or you could cut your hand and badly.

30. Etched Glass

Materials

- Cricut machine
- Stencil vinyl
- Rubbing alcohol
- Gloves
- Plastic spoon
- Paper towel
- Etching cream
- Transfer tape
- Scrapper tool
- Weeding tool

Where To Find Materials

- Express vinyl
- Craft stash
- Happy crafter
- amazon
- Esty
- Cricut.com
- Swing design

Illustration

- ✓ Log in to the Cricut Design Space.
- ✓ Create your stencil.
- ✓ Click on the Text icon and input your text.
- ✓ Highlight the font and change the font.
- ✓ Ungroup the text.
- ✓ Adjust the spacing and let them overlap slightly.
- ✓ Highlight and group the text.
- ✓ Adjust the text size to the size of the stencil you want to make.
- ✓ Highlight the text and "attach" to keep them together.
- ✓ Click on the Insert Shape icon.
- ✓ Insert a square shape.
- ✓ Unlock the shape and make it a rectangle.
- ✓ Move the new shape over the text.
- ✓ Right-click on the box and select Move to the Back.
- ✓ Change the color of the shape to whatever color you want.
- ✓ Highlight the whole project and Attach it.
- ✓ After attaching it all, the cut line should be shown.
- ✓ Press the Make It button on your machine.
- ✓ Place the stencil vinyl onto the cutting mat.
- ✓ Load the cutting mat into the machine.
- ✓ Let the machine cut out the design on the stencil.

- ✓ Weed out the excess vinyl with the weeding tool.
- ✓ Apply a layer of transfer tape on the stencil.
- ✓ Put on the gloves.
- ✓ Prepare the glass by cleaning it with rubbing alcohol.
- ✓ Apply the transfer tape on the glass.
- ✓ Brush over with a scraper tool to remove the air bubble.
- ✓ Use the plastic spoon to apply a thin layer of etching cream on the stenciled glass.
- ✓ Let it dry out for twenty minutes.
- ✓ Scrap off the etching cream.
- ✓ Remove stencils and wipe the body with rubbing alcohol.
- ✓ Rinse with water.
- ✓ Your etched cup is ready.

Tips and Tricks

If you are working with glass, mugs, or anything else that shows fingerprints easily then you should clean the surface evenly with rubbing alcohol. This will make sure that your vinyl will adhere properly to the surface.

You can get up to four or five uses out of transfer tape if your careful. Reuse it to save supplies and money.

Use a small box for your weeding scraps and place them inside. No more little pieces in your hair or shoes. This is a great tip for people because you honestly can find little scabs everywhere and it is dangerous in a house with children and pets.

31. Wooden Sign

Materials

- Acrylic paint for whatever colors you would like
- Vinyl
- Cricut Explore Air 2
- Walnut hollow basswood planks
- Transfer Tape
- Scraper

- An SVG file or font that you wish to use
- Pencil
- Eraser

Where to Find Materials

- Happy crafter
- amazon
- Esty
- Cricut.com
- Swing design

Illustration

- ✓ You will need to start by deciding what you will want to draw onto the wood.
- ✓ Then, place some lines on the plank to designate the horizontal and vertical axis for the grid. Set this aside for later.
- ✓ Upload the file that you wish to use to the Design Space. Then, cut the file with the proper
- ✓ Weed out the writing or design spaces that are not meant to go on the wood.
- ✓ Using the transfer tape, apply the tape to the top of the vinyl and smooth it out. Using the scraper and the corner of the transfer paper, slowly peel the backing off a bit at a time. Do it carefully.
- ✓ Remove the backing of the vinyl pieces, aligning the lettering or design so that it is fully centered. Place it carefully on the wooden plank.
- ✓ Again, use the scraper to smooth out the vinyl on the plank.

- ✓ Take off the transfer tape by smoothing off the bubbles as you scrape along the wood sign. Discard the transfer tape at that time.
- ✓ Continue to use the scraper to make the vinyl smoother. There should be no bumps since this creates bleeding.
- ✓ Now, paint your wood plank with any color of your choice. Peel the vinyl letters off. Once the paint has completely dried, you are able to erase your pencil marks.

Tips and Tricks

Label your scraps, particularly if they are vinyl, because if you have waited a little while between your projects

Pay attention to your box. If you see a number one, there will be a note that says sold separately. You might find that it is something that you want, which is why they offer the option of bundling in case there is something that you wanted that wasn't able to be found with the machine.

Watching videos can help you learn as well and it is a great way to learn about your machine and become accustomed to the bells and whistles

32. Clutch purse

Materials

- Two fabrics, one for the exterior and one for the interior
- *Fusible fleece*
- Fabric cutting mat
- *D-ring*
- *Sew-on snap*
- *Lace*
- *Zipper*
- *Sewing machine*

- *Fabric scissors*
- Keychain or charm of your choice Instructions

Where to Find Materials

- Express vinyl
- Craft stash
- Happy crafter
- amazon
- Esty
- Cricut.com
- Swing design

Illustration

- ✓ Open Cricut Design Space and create a new project.
- ✓ Select the "Image" button in the lower left-hand corner and search for "essential wallet."
- ✓ Select the essential wallet template and click "Insert."
- ✓ Place the fabric on the mat.
- ✓ Send the design to the Cricut.
- ✓ Remove the fabric from the mat.
- ✓ Attach the fusible fleecing to the wrong side of the exterior fabric.
- ✓ Attach lace to the edges of the exterior fabric.
- ✓ Assemble the D-ring strap.
- ✓ Place the D-ring onto the strap and sew into place.
- ✓ Fold the pocket pieces wrong side out over the top of the zipper, and sew it into place.
- ✓ Fold the pocket's wrong side in and sew the sides.
- ✓ Sew the snap onto the pocket.
- ✓ Lay the pocket on the right side of the main fabric lining so that the corners of the pocket's bottom are behind the

curved edges of the lining fabric. Sew the lining piece to the zipper tape.
- ✓ Fold the lining behind the pocket and iron in place.
- ✓ Sew on the other side of the snap.
- ✓ Trim the zipper so that it's not overhanging the edge.
- ✓ Sew the two pocket layers to the exterior fabric across the bottom.
- ✓ Sew around all of the layers.
- ✓ Trim the edges with fabric scissors.
- ✓ Turn the clutch almost completely inside out and sew the opening closed.
- ✓ Turn the clutch all the way inside out and press the corners into place.
- ✓ Attach your charm or keychain to the zipper.
- ✓ Carry your new clutch wherever you need it!

Tips and Tricks

There are many projects that will eat up your scraps of vinyl so save them. Vinyl is expensive so make sure you use as much as you can. Weeding on the mat will keep your design secure and the weeding will be much easier.

If you are using light cardstock or vellum, do not use more pressure. It will damage the materials.

Using too much pressure on your mats can damage your mats as well and cause you to have to gain new ones.

If you're doing an intricate design, especially a very intricate one, you should cut on standard pressure.

33. Thank You Card

Materials

- Cardstock in the main color of your wedding
- Sparkling cardstock, if matches your wedding theme, or cardstock in your secondary color
- Acetate paper liners for the envelope liners
- Adhesive runner used for scrapbooking

Where to Find Materials

- Craft stores
- Superstores
- Vinyl/Heat Transfer Vinyl
- Amazon.com
- ExpressionsVinyl.com

- MyVinylDirect.com
- Craft stores
- Amazon.com
- PaperAndMore.com
- Craft stores

Illustration

- ✓ In Design Space, open the card and envelope template. Place your main color cardstock on your cutting mat and the scoring blade into the machine next to your cutting blade and cut your card. Use your weeding tool to remove any parts that remain that you do not want.
- ✓ Trim your sparkling cardstock to the size of the thank you card top part and attach it to the underside of your card top with adhesive scrapbooking tape. You want to put this piece of cardstock under your cut-out design so the sparkle shows through.
- ✓ Add the cardstock for your envelope to your cutting mat. If you are using the same cardstock as your card, keep your dial set to "light cardstock." If you choose something sturdier, adjust your dial to "Cardstock +." Cut your design.
- ✓ Fold the envelope's edges up and use adhesive scrapbooking tape to secure the edges. Use your scoring tool to enhance the crease of the envelope flap, if you deem it necessary.

Tips and Tricks

You can also edit your cut settings for any material so you can have fun doing this as well so that you can get used to the custom options.

You can also adjust your cut pressure and this can save your money on mats as you will not be ruining them.

Do not use an iron for iron-on projects. If you are using an iron for adhering your HTV there is better technology available to you and it will work much better.

Chapter 3: Project ideas for advanced

34. Coloring Pages

Materials

- whitekraft paper or a big sheet of white paper
- Cricut Explore or Maker
- Cricut Pens
- 1224 mat

Where to Find Materials

- Express vinyl

- Craft stash
- Happy crafter
- Esty
- Cricut.com
- Swing design

Illustration

- ✓ Open Design Space and pick your design, to begin with. I searched for "draw Christmas" and chose these adorable woodland creatures, ideal for drawing with pens.
- ✓ Once I had about a 12x12 section filled with animals and holly, I hit CTRL+A to select everything and copy and paste the entire design below. It saved me much work, not having to move and replace each object.
- ✓ Hit the Make It button once you have everything in location. The software reminds you you need a larger mat since your project is larger than 11.511.5".
- ✓ Now comes the fun part: wait. The black will take at least an hour, but I didn't. You can switch the pen, get the quick parts out of the way, and do something else while Cricut draws the designs.
- ✓ Once finished, remove it thoroughly and wrap your donation.

Tips and Tricks

When you want to layer to pop out a bit from another layer that you have either use a product like Zits or what is called Pop Dots. You could even make little circles using craft foam or cardboard and glue it between your layers.
If a Brightpad is out of your budget, you can hand your vinyl on a window and achieve an effect that is similar.

Make sure that your following the prompts when you're making a project.

Experiment with your search terms. It can be a little touchy so have fun changing things around and seeing what it can come up with for you. In some cases, you should take of the letter S or add one because it can change the search terms completely. It can also change the results.

Save your most commonly used materials that you cut. It has the option to do this and it is a good one to use because it will be more customized to you.

35. Luggage tags

Materials

- Cricut Faux Suede or other substantial material of your decision
- Cricut Pen
- Shower Adhesive

- Cowhide line
- Cricut Explore Air, Cricut Explore Air 2, or Cricut Maker
- Solid Grip Cutting Mat

Where to Find Materials

- Express vinyl
- Craft stash
- Happy crafter
- amazon
- Esty
- Cricut.com

Illustration

- ✓ This venture is in fact a Make It Now venture in the Cricut Design Space, however in the event that you go straightforwardly there you can't tweak it with your name and contact data. So all things considered, click the Images tab in the left sidebar and quest for "gear tag."
- ✓ Look down until you discover this gear tag and addition it into your canvas. You'll see that there's space to include your own content over the plane on the rear of the tag.
- ✓ Change the textual style by utilizing the drop-down menu on the correct side. You can sort by "expressing" style to discover the text styles that work with the pen instrument.
- ✓ When you have your name put, select everything on your canvas and snap "append" this is guarantee your contact data writes in the right spot on your gear tag.
- ✓ Hit Make It and follow the on-screen prompts to compose and cut your baggage tag! Utilize splash glue to stick the two sorts out, and bind to your pack with a cowhide rope or

other strip on cording! Such a simple undertaking, that will assist you with monitoring your sacks when you travel.

Tips and Tricks

When you can no longer make a smooth cut or an effective cut, you need new blades. Be careful when replacing them because you can cut yourself pretty badly.

You can clean your cutting mats with baby wipes as well. They need to be water based and using them to keep your mats clean can help them stay sticky longer. Make sure that these baby wipes have no fragrance. If they are not water based, they will damage the mat and you will not be able to use it again.

Keep the plastic sheets that come with your mats and you can protect the mats between uses. This helps your mats last longer so that you can use them repeatedly.

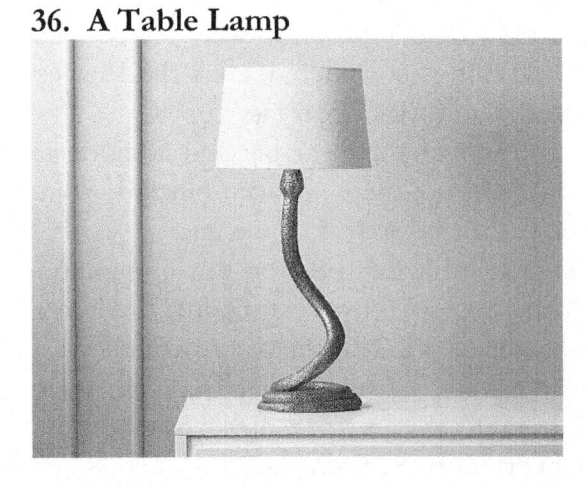

36. A Table Lamp

Materials

- Set of 6 Scrapbooking paper sheets - Tropical Paradise

- Slate scrapbooking sheet - Mahé - 30x30cm
- Sheet of 34 epoxy stickers - Tropical Paradise
- 8 card stock polaroid frames - Tropical Paradise
- 100m two-tone spool - Sky blue
- 16 mini clothespins 35 mm
- Vivaldi smooth sheet A4 240g - Canson - white n ° 1
- Precision cutter and 3 blades
- Blue cutting mat - 2mm - A3
- Black acrylic and aluminum ruler 30cm
- Precision scissors 13.5cm blue bi-material rings
- 3D adhesive squares
- Pack of 6 HB graphite pencils

Where To Find Materials

- Express vinyl
- Craft stash
- Happy crafter
- amazon
- Esty
- Cricut.com
- Swing design

Illustration

- ✓ Gather the materials.
- ✓ Using the template and a pencil, reproduce the palm tree on the papers in the collection.
- ✓ Cut out with a cutter or scissors.
- ✓ Assemble the trunk of the palm tree. Glue the foliage. Using the template, reproduce the traces of the cocktail support on

thin cardboard, following the dimensions indicated. Cover it with the collection paper.
- ✓ After having cut in the slate sheet: 1 x (8.5 x 8.5 cm). Choose a Polaroid. Glue the slate sheet to the back of the Polaroid. Using a chalk pen, write "Cocktail of the day". Decorate with the stickers. Fold the support at the dotted lines.
- ✓ Using the templates and a pencil, draw the leaves and flowers on the Mahé paper and on the collection paper. Draw.
- ✓ Choose photos. Cut them to size: 8.5 x 8.5 cm. Stick to the back of the Polaroids.
- ✓ Glue the leaves and flowers together. Cut the string to the desired dimensions and glue it to the back of the flowers. Glue the birds on the string and hang the photos using mini clips.
- ✓ And here is a pretty summer and tropical decoration! Beautiful evenings in perspective!

Tips and Tricks

Clear contact paper works like transfer sheets and you can usually find this for a dollar as well.

You can store vinyl rolls in organizers from Ikea. They are great to use and you can put them on a Lazy Susan or onto a wall. This really helps you see the items that you have on hand as well which means that you will not be doubling unnecessarily or on accident.

Pegboards are amazing for your tools and it is great for not losing your tools when you need them the most and you can put them in a high place so children do not get hurt.

37. Xmas Decoration

Materials

- *Cricut machine*
- Cricut glitter vinyl
- *Transfer tape*
- *Scraper tool*
- *Weeding tool*
- *Ribbon*

Where to Find Materials

- Express vinyl
- Craft stash
- Happy crafter
- Amazon
- Esty

- Cricut.com
- Swing design

Illustration

- ✓ Log in to the Cricut design space and start a new project.
- ✓ Click on the Input icon.
- ✓ Type in your Christmas greetings.
- ✓ Change the text font.
- ✓ Ungroup and adjust the spacing.
- ✓ Highlight and "weld" to design the overlapping letters.
- ✓ Select the parts of the text you do not want as part of the final cut.
- ✓ Readjust the text size.
- ✓ Select the file as a cut file. You will get to preview the design as a cut file.
- ✓ Approve the cut file.
- ✓ The text is ready to cut.
- ✓ Place the vinyl on the cutting mat shiny side down.
- ✓ Load the mat into the machine.
- ✓ Custom dial to vinyl.
- ✓ Cut the image.
- ✓ Use the weeding tool to remove excess vinyl after the image is cut.
- ✓ Apply a layer of transfer tape to the top of the cut vinyl.
- ✓ Peel back the vinyl paperback.
- ✓ Apply the vinyl onto the glass ornament.
- ✓ Go over the applied vinyl with a scraper tool to remove air bubble underneath the vinyl.
- ✓ Slowly peel away the transfer tape from the glass ornament.

Tips and Tricks

If you want to use a pen that is too thin, pencil grips might help this issue.

Remember that the app has free weekly designs. But they are only free for that one week. Use it or you may lose it.

If you notice that your Design Space is not working with one internet type, try another. Firefox, Chrome, and Safari are usually considered to be good ones to choose from.

If you have leftover debris stuck to your mat, an old gift card will scrape it off easily. It is better to use an old gift card than a credit card because you could get items stuck to your credit card or damage it depends on how you scrape it across the mat.

If you accidentally cut through your mat, you can fix it by placing a duct tape or gorilla tape onto the back of your mat.

38. Wall Art

Materials

- Adhesive vinyl
- Cricut machine
- Weeding tool
- Scrapper tool

Where to Find Materials

- Express vinyl
- Craft stash
- Happy crafter
- Esty
- Cricut.com
- Swing design

Illustration

- ✓ Log in to the Cricut design space.
- ✓ *Create a* 'New Project'.
- ✓ *Click on* 'Upload Image'.
- ✓ Drag the image to the design space.
- ✓ Highlight the image and *'Flatten'* it.
- ✓ Click on the *'Make It'* button.
- ✓ Place vinyl to the cutting mat.
- ✓ Custom dial the machine to vinyl.
- ✓ Load the cutting mat into the machine.
- ✓ Push the mat up against the rollers.
- ✓ Cut the design out of the vinyl.
- ✓ Weed out the excess vinyl with a weeding tool.

- ✓ Apply a thin layer of transfer tape on the vinyl.
- ✓ Peel off the backing.
- ✓ Apply the transfer tape on the wall.
- ✓ Smoothen with a scraper tool, to let out the air bubble

Tips and Tricks

You can clean your cutting mats with baby wipes as well. They need to be water based and using them to keep your mats clean can help them stay sticky longer. Make sure that these baby wipes have no fragrance. If they are not water based, they will damage the mat and you will not be able to use it again.

Keep the plastic sheets that come with your mats and you can protect the mats between uses. This helps your mats last longer so that you can use them repeatedly.

If you are not sure about the correct cut setting, run a small test cut first. This is especially true if you have a larger project. Doing this is going to make sure that you are not wasting expensive materials that you want and need. It will also make sure you understand what cuts can do to materials.

39. Print socks

Materials

- Socks
- Heat transfer vinyl
- Cutting mat
- Scrap cardboard
- Weeding tool or pick
- Cricut EasyPress or iron

Where to Find Materials

- Express vinyl
- Craft stash
- Happy crafter

- amazon
- Esty
- Cricut.com
- Swing design

Illustration

- ✓ Open Cricut Design Space and create a new project.
- ✓ Select the "Image" button in the lower left-hand corner and search "paw prints."
- ✓ Select the paw prints of your choice and click "Insert."
- ✓ Place the iron-on material on the mat.
- ✓ Send the design to the Cricut.
- ✓ Use the weeding tool or pick to remove excess material.
- ✓ Remove the material from the mat.
- ✓ Fit the scrap cardboard inside of the socks.
- ✓ Place the iron-on material on the bottom of the socks.
- ✓ Use the EasyPress to adhere it to the iron-on material.
- ✓ After cooling, remove the cardboard from the socks.
- ✓ Wear your cute paw print socks!

Tips and Tricks

If you are finding that your cutting something tricky, your machine will cut it several times. But when it does this, keep the mat in the position, and do not hit the arrows buttons to eject it. Press C instead. It will make it cut again.

When you are going to print and cut, you need to use an inkjet printer. It works better than a laser. A laser can heat the toner and cause it not to be read.

40: Jam Jar Labels

Materials to Use

- Mason jar with lid ring
- Red glitter ribbon
- White cardstock or sticker paper
- Double-sided tape
- Scissors
- Assorted holiday candies

Where to Find Materials

- Craft stores
- Superstores
- Vinyl/Heat Transfer Vinyl

- Amazon.com
- ExpressionsVinyl.com

Illustration

- ✓ Follow the on-screen instructions to print and cut each character's design.
- ✓ Wrap the jar with a ribbon and use the tape to stick. The glitter ribbon is slightly tricky, so use hot glue to work better. Or go with a non-glitter ribbon.
- ✓ Apply a beautiful design on top to cover where the overlapping ends in your ribbon seam.
- ✓ Fill your jars with candies and top with a mini bow.
- ✓ Optionally, you can **create a gift tag** to coordinate with your treat jar. Here are some gift tag ideas, printable and project tutorials to help get you started.
- ✓ Gingerbread Man treat jar for Christmas parties and neighbor gifts

Tips and Tricks

A trick for installing fonts into your computer, you may need to sign out of the app and then back in before your new font will show up. If this does not work, then be sure to restart your computer.

The deep cut blade is a handy tip here as well. Having the deep blade means you can cut through thicker materials like chipboard, felt, and leather. It is compatible with the Explore Air 2. Just make sure when you get this blade, you get the housing for it as well.

41. Monogrammed Drawstring Bag

Materials

- Two matching rectangles of fabric
- *Needle and thread*
- *Ribbon*
- Heat transfer vinyl
- Cricut EasyPress or iron
- *Cutting mat*
- Weeding tool or pick

Where to Find Materials

- Express vinyl
- Craft stash

- Happy crafter
- amazon
- Esty
- Cricut.com
- Swing design

Illustration

- ✓ Open Cricut Design Space and create a new project.
- ✓ Select the "Image" button in the lower left-hand corner and search "monogram."
- ✓ Select the monogram of your choice and click "Insert."
- ✓ Place the iron-on material shiny liner side down on the cutting mat.
- ✓ Send the design to the Cricut.
- ✓ Use the weeding tool or pick to remove excess material.
- ✓ Remove the monogram from the mat.
- ✓ Center the monogram on your fabric, then move it a couple of inches down so that it won't be folded up when the ribbon is drawn.
- ✓ Iron the design onto the fabric.
- ✓ Place the two rectangles together, with the outer side of the fabric facing inward.
- ✓ Sew around the edges, leaving a seam allowance. Leave the top open and stop a couple of inches down from the top.
- ✓ Fold the top of the bag down until you reach your stitches.
- ✓ Sew along the bottom of the folded edge, leaving the sides open.
- ✓ Turn the bag right side out.
- ✓ Thread the ribbon through the loop around the top of the bag.
- ✓ Use your new drawstring bag to carry what you need!

Tips and Tricks

Make sure that your blade is placed correctly. If it is placed to high, it may only cut part of the way through, but if it is down to low, it will ruin your mat. Doing a test cut to make sure it is in the right spot therefore could save you a lot of frustration.

Keeping some supplies on demand is a good idea as well, particularly if your going to be working with vinyl and cardstock. Since most projects use vinyl, you could have some of that on hand along with a pack of cardstock and things of that nature.

Know which machine has which options on it. The machines are different and can come with different settings as well.

42. Drinks Coasters

Materials

- 3mm thick balsa wood
- inexpensive "silver" hoop earrings in the number of charms you want to make
- Variety of paints, such as brown, green, orange, etc.

Where to Find Materials

- Express vinyl
- Craft stash
- Happy crafter
- Cricut.com
- Swing design

Illustration

- ✓ Open Design Space and insert various images you want to turn into wine charms. Keep the size smaller so that they will not interfere with someone holding the wine glass, but large enough to be able to identify easily. Add a small circle to each shape that will be cut out and where you will end up attaching the earring too.
- ✓ Cut the shapes onto the balsa wood. You may need to send it to cut a few times to make sure it has cut all the way through your wood.
- ✓ Paint your shapes or stain them in the colors you want. Allow them to dry completely.

- ✓ Once dry, thread one earring through the hole and get ready to dress up your next beverage! Consider adding initials, monograms, images, and patterns to the wine charms for different occasions.

Tips and Tricks

Your vinyl needs to be placed the right way up on the cutting mat.
The heat transfer vinyl
When you are cutting heat transfer vinyl, you need to remember to mirror the design. This is crucial because if you do not, then you will be cutting incorrectly and your project could be ruined as a result.

The Cricut tool set is not a necessity, but it can certainly help and it can be a great thing to have on hand for when your mastering your machine. It also has many different items that can make your crafting easier and less of a hassle.

Many card projects require that you have a stylus. If you bought your machine a part of a bundle it can have the stylus inside it already, but some may not. This is something to ask the person at the store when you are buying one because the stylus can really help.

43. Baby Blanket

Materials

- Cricut Machine
- Cricut EasyPress or Iron
- 23 sheets press on
- 1 1/4 yard white bandage texture
- Cricut Configuration Space document
- Autumn in November textual style

Where to Find Materials

- Express vinyl
- Craft stash
- Happy crafter
- Cricut.com
- Swing design

Illustration

When utilizing Cricut Press On, it's imperative to make sure to reflect the picture. You'll put it glossy side down on the tangle and cut utilizing the iron-on setting. Try not to utilize the HTV setting with your Creator. For reasons unknown, it is slicing through. You simply need it to cut the vinyl and keep the transporter sheet unblemished.

You'll evacuate all the negative space and after that cut every month number with the goal that you can space them on your cover. When utilizing the Cricut EasyPress, you require a hard surface and afterward a collapsed towel on that hard surface. You require something that will give a little with the goal that every one of the edges will be safely followed. You know you've got an awesome grip when you can see the material's surface.

For IronOn Lite, you'll require a temperature of 305F and afterward press for 2530 seconds. Give your things a decent warm-up in advance and after you're finished squeezing, turn your material over and press again for a couple of more seconds.

Now you're finished. So super simple yet it requires a tad of investment to get your numbers equitably dispersed and to complete the edges of your material. You'll never need to spend $40+ on a Milstone infant cover again.

Tips and Tricks

When you can no longer make a smooth cut or an effective cut, you need new blades. Be
Keep the plastic sheets that come with your mats and you can protect the mats between uses. This helps your mats last longer so that you can use them repeatedly.
Your vinyl needs to be placed the right way up on the cutting mat. The heat transfer vinyl should always be placed shiny side down.

44. Shoe Decals

Materials

- Shoes to embellish - Canvas is not necessary unless you want to iron on something to the top.
- Adhesive vinyl or iron-vinyl, depending on your design and shoe
- Transfer tape and scraper tool
- Iron, if required for iron-on

Where to find Materials

- Craft stores
- Superstores
- Vinyl/Heat Transfer Vinyl
- Amazon.com
- Craft stores

Illustration

- ✓ In Design Space, create your image or phrase and send the file to cut out of the vinyl. You can use the phrase for one shoe and the negative vinyl for the other, or you can send the file to cut two times.
- ✓ Use the transfer tape to remove the vinyl design and line it up on the shoe where you want to put it. Using the scraper tool, smooth the vinyl onto the shoe. If you are adding an iron-on design, heat your iron and place your vinyl on the canvas portion of the shoe. Place a cloth over the top and iron it on.
- ✓ peel away the backing of the vinyl, making sure it has completely attached to the shoe. You can go back over your vinyl with the iron or scraper tool to make sure everything is securely in place.

- ✓ Throw on your new custom shoes and show them off to the world!

Tips and Tricks

Vinyl can also be used to make personalized items, such as water bottle decals. First, design the text – you can pretty much use whatever you want for this. From here, create a second box and make an initial, or whatever design you want. Make sure that you resize this to fit the water bottle, as well.

Finally, when you adhere the lettering to the bottle, go from the center and then push outwards, smoothing as you go. It takes a bit, but there you have it – simple water bottles that children will love! This is a wonderful, simple project for those of us who aren't really that artistically inclined but want to get used to making Cricut items.

45. Leather foil

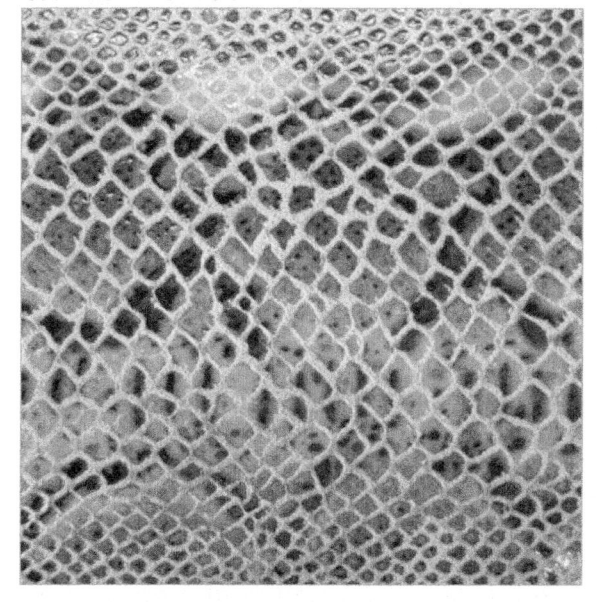

Materials

- Cricut Iron-on Foil in rose gold
- Cricut EasyPress 2 Small
- Cricut EasyPress Mat
- *Cricut Tools*
- Cricut True Control Knife
- Cricut Self-Healing Mat
- Keychain Lanyards
- Cricut Normal and Strong Grip Cutting
- Cricut Self-Healing
- Criciut EasyPress

Where to Materials

- Express vinyl
- Craft stash
- Happy crafter
- amazon
- Esty
- Cricut.com
- Swing design

Illustration

- ✓ Start by opening up Cricut Design Space
- ✓ Design Space comes complete with many font, pictures and characteristics so that it can be used immediately after you plug into it. You can easily upload your own images, but the project today will only use a Cricut fountain.
- ✓ You can check out my project here, but your own custom names must be created.

- ✓ Make it visible to both layers.
- ✓ Changing the iron-on vinyl color from the top layer to the color... or closing.
- ✓ Double every name now.
- ✓ The background of one version must be visible, the other the front.
- ✓ Select and solder every single name. All letters will be merged into one solid piece.
- ✓ After soldering, the background is solid and each name is solid. Choose and sweat or join all the blue names. Repeat the yellow names soldering.
- ✓ Click on the button to make it.
- ✓ On two separate mats you will bring up the sold or attached words.
- ✓ Mirror the front-end mat picture. Then, with a glittering side, place the iron-on vinyl on your mat. Set the Iron on Foil configuration of the machine.
- ✓ Click on the "C" button and insert it into the Cricut Maker. It will cut the picture with the fine dot blade beautifully.
- ✓ Remove the vinyl iron and trim the edges once cut. Set it above your Bright Pad Cricut and see where you should weed. It has a breeze. To remove excess vinyl, use the weeding tool.
- ✓ Get the leather ready for the second mat. Leather cutting was never so easy with the Blade and the Builder Knife.
- ✓ To help protect your cutting mat against leather, use the contact paper. Remove the leather packaging and turn it roughly onto it.
- ✓ Place the paper and securely paste it on clear contact paper. Cut the leather in plastic.
- ✓ Slide onto the machine and put the chrome blade in the machine to the right.

- ✓ Make certain you have calibrated the blade beforehand.
- ✓ Put the leather-covered contact paper right on the strong grip mat.
- ✓ Place the blade in the Cricut Maker and have a chrome blade easily cut the leather.

Tips and Tricks

When you are cutting heat transfer vinyl, you need to remember to mirror the design. This is crucial because if you do not, then you will be cutting incorrectly, and your project could be ruined as a result.

The Cricut tool set is not a necessity, but it can certainly help, and it can be a great thing to have on hand for when your mastering your machine. It also has many different items that can make your crafting easier and less of a hassle.

46. Leftover Boxes

Materials

- Sticker paper for labels or stickers
- Cardstock
- Hot glue gun or glue dots

Where to Find Materials

- Express vinyl
- Craft stash
- Happy crafter
- amazon
- Esty
- Cricut.com
- Swing design

Illustration

- ✓ If you are going to add labels of stickers to your boxes, design them in Design Space with the image or text that you prefer. Consider adding the title of the event and the date to the label so guests know right away how long they have the leftovers for in their fridge. Create a variety of sizes so they will fit over the cardstock boxes you are about to create or other containers you might need to use.
- ✓ Once your stickers or labels are created, send the file to print and cut.
- ✓ Search in the Design Space library the template for Chinese Take Out Boxes and load it into a new workspace. Choose a variety of sizes. Load your cardstock onto your cutting mats and send the file to cut.

- ✓ Fold your cut cardstock along the score lines. Apply glue along the edges to assemble the box and reinforce the seams.
- ✓ If you are adding stickers to your boxes, add them now. For other containers, keep the stickers nearby or apply them onto them as well. You are ready to send your guests away in style now!

Tips and Tricks

Load your mat correctly. Both sides of the mat need to be able to slide under the rollers or the mat will not cut in the correct manner. When you can no longer make a smooth cut or an effective cut, you need new blades. Be careful when replacing them because you can cut yourself pretty badly.

Keep the plastic sheets that come with your mats and you can protect the mats between uses. This helps your mats last longer so that you can use them repeatedly.

47. Photo Envelope Liners

Materials

- Envelopes to address
- Cricut Pen Tool
- Lightstick cutting mat

Where To Find Materials

- Express vinyl
- Craft stash
- Happy crafter
- amazon
- Esty
- Cricut.com
- Swing design

Illustration

- ✓ Open Cricut Design Space and create a new project.
- ✓ Create a box the appropriate size for your envelopes.
- ✓ Select the "Text" button in the lower left-hand corner.
- ✓ Choose one handwriting font for a uniform look or different fonts for each line to mix it up.
- ✓ Type your return address in the upper left-hand corner of the design.
- ✓ Type the "to" address in the center of the design.
- ✓ Insert your Cricut pen into the auxiliary holder of your Cricut, making sure it is secure.
- ✓ Place your cardstock on the cutting mat.
- ✓ Send the design to your Cricut.
- ✓ Remove your envelope and repeat as needed.
- ✓ Send out your "hand-lettered" envelopes!

Tips and Tricks

Keeping your mats clean is also going to be a great way to make them last longer so you do

Keeping your blades separate and organized will help too. Having separate blades for vinyl or fabric will help the blades stay sharp and the way you need them to longer. Keeping the blades separate is also going to help you be more organized. You can also spray paint your vinyl if you need a color and you do not have it just make sure that it is Rustoleum metallics spray and give it a quick spray. Make sure that the vinyl is uncut and that you dry it before

Make sure that you do a trial run of your materials that you are going to use for your project first. This is going to help ensure that you have the proper cutting techniques and you have the proper settings in place. This also ensures that you are not wasting materials, time or money.

48. Burlap

DIY BURLAP SUCCULENT

Materials

- Burlap (a genuinely tight weave works best)
- Shabby Glue
- Pouncer brush
- Wax paper
- Cricut Strong Grip move tape
- Cricut green tangle
- Earthenware pot
- Styrofoam ball
- Craft glue and paste firearm
- Cricut delicious document

Where to Find Materials

- Express vinyl
- Craft stash

- Happy crafter
- amazon
- Esty
- Cricut.com
- Swing design

Illustration

- ✓ Start with a 12 x 12 square of burlap and lay it on certain was paper to ensure your work surface. Blend tasteless paste creamer in with water. At that point utilize a pouncer brush to apply this blend all over your burlap.
- ✓ Permit to dry. This will take in any event for the time being. At that point simply strip your hardened burlap from the wax paper sheet. Presently we need to get this solid material to adhere to a Cricut tangle. Apply solid grasp move tape to the rear of your burlap. At that point place the non-clingy side of your exchange tape down onto your tangle. Press it down truly well. You can even utilize a brayer or moving pin here.

49. Model Airplane

Materials

- Two pieces of 1/32-inch thick balsa wood
- Dark stain
- Ivory adhesive vinyl
- Super glue or wood glue

Where to Find Materials

- Express vinyl
- Craft stash
- Happy crafter
- amazon
- Esty
- Cricut.com
- Swing design

Illustration

This is a "Make it Now" project in Design Space so open the library, search for the project, and open the project in a new workspace. Using a StrongGrip cutting mat, lay your balsa wood pieces on and make sure to adjust your settings to "custom" on your machine. When you are ready, send your project to cut. If the machine does not cut through the first time, repeat cutting, without moving your mat, three or four more times.

Gently remove the wood pieces from your mat. This is a fragile wood, so be very careful removing the pieces so you do not break them. Lay your pieces to the side for now.

- ✓ Go back to Design Space and write out the name or message you want to appear on the side of the plane. Make sure the size is correct for the size of the plane. Add your vinyl to your StandardGrip cutting mat and tell your machine to cut the image. Follow the prompts on your computer.
- ✓ Weed out the insides of your vinyl as necessary and remove the unnecessary exterior vinyl that is not part of your design. When it is ready, lay the design on your airplane and use the
- ✓ You can offer the pieces of the plane with instructions as a gift, or you can assemble the plane yourself. If you are making it, use your super glue or wood glue to securely attach all the pieces to one another and allow them to dry fully. Place this design somewhere people can enjoy your handiwork!

Tips and Tricks

Besides Cricut pens, there are a variety of other options that work for Explore machines. They include American Crafts, Recollection, Sharpies, or even Crayola.

If you have a smaller or more intricate design you can use a weeding box. This is especially helpful if your cutting multiple designs on one mat.

Make sure that your dial is set to the correct setting for materials. It is very easy to forget that this is on the wrong setting and then the cut can be wrong.

50. Wedding invitation

Materials

- Cricut Maker
- Cutting mat
- Decorative paper
- Crepe paper
- Fabric,
- Home printer

Where to Find Materials

- Craft stores
- Superstores
- Vinyl/Heat Transfer Vinyl
- Amazon.com

Illustration

- ✓ Log into the "Design Space" application and click on the "New Project" button on the top right corner of the screen to view a blank canvas.
- ✓ Let's customize an already existing project by clicking on the "Projects" icon on the "Design Panel" and selecting "Cards" from the "All Categories" drop-down then type in "wedding invite" in the search bar.
- ✓ For example, you could select the project shown in the picture below and click "Customize" at the bottom of the screen to edit and personalize the text of your invite.
- ✓ Click "Text" on the "Designs Panel" and type in the details of the invite. You can change the font, color and alignment of the text from the "Edit Text Bar" on top of the screen and remember to change the "Fill" to "Print" on the top of the screen.
- ✓ Select all the elements of the design and click on "Group" icon on the top right of the screen under "Layers panel". Then, click on "Save" to save your project

Tips and Tricks

When your mat loses its stickiness, you may think that you have to buy a new one. You do not, however, at least in most cases, because there are tips you can use here too. Clean your mat and see if that works and then tape your project down to hold it in place. Not over an area that needs to be cut but just over a few edges. A tack paint that is medium tape is good for this and shouldn't damage the cardstock.

A trick for installing fonts into your computer, you may need to sign out of the app and then back in before your new font will show up. If this does not work, then be sure to restart your

If you have a project that cuts on two different materials (such as a pink cardstock and a purple cardstock), you can do this at the same time by positioning the designs you will be cutting in different areas of the canvas on your app. Click Attach, then position the materials in the same spot on the map. This tip can be applied to Design Space for desktop and web.

Conclusion

This guidebook has been written to help you appreciate the power of your Cricut machine in terms of the projects that can be done with it. The step-by-step approach used to describe these projects will inspire your creative mind and produce designs that are even better than the ones described in this book.

You will be able to turn even the most unlikely and seemingly unrealistic ideas into beautiful craft projects in no time. You have learned all about the free resources including images, fonts, and projects that are available through the "Cricut" library so you can save money as you learn and sharpen your craft skills.

The detailed instructions with step-by-step process including pictures are written in an easy to understand language so you can have this book with you as you work to design your projects using the "Design Space" application, cut them using the "Cricut" cutting machine and then use the "Cricut Easy Press" for professional-looking projects. The 60+ project ideas covered in this book are only a tiny fraction of what you can do with your "Cricut" devices. It would be wise to sharpen your crafting skills by exploring and playing with the "Design Space" application in your spare time before you start creating some of the more advanced level projects.

Cricut machines are getting more popular every day. A lot of people have a preference for Cricut machines for many reasons. User-friendliness is one of the major reasons that people choose Cricut machines to do their cutting job. It's easy to use and also easy to learn if you have the right resources. Almost anyone can set up a Cricut machine because it is not too complicated. All that a new user has to do is to follow the straightforward instructions that come with the box.

You've just become a professional Cricut user! However, it would help if you did not forget the most important things discussed in this book. If you forget things quickly, have this book with you every time you want to work on your Cricut machine.
If you have worked your way through the projects in this book, you are well on your way to becoming a Cricut pro. Like a recipe book, the projects, along with the ideas in this book, can be adjusted, adapted, and added to, so that you can make each one uniquely yours.

With the Cricut, you are going to find birthdays, special occasions, seasonal holidays, and even school projects to be a lot easier, as well as more personalized. Everyone loves receiving gifts, cards and so on, that have been designed especially for them.

.

Made in the USA
Monee, IL
05 January 2021